BLOOD RIVER

Born in 1967, Tim Butcher has worked for the *Daily Telegraph* since 1990 as the paper's chief war correspondent and Africa Bureau Chief. He is currently their Middle East correspondent, based in Jerusalem.

TIM BUTCHER

Blood River

A Journey to Africa's Broken Heart

VINTAGE BOOKS
London

Published by Vintage 2008

4 6 8 10 9 7 5 3

Copyright © Tim Butcher 2007

Tim Butcher has asserted his right under the Copyright, Designs and Patents Act 1988 to be identified as the author of this work

This is a work of non-fiction based on the experiences of the author. In some limited cases names of people have been changed to protect their privacy. The author has stated to the publishers that, except in such minor respects, the contents of this book are true.

First published in Great Britain by Chatto & Windus in 2007

Vintage
Random House, 20 Vauxhall Bridge Road,
London SW1V 2SA

www.vintage-books.co.uk

Addresses for companies within The Random House Group Limited can be found at: www.randomhouse.co.uk/offices.htm

The Random House Group Limited Reg. No. 954009

A CIP catalogue record for this book is available from the British Library

ISBN 9780099494287

The Random House Group Limited supports The Forest Stewardship Council (FSC), the leading international forest certification organisation. All our titles that are printed on Greenpeace approved FSC certified paper carry the FSC logo. Our paper procurement policy can be found at www.rbooks.co.uk/environment

Mixed Sources
Product group from well-managed forests and other controlled sources
www.fsc.org Cert no. TT-COC-2139
© 1996 Forest Stewardship Council
FSC

Printed in the UK by CPI Bookmarque, Croydon, CR0 4TD

For Jane

Contents

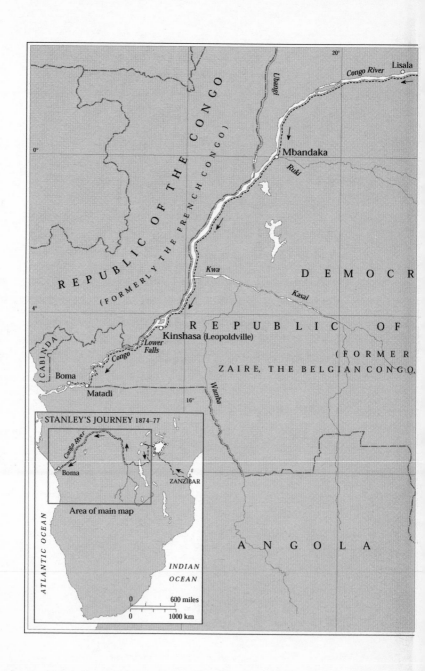

REPUBLIC OF THE CONGO (FORMERLY THE FRENCH CONGO)

20°

Congo River   Lisala

Ubangi

0°

Mbandaka

Ruki

Kwa

Kasai

D E M O C R

4°

R E P U B L I C   O F

Kinshasa (Leopoldville)

Lower Falls

(F O R M E R

Congo

Z A I R E,   T H E   B E L G I A N   C O N G O,

Boma

Matadi

Wamba

16°

STANLEY'S JOURNEY 1874-77

Congo River

Boma

ZANZIBAR

Area of main map

ATLANTIC OCEAN

A N G O L A

INDIAN OCEAN

0 ———— 600 miles

0 ———— 1000 km

CABINDA

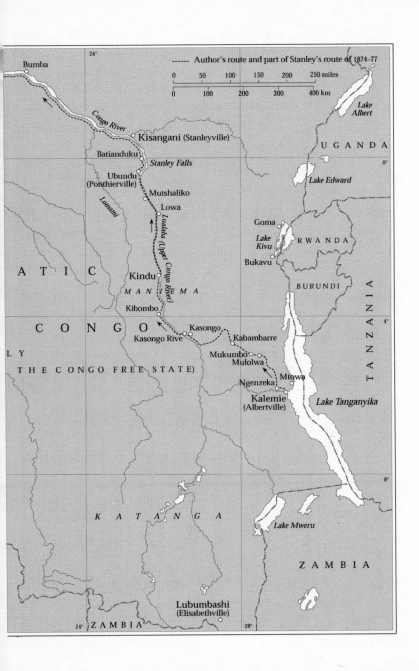

Bumba

Congo River

24°

------ Author's route and part of Stanley's route of 1874–77

| 0 | 50 | 100 | 150 | 200 | 250 miles |
| 0 | 100 | 200 | 300 | 400 km |

Kisangani (Stanleyville)

Batianduku

Stanley Falls

Ubundu
(Ponthierville)

Mutshaliko

Lowa

Lomami

Lualaba (Upper Congo River)

Kindu

M A N I E M A

Kibombo

A T I C

C O N G O

L Y

T H E   C O N G O   F R E E   S T A T E)

Kasongo

Kasongo Rive

Kabambarre

Mukumbo

Mulolwa

Ngenzeka

Mtowa

Kalemie
(Albertville)

K A T A N G A

Lake Mweru

Lubumbashi
(Elisabethville)

24°   **Z A M B I A**

28°

U G A N D A

*Lake
Albert*

0°

Lake Edward

Goma

*Lake
Kivu*

R W A N D A

Bukavu

B U R U N D I

T A N Z A N I A

Lake Tanganyika

4°

8°

Z A M B I A

Preface

I stirred in the pre-dawn chill, my legs pedalling for bedclothes kicked away earlier when the tropical night was at its clammiest. I could hear African voices singing to a drum beat coming from somewhere outside the room, but my view was fogged by the mosquito net, and all I could make out around me were formless shadows. Slowly and carefully, so as to not to anger them, I reached for the sheet balled next to my knees. It stank of old me and insect-repellent as I drew it over my shoulders. I was not just looking for warmth. I wanted protection. Outside was the Congo and I was terrified.

On the grubby floor next to the bed, my kit lay ready in the dark. There were my boots with their clunky tread and sandy suede uppers. Two thousand dollars were hidden in each, counted carefully the day before, folded into plastic bags and tucked under the insoles. There was my rucksack, packed and repacked several more times for reassurance with my single change of clothes, a heavy fleece, survival bag and eight bottles of filtered water. Explorers who first took on the Congo in the nineteenth century brought with them small armies bearing the latest European firearms and the best available medicines to protect against ebola, leprosy, smallpox and other fatal endemic diseases. The only protection I carried was a penknife and a packet of baby-wipes.

I was in a large town called Kalemie, but all was dark outside. It lies on the Congo's eastern approaches, a port city on the edge of Lake Tanganyika, once connected by boat with Tanzania, Zambia and the world beyond. Forty years of decay have turned it into a disease-ridden ruin and its decrepit hydroelectric station could barely muster a flicker. As with the rest of this huge country, the locals in Kalemie have long since learned to regard electrical power as a rare blessing, not a permanent right.

Now too anxious to sleep, I got up and dressed, taking special care not to ruck the dollars as I slipped on my boots. The charcoal burner, used to warm the gluey brick of rice I had eaten the previous night, glowed as I unlocked the double padlock on the back door and pushed open the crudely-welded security gate. I was staying in a bleak building, cloudy with mosquitoes and lacking running water, but the fact that it housed an American aid group made it a target in a country where acute poverty makes lawlessness routine. Against the lightening sky in the east I could make out a crude line of jagged bottle fragments cemented to the top of the high perimeter wall.

'Is anyone there?' My voice set off a dog barking outside the compound. The night watchman stepped out smartly from shadows.

'Present, patron.' The tone of his reply made him sound like a soldier answering roll call: subservient, militaristic and deferential. It was the tone of the Congo, drilled into its people first by gun-wielding white outsiders and then by cruel local militia.

As I checked over the motorbikes I had lined up for my journey, I could feel that the guard was anxious to reassure me. 'Don't worry, patron, everything is okay' he told my arched back as I bent over a rear wheel. 'I was awake all night long and nobody came over the wall.' He was a trained teacher, but the collapse of the Congolese state meant there was no money in teaching. The $30 he earned for a month of nights spent swatting mosquitoes in this compound was enough to keep him from his pupils.

The eastern sky was slowly growing more pale, but I turned to face west. Out there the darkness remained absolute. I felt a presence. Between me and the Atlantic Ocean lay a primeval riot of jungle, river, plain and mountain stretching for thousands of kilometres. For years I had stared at maps dominated by the Congo River, a silver-bladed sickle, its handle anchored on the coast, its tip buried deep in the equatorial forest, but now I could feel its looming sense of vastness. It scared me.

I have come to know well my own symptoms of fear. In ten years as a war correspondent I have crossed enough active frontlines and stared at enough airily-waved gun barrels to recognise how my subconscious reacts. For me terror manifests itself through clear physical symptoms, an ache that grows behind my knees and a choking dryness in my throat.

I had spent three years preparing for this moment, planning and researching, and it had already taken a week of delays and hassle just to reach this spot, but the most dangerous part of my journey was only now beginning. Feeling as if my legs were about to collapse, I croaked a faint curse against the obsession that had drawn me to the most daunting, backward country on Earth.

I fingered a piece of paper folded in my pocket. It was a travel pass bearing the smudgy ink stamps of the local district commissioner, granting permission for 'Butcher, Timothi' to make a journey overland to the Congo River 500 kilometres away. It spelled out the modes of transport authorised for the trip: bicycle, motorbike and dugout canoe. To reach the river I would have to travel west, crossing Katanga, a province that has been in a state of near-permanent rebellion for more than forty years, and Maniema, a province where cannibalism remains as real today as it was in the nineteenth century, when bearer parties refused to take explorers there for fear of being eaten. Even if I made it to the river, I would still have 2,500 kilometres of descent before reaching my final goal, close to where the Congo River spews into the Atlantic.

I remembered the reaction of the commissioner's secretary in Kalemie when I had collected the pass a few days earlier. After reading my itinerary he stopped writing, put his pen down very deliberately and raised his head to look at me. The lenses of his thick-framed glasses were misty with scratches, but I could still see his pupils pulse with disbelief.

'You want to go where?'

'I want to go to the Congo River.'

'You want to go overland?'

'Yes.'

'My family comes from a village on the way to the river, but we have not been able to go there for more than ten years. How do you think you will get there?'

'With a motorbike and some luck.'

'You are a white man, you will need something more than luck.'

Shaking his head slowly, his gaze dropped back to the travel pass, which he stamped with the seal of office of the District Commissioner for North Katanga. As I turned to leave I looked round the office. It had a crack in one wall so wide I could see blue sky through it, an old Bakelite telephone connected to nothing, and a tatty air that spoke of regular bouts of looting.

Commissioner Pierre Kamulete had hidden his surprise rather better when I approached him for permission to travel. He listened politely to my request, then gestured for me to join him over at the cracked wall where a large map hung. It was foxed with damp patches and bore place names that had not been used for decades. He pointed at the gap between Kalemie and the headwaters of the Congo River.

'You see this road that is marked here?' His finger traced what was shown as a national highway running due west from the lake. 'It does not exist any more. And the railway here. That does not work, either. A storm washed away the bridge. I don't know what route you will use, but it will take you a long time.'

But it wasn't the lack of roads that really worried me. It was the rebels, especially the mai-mai.

Mai-mai is a corruption of 'water-water' in the local language of Swahili and refers to the magical water with which rebels douse themselves after it has been imbued with special properties by sorcerers. Believers will tell you that bullets fired at anyone sprinkled with the special water will fall harmlessly to the ground. Non-believers will tell you that mai-mai are well-armed, dangerous killers who answer to nobody but themselves.

I had seen my first mai-mai soldier earlier that day. He was sidling along the potholed main road in Kalemie. He had the swagger you see all over Africa when possession of a weapon transforms a boy into a man. His uniform was typically hotch-potch, his beret was cocked at a fashionable angle and his eyes were hidden by dark glasses. But the thing that marked him out as mai-mai was that he was carrying a bow and arrow.

'The traditional belief system is very strong, and for the mai-mai a bow and arrow is every bit as good a weapon as a modern assault rifle. The arrow tip is dipped in poison made from plants found in the bush and the poison is highly toxic. Believe me, it works.' My security briefing had come from Wim Verbeken, a human-rights specialist at the local United Nations headquarters built in the ruins of Kalemie's abandoned cotton mill.

He explained how all the mai-mai in the Congo were meant to have put away their bows and arrows a year earlier under the terms of the ceasefire that supposedly ended the country's latest civil war. But he also explained how outside the major towns like Kalemie it was impossible to enforce the agreement and how the killing, rape and violence continued in the area I wanted to travel through.

'If we get reports of mai-mai activity, we are supposed to send a patrol to check it out. But then we also have a strict policy that we only patrol roads that are "jeepable", that we can drive down in a jeep. Here in Kalemie the jeepable roads stop just a few kilometres outside town. I come from Belgium and this province alone is fifteen times bigger than my own country. Nobody really knows what is going on out there.'

I was grateful for his candour as he spelled out the hazards. He said there was a particular mai-mai leader who liked to be known by his radio call sign Tango Four. Wim described him in somewhat undiplomatic language as a 'psychotic killer' and warned me that he was still out there in the bush. But Wim hadn't finished. He said there were also reports of activity involving the interahamwe, Hutu fugitives from Congo's troubled neighbour, Rwanda. These were the murderers responsible for the 1994 genocide of Tutsis in Rwanda and they had spent the last decade surviving in the lawless forests of eastern Congo. At this point Wim leaned right across the table for emphasis.

'Believe me, you don't want to meet the interahamwe.'

Thoughts of rebels and poisoned arrows swirled through my mind as I tucked the travel pass safely into a pocket. Someone could be heard running outside the compound and then came a pounding on the gate. It swung open and the sweating face of Georges Mbuyu appeared, gasping an apology.

'I thought I was going to be late. Let's go.'

Georges was a pygmy. A man just five foot tall and half my body weight was to be my protector through the badlands of the Congo. It was then that the backs of my knees really began to throb.

1.

Africa's Broken Heart

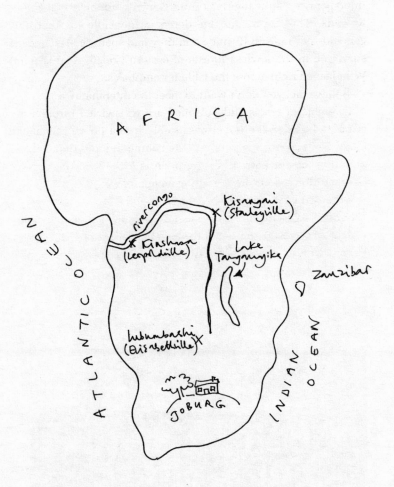

AFRICA

ATLANTIC OCEAN

river congo

Kisangani
(Stanleyville)

Kinshasa
(Leopoldville)

Lake
Tanganyika

Zanzibar

Lubumbashi
(Elisabethville)

JOBURG

INDIAN OCEAN

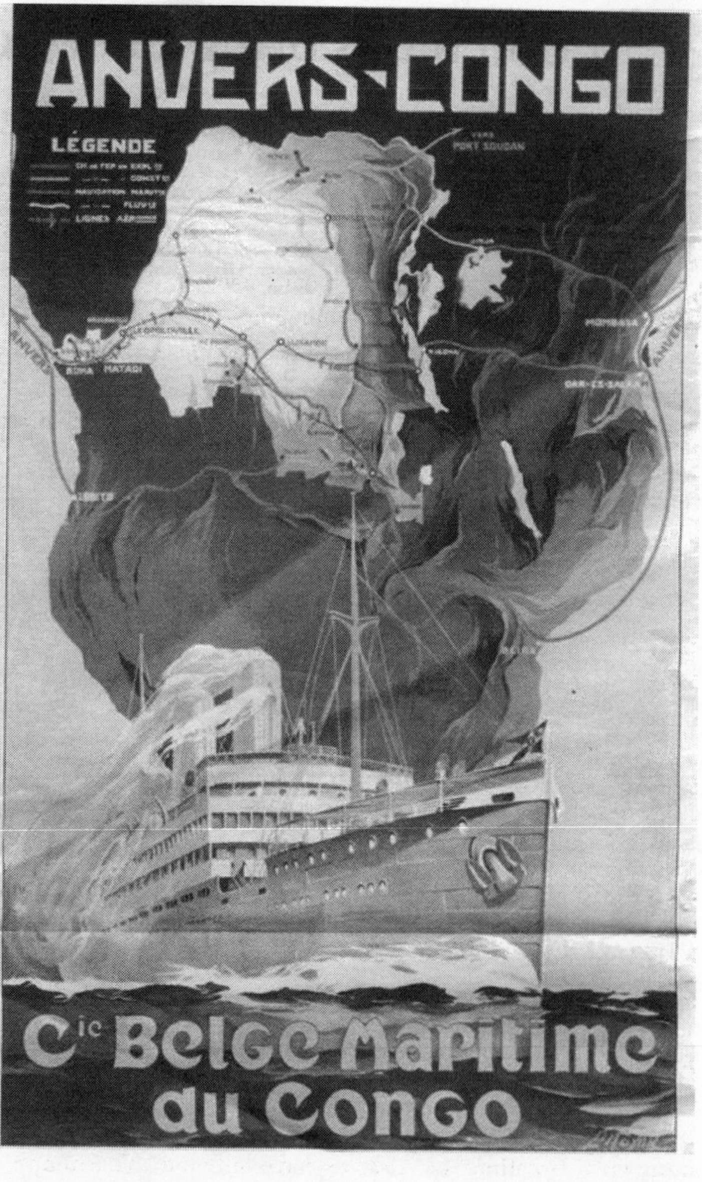

ANVERS-CONGO
LÉGENDE
PORT SOUDAN
BOMA MATADI
Cie Belge Maritime du Congo

It was a strange setting for a revelation. I was sunbathing on the beach of a luxury hotel next to the Indian Ocean, wearing nothing but blue swimming trunks and sunglasses, reading a book on African history. I know exactly what I had on, because around that moment someone took a photograph of me. It shows me concentrating hard, my fingers, slimy with sun-cream, splaying the pages. What it cannot show, though, is the racing surge in my heartbeat. I had just read something about the Congo that was going to change my life.

Recently appointed as Africa Correspondent for *The Daily Telegraph*, I was doing what every new foreign correspondent must: cramming. My reading list was long. After Africa's early tribal history came the period of exploitation by outsiders, starting with centuries of slavery and moving on to the Scramble for Africa, when the white man staked the black man's continent in a few hectic years at the end of the nineteenth century to launch the colonial era. Then came independence in the late 1950s and 1960s when the Winds of Change swept away regimes that some white leaders had boasted would stand for ever. And it finished with the post-independence age of economic decay, war, coup and crisis, with African leaders manipulated, and occasionally murdered, by foreign powers, and dictatorships clinging to power in a continent teeming with rebels, loyalists and insurgents.

The one constant through each of these episodes was the heavy undertow of human suffering. It gnawed away at every African epoch I read about, no matter whether it was caused by nineteenth-century colonial brutes or twenty-first-century despots. Generations of Africans have suffered the triumph of disappointment over potential, creating the only continent on the planet where the normal rules of human development and advancement simply don't apply.

It was this sense of stagnation that troubled me most as I worked through my reading list. Sub-Saharan Africa has forty-one separate countries of stunning variety – from parched desert to sweaty rainforest, from wide savannah to snow-tipped volcano – and yet as I did my background research, the history of these varied countries merged into a single, pro-forma analysis. I came to focus on which Western country exploited them during the colonial period and which dictator abused them since independence. The analysis was as crude as the underlying assumption: that African nations are doomed to victim status.

Things had been different when I was younger. I grew up in Britain in the 1970s and collected milk-bottle tops so that my *Blue Peter* children's television heroes could dig wells for Kenyan villagers. My last day at school in 1985 was the day when the Live Aid concert rocked the world for victims of the Ethiopian famine. And as a student in the late 1980s I did my bit to bring down the apartheid regime in South Africa, boldly refusing to use my cash-point card in British banks linked to the white-only government.

But by the time I started working in Africa as a journalist in 2000, its patina of despair had thickened to impenetrability. An old newspaper hand took me to one side shortly before I flew out to Johannesburg and gave me some advice. This man was no fool and no brute. He had stood on a beach in west Africa twenty years earlier and watched thirteen members of the Liberian cabinet shot by rebel soldiers wearing grubby tennis shoes, a horror that scarred his soul until the day he died. But his only advice to me, the novice, was: 'Just two things to remember in Africa – which tribe and how many dead.'

The Congo was prominent in every African era. As a child I had prided myself on knowing some of its history, about how Joseph Conrad used his time as a steamboat skipper on the mighty Congo

River as the basis for his novel *Heart of Darkness*. I am of the *Apocalypse Now* generation and can remember earnest conversations in school common rooms about how film-maker Francis Ford Coppola had borrowed directly from Conrad to create his cinematographic masterpiece on the depths the human soul can plumb. My friends and I would argue about whether Conrad was being racist, suggesting that black Africa was in some way inherently evil, or whether he used equatorial Africa simply as a backdrop for a novel about how wicked any human can become.

In my early months working in Africa, the Congo's contemporary woes soon became clear. It was in the Congo that the world's bloodiest war was raging. It began in 1998 and, by the time I started work, it was claiming more than 1,000 lives a day. But the truly staggering thing was how this loss of life barely registered in the outside world. Like so many other places in Africa, the Congo had come to be seen as a lost cause, and the costliest conflict since the Second World War passed largely unnoticed.

Before my moment of revelation, I found all of this a curiosity. What drove my interest up a quantum level was when, lolling on my sun lounger, I discovered a direct, personal link to the Congo and its turbulent history. I read that it had all been started by another reporter sent to Africa by the *Telegraph* more than a century before me. His name was Henry Morton Stanley.

In the Victorian era, Stanley was the world's best-known journalist, famous for the scoop of the century – tracking down the Scottish explorer, David Livingstone, in November 1871. The soundbite he came up with was as glib and memorable as any a modern spin doctor could conjure. Stanley's 'Dr Livingstone, I presume,' greeting remains so dominant that it has overshadowed his much greater and more significant achievement.

It came on his next epic trip to Africa between 1874 and 1877, when he solved the continent's last great geographical mystery by mapping the Congo River. Commissioned jointly by the *Telegraph* and an American newspaper, *The New York Herald*, he hacked his way through a swathe of territory never before visited by a white man, crossing the Congo River basin and proving that the continent's previously impenetrable hinterland could be opened up by steamboats on a single, huge river. He presumed to name the river Livingstone, in honour of his mentor, but it is now known as the Congo. His methods were brutal, opening fire on tribesmen who did not instantly obey, pillaging food and supplies. And his brazenness in describing his methods when he eventually reached home stirred angry controversy among humanitarian activists of the day. But their complaints were deafened by the hero's welcome Stanley received when he returned to London in 1878.

His Congo fame was fleeting. At the *Telegraph*'s London head-quarters today there is a modest collection of paintings and busts of the paper's luminaries. But there is no mention of Stanley or his Congo trip, even though it changed history more dramatically than anything the newspaper has ever been involved with.

Stanley's adventure caught the eye of a minor European monarch, Leopold II, King of the Belgians. Leopold read about Stanley's expedition in the newspaper, seeing past the reporter's colourful account of cannibals, man-eating snakes and river rapids so ferocious they devoured men by the canoe-load. Desperate for a colony that would mark Belgium's arrival as a world power, Leopold saw rich potential in Stanley's story. The explorer had found a river that was navigable across much of central Africa and Leopold envisaged it as the main artery of a huge Belgian colony, shipping European manufactured goods upstream and valuable African raw materials downstream.

Stanley's Congo expedition fired the starting gun for the Scramble for Africa. Before his trip, white outsiders had spent hundreds of years nibbling at Africa's edges, claiming land around the coastline, but rarely venturing inland. Disease, hostile tribes and the lack of any clear commercial potential in Africa meant that hundreds of years after white explorers first circumnavigated its coastline, it was still referred to in mysterious terms as the Dark Continent, a source of slaves, ivory and other goods, but not a place white men thought worthy of colonisation. It was Leopold's jostling for the Congo that forced other European powers to stake claims to Africa's interior, and within two decades the entire continent had effectively been carved up by the white man. The modern history of Africa – decades of colonial exploitation and post-independence chaos – was begun by a *Telegraph* reporter battling down the Congo River.

Reading about this epoch-changing journey seeded an idea in my mind that soon grew into an obsession. To shed my complacency about modern Africa and try to understand it properly, it was clear what I had to do: I would go back to where it all began, following Stanley's original journey of discovery through the Congo. The historical symmetry of working for the same paper as Stanley was appealing, but this alone was not enough. What really stirred me was the sense of challenge that the Congo represented. I had covered wars in Croatia, Bosnia, Kosovo, Sierra Leone, Iraq and elsewhere, but the work had started to feel routine. I wanted to leave the journalistic herd, to find a project that would both daunt and inspire me. Facing down the Congo was just such a project.

I don't need that beach photograph to remind me how excited I felt at that moment. And I don't need it to remind me how fear overwhelmed the excitement. It was not just the war that made the idea of crossing the Congo dangerous. There was something far more sinister.

For me the Congo stands as a totem for the failed continent of Africa. It has more potential than any other African nation, more diamonds, more gold, more navigable rivers, more fellable timber, more rich agricultural land. But it is exactly this sense of what might be that makes the Congo's failure all the more acute.

Economists have no meaningful data with which to chart its decline. Much of its territory has long been abandoned to a feral state of lawlessness and brutality. With a colonial past bloodier than anywhere in Africa, the Congo represents the sum of my African fears and the root of my outsider's shame.

Decay has hollowed the Congo name. It has a rich history, but of its present, precious little is known. People remember flickers from its past – the brutality of the early colonials, the post-independence chaos of elected leaders beaten to death, corrupt dictators whittling away the nation's wealth, mercenaries running amok in wars too complex for the outside world to bother with, rebels who rely on cannibalism and fetishism. Foreign journalists smirk at an old Congo story dating from the 1960s when rape was so common that a British reporter approached a column of refugees demanding, 'Is there a nun here who's been raped and speaks English?'

Travellers have long since stopped venturing there and the remnants of a once-booming African economy are regarded as too murky and risky for most conventional business travellers. Today, only a handful of aid workers, peacekeepers and journalists dare visit, but the vast scale of the place – from one side to the other is greater than the distance from London to Moscow – and the depth of its problems make it difficult to focus on much beyond a particular project in a particular place. I wanted to do something more complete, something that had not been done for decades, to draw together the Congo's fractious whole by travelling Stanley's 3,000-kilometre route from one side to the other.

In part my obsession came from another Congo journey that had nothing to do with Stanley. In late 1958 two young, middle-class English girls, lugging trunks full of souvenirs and party frocks, crossed the Congo. My mother and a close school friend were in their early twenties and, for them, the Congo was simply another leg in a rich travel adventure. Sent to colonial Africa as a sort of unofficial finishing school, they had worked, danced, giggled and charmed their way through a series of jobs and house parties, from Cape Town in South Africa to Salisbury, then the capital of Rhodesia.

They were nearing the end of their journey when they entered the Congo. Within a year the country would be at war, but today my mother recalls no sense of that impending doom. In all honesty, she remembers little about the trip by rail and steamboat, and it was only after I began my Congo research that she let me in on a family secret she had not talked about for decades. She was only twenty-one at the time, but while in Salisbury she had fallen in love and become engaged to a retired officer. The fact that he was divorced with three children was too much for my maternal grandmother, a woman so unutterably proper that she talked of 'gells' rather than 'girls'. My granny flew all the way to Rhodesia to bully her daughter into breaking off the engagement. 'I howled all the way through the Congo' is how my mother describes the trip, which she otherwise remembers as being no trickier than any other part of her 1950s African journey.

And that really was the point. Half a century ago there was nothing out-of-the-ordinary about the Congo. It was integrated, not just with the rest of the continent, but with the rest of the world. The Congo's colonial capital, Leopoldville, named after the acquisitive Belgian monarch, was the hub of one of Africa's largest airline networks, and the country's main port, Matadi, was served by a fleet of ocean-going liners. I have a picture of a poster from a Belgian shipping line that overlays an image of a ship on an outline of a very tame-looking Congo. The image was not of a sinister place at all, but of a swathe of African territory accessible by railways represented with cross-hatching, or by shipping routes depicted by elegant red arrows. Trains from the neighbouring Portuguese colony that later became Angola shuttled in and out of the Congo through its copper-rich Katanga province.

There were bus links with Rhodesia and across Lake Tanganyika a fleet of ferries moved goods and people to the former colony of German East Africa.

A flavour of that era comes from a guidebook I discovered in a second-hand bookshop in Johannesburg. The 1951 *Travel Guide to the Belgian Congo* runs to 800 pages of information for visitors. Some of the detail is wonderfully mundane. The names and location of scores of guest houses are listed, along with prices of meals and journey times between local towns. The procedure for buying a hunting licence is spelled out, along with lists of the national parks and their viewing hours. Maps show, in precise detail, the country's road network, spreading right across the rainforest and climbing over mountain ranges, and the book lists itineraries with helpful hints about turning left at Kilometre 348 or buying pottery from the natives, *les indigènes*. It has hundreds of black-and-white photographs that show a functioning country – bridges, churches, schools, post offices and towns. And, in blue ink, the inside cover is inscribed 'Annaliesa'. In my imagination, Annaliesa used it to plan genteel trips to visit waterfalls or go on safari. Today those same journeys would be impossible.

The book conveys the sort of normality my mother recalled. Mum described her steamboat journey through virgin rainforest and how she would lean over the rail to point at sparring hippos, and spot the breaks in the bush where fishing villages of thatched huts stood on the river bank. You could always identify the villages, she said, because of the cluster of needle-thin canoes hanging in the river's current beneath each settlement. She remembered how the boat dropped her off, apparently in the middle of nowhere, only for her to scramble up the muddy river bank and find, half-hidden by towering elephant grass, a steam-train waiting to take its passengers on the next leg of their journey, with a steward, clad in a peaked cap of rail-company livery, anxious to keep to the timetable.

On the wall of our home in a Northamptonshire village she

hung some of the souvenirs she bought from Congolese hawkers. There were brightly coloured crayon pictures of tribal stickmen dancing and hunting against an elegant background of grass huts or canoes. On a rainy day in the British Midlands in the 1970s they took a child's mind far away to equatorial Africa, to a country my mother still cannot bring herself to call anything but 'The Belgian Congo'.

She still has packs of unsent postcards produced in Leopoldville. The cards, printed in 1950s Technicolour, show naive Congolese scenes – tribal hunters in headdresses, jungle elephants glaring at the camera and loincloth-clad fishermen. My mother's view was just as rose-tinted. She knew nothing of the brutality that the Belgians used to maintain their rule, or of the turbulent currents then drawing the Congo towards independence. As a child, I would ask her what had happened to this place where officials stamped her passport with funny French messages in red ink, but she knew little and cared even less.

'A year or so after we passed through, there was all that beastliness in the Congo,' was her understated way of putting it. My route would take me through some of the places she visited in 1958, but when I started seriously planning the journey it was clear I would face a great deal of 'beastliness'.

'It cannot be done. For many years it has been impossible for an outsider to travel through the east of this country.' This doom-laden analysis on the Democratic Republic of Congo, the modern name of the territory colonised by the Belgians, came from Justin Marie Bomboko. We met in his once grand but now tatty apartment in the capital, Kinshasa, formerly Leopoldville. A tidemark of white spittle flecked the crease of his mouth, and his eyes were emotionless behind thick-framed glasses, identical to those worn by his former sponsor, Mobutu Sese Seko. From 1965 until 1997 Mobutu had ruled the Congo as an African emperor, plundering the country's mining revenues and surrounding himself with a wealthy elite, known in Congolese street patois as *Les Grosses Légumes*, a euphemism for Fat Cats. Mr Bomboko was one of the fattest. Twice he had served as Foreign Minister, during the period when Mobutu had the country's name changed to Zaire, and for a long time back in the 1960s this now elderly and frail man was kingmaker in the Congo, chairman of an unelected, executive committee of young men, mostly in their thirties, running a country larger than western Europe.

It was January 2001 and I was visiting the Congo for the first time. I had flown to Kinshasa which lies on the southern bank of the Congo River in the west of the country, to cover the aftermath of the assassination of Laurent Kabila, the rebel who ousted Mobutu in 1997. Diplomats, world leaders and African experts had expressed a degree of optimism about Mr Kabila's arrival, confident that he could do no worse than Mobutu. They were disappointed. Mr Kabila had morphed into the worst type of African dictator – greedy, petty and brutal – and under his reign the Congo's collapse continued. His murder (shot at point-blank range by a bodyguard, who was mown down seconds later by more loyal bodyguards at the presidential palace in Kinshasa) gave me the first real opportunity to sound out the possibility of crossing the Congo.

Even though Mr Bomboko lived in the capital of the Democratic Republic of Congo, technically he had opted out of sovereign Congolese territory. He had taken the precaution of moving inside the Belgian diplomatic compound. When I saw the high security fence and well-armed guards that protected both the embassy and his home from the chaos of Kinshasa, I did not need to ask why.

Mr Bomboko was more than seventy years old when I met him. In a sombre voice, he described, in painstaking detail, the series of rebellions and invasions that had gripped his country for forty years. Listing them took over an hour and by the time he finished his declaiming, the flecks of spittle round his mouth had formed into two distinct splodges.

'The big mistake that Mobutu made was becoming friends with the Hutus to the east of our country.' His voice was steady and dispassionate. 'By allying Congo with the Hutus in the late 1980s and early 1990s, Mobutu laid the foundations for today's crisis.'

Mobutu's relationship with the Hutu leaders of Rwanda went beyond mere friendship. He had been so close to Juvénal Habyarimana, the Hutu president of Rwanda whose assassination in 1994 triggered the Rwandan genocide, that the body of his friend had been flown to Kinshasa for burial. And days before Mobutu himself was ousted, he had the remains of Habyarimana exhumed and cremated, so that he could flee the country with the ashes of his old ally.

'When the genocide ended in Rwanda, the Hutu gunmen responsible for the killings, the interahamwe, were invited by Mobutu to flee into the Congo. They came by the thousand and ten years later they are still there, hiding in the forests near our eastern borders. They are the biggest single source of instability in the country,' Mr Bomboko explained.

It was the presence of those Hutu gunmen after 1994 that led to Mr Kabila's early success in ousting Mobutu, ally of the Hutus. The Tutsi regime that had taken over Rwanda, and driven the Hutu killers into the Congo, were happy to exploit Mr Kabila's ambitions to replace Mobutu. The Tutsi-dominated Rwandan government sent troops, arms and money to support Mr Kabila's insurgency against Mobutu. And Mr Kabila received similar support from Uganda, anxious to silence its own rebel enemies lurking across the border inside the Congo, staging raids into Ugandan territory. With Rwandan and Ugandan military backing, Kabila swept away Mobutu's regime in a few heady months in early 1997. Mobutu fled and a few months later, in September 1997, died a painful death from prostate cancer in Morocco, far from the homeland he had misruled for so long.

Kabila's close relationship with Uganda and Rwanda did not last. Both insisted on keeping troops on the Congolese side of the border, stating that they had not mopped up the rebels they had been so interested in silencing. In reality, the motives of Rwanda and Uganda in maintaining a presence in the Congo were more grubby. They wanted to keep the easy money they were earning from various Congolese mines producing gold, tin and other minerals in the east of the Congo.

Within a year, the relationship between Kabila and his two erstwhile allies, Rwanda and Uganda, had deteriorated into all-out war. Without any meaningful army of his own, Kabila effectively bribed local countries to fight on his behalf. Zimbabwe sent troops to support Kabila, but only as long as Zimbabwean generals were allowed to keep the profits from cobalt and diamond mines in the south of the country. Angola sent troops to help Kabila, but only if deals were agreed to share offshore oil. The war was complex – at one point it drew in the armies of Rwanda, Uganda and Burundi, against the armies of the Congo, Zimbabwe, Chad, Angola and Namibia – and it was very bloody, with a death toll that would eventually exceed four million.

This was the background to Mr Bomboko solemnly shaking his head when I asked him about the possibility of travelling across the country.

'The problem you face is that the country is split in so many parts. The government barely controls the capital, as you can see outside.'

Mr Bomboko did not have to explain further. A few hours earlier I had been dragged out of a car by soldiers in broad daylight and threatened at gunpoint, while my local driver was cuffed viciously about the head with the butt of a rifle. We were only a few yards from the British Embassy, in the city's upmarket diplomatic quarter, but at that time nowhere was safe in the city. The British Ambassador's staff had even readied the motorboat that was kept not just for Sunday jaunts, but as a means of escape. While Leopold staked most of the Congo River basin as his colony, the French claimed a much smaller slice of territory for themselves on the north bank of the river. The former French colony is today known as Republic of the Congo and its capital, Brazzaville, lies just two kilometres from Kinshasa on the other side of the river.

In the chaotic days after Laurent Kabila's death, Kinshasa was a very scary place. Even though he was already dead, his supporters had his body smuggled to Harare on a private jet owned by a friendly Zimbabwean businessman and then made public statements that he was still alive. It was a ploy to buy enough time to arrange a suitable succession, and in the meantime loyalist vigilantes were out on the streets searching for culprits, and looters were helping themselves to whatever they could find. The soldiers were the most dangerous of all. Most of the senior ranks defending Kabila's regime did not even come from Kinshasa, but from his home province of Katanga, almost 2,000 kilometres away to the east. Swahili-speakers by birth, they could not communicate with the capital's Lingala-speaking population. These soldiers were a long way from home and their patron had just been killed – they were scared, jumpy and aggressive.

I had joined the small group of foreign journalists who flew to Kinshasa after news emerged of Kabila's shooting. All scheduled flights were cancelled, so we chartered planes and scrambled for visas. The Congo's reputation made that flight unique, even for seasoned hacks. Instead of the excited chatter and world-weary cockiness that I had experienced among colleagues on other journeys to major news stories, that flight was deafeningly quiet. We sat in silence as the plane dipped down through thick tropical cloud cover and I caught my first glimpse of the Congo River, a wide smear of gun-metal grey under rainy-season skies. Near Kinshasa, the river balloons to twenty kilometres in breadth, a reach still named Stanley Pool after the explorer. The city below us is home to nine million people, but from the air it seemed as small as a riverside village next to the vast expanse of water. I tried to imagine how Stanley felt when, at the end of his three-year-long journey, he reached this sea-like stretch.

My own feelings were perfectly clear as I reached the scruffy arrivals hall at the airport. I was terrified. I can still picture the pudgy face of the airport security official as he spotted a Ugandan visa in my passport. Like the reels of a slot-machine shuddering to a jackpot, his pupils flickered both with suspicion and greed. Uganda was still at war with the Kabila regime and, seeing that I had been there only a few months earlier, the official started whispering to his boss. The only word I could make out was *espion*, spy, but it was enough to make my heart stand still.

I was bundled into a side-room. My passport disappeared and I was left alone. Over the next few hours a series of officials traipsed in and out, alternately threatening and then reassuring me. It was ghastly. In the end, I was forced to pay a 'recovery fee' for my passport, ushered out of the office and told to get lost.

It set the tone of the trip. Even in Africa, the Congo has few rivals for corruption. A hanger-on at the airport jumped into my wreck of a cab before coolly informing me that he was a government-approved minder and must be paid hundreds of dollars for his services. Once I had reached one of only two hotels still functioning for outsiders, I bundled my bags onto the pave-ment at the feet of a security guard and felt bold enough to brush him off. But when it came to the 'journalist's accreditation fee' demanded by officials at the Ministry of Information, I was more feeble. Along with all the other foreign reporters. I had been made to stomp sweatily up to the ministry's seventeenth-floor offices, in a government building where the lift had not worked properly for years, and along with the rest of my colleagues I dutifully handed over hundreds of dollars for my 'press pass' for Kabila's state funeral.

All of this I viewed as par for an African country in crisis. What made that trip so memorable was that never had I been so professionally out of my depth. As a reporter I had worked in

Baghdad during Saddam Hussein's rule, in Sarajevo under Serbian siege and in Algiers when its people were being slaughtered by Muslim fundamentalists, but I have never been as petrified, disorientated and overwhelmed as I was during that first trip to the Congo. None of us could find out who was behind the assassination, why it had happened or what it really meant for the Congo, but at least we were not alone in our ignorance. Nobody seemed to know what was going on – not the local army officers, not the diplomats and certainly not the country's political leadership. Writing now, four years later, there is still no clear account of who killed Kabila. There are plenty of conspiracy theories and rumours: the most colourful suggests that the dictator was killed for welshing on a diamond deal with Lebanese gangsters. But the mystery surrounding Kabila's death remains intact.

Back then, the reporters barely ventured outside Kinshasa's functioning hotels and, when we did, we soon hurried back to swap stories of how we had been detained by rogue army units, had our press passes sold back to us by corrupt officials or been set upon by angry crowds of Congolese people whipped into xenophobic hysteria by the local media.

On Friday 26 January 2001 the Democratic Republic of Congo failed spectacularly to live up to its name when it installed Kabila's son, Joseph, as head of state without bothering with any election. We journalists struggled for information about the new leader. It was almost impossible. We could not even find out his age. Within hours of his accession, I joined all the other foreign reporters scurrying home on the first flight after the funeral, shaking our heads at the chaos in the country and taking solace in the advice of the older, more experienced hands, who said this was quite normal for the Congo.

It was deeply unsettling to be so completely beaten by a story. My journalistic vanity had been pricked and I was too proud to let it pass. Crossing the Congo was now my personal obsession, and it was clear that if the Congolese government could not help, then I would have to get to know some of the rebels.

It took a volcanic eruption to cement my relationship with one of the Congo's most important rebel leaders. I was walking my dogs early one morning in Johannesburg when my mobile phone rang. The echo on the line told me it was a call from a satellite phone, and the booming voice with a heavy French accent told me I was speaking to Adolphe Onusumba, the leader of the main rebel group based in Goma, Congo's most easterly town on its border with Rwanda.

'The volcano has erupted above Goma and the whole town is being consumed. You must come quickly and tell the world we need help.' Adolphe sounded frantic.

Six months earlier I had first approached Adolphe about crossing the Congo. As president of the RCD (*Rassemblement Congolais pour la Démocratie*), the principal pro-Rwanda rebel group involved in the war, he had influence over some of the gunmen active in the east of the country. After the disappointment of my visit to Kinshasa, these were the groups I had to get to know.

Throughout the war he and the other major rebel leaders were flown from time to time to peace talks sponsored by the United Nations. I arranged an appointment with Adolphe during one of his stops in South Africa. It was mid-winter and we met in a modest hotel, where he was being put up by the UN. He was the leader of one of the largest unofficial Congolese militias responsible for atrocities that many describe as war crimes, so I admit I was rather apprehensive. I expected a man with military bearing and a cold demeanour. Instead, the figure who greeted me in the hotel coffee shop was young, jolly and shambling, with rather a friendly smile.

He listened closely as I explained my historical connection to Stanley through the *Telegraph* and how his Congo trip changed Africa. I had already delivered the same pitch to aid workers, journalists and diplomats, so I treated him to my party trick, rolling out an old map of the Congo that I had bought from a hawker in Kinshasa and on which I had traced my rough route all the way from Lake Tanganyika on the country's eastern approaches to its western edge where the Congo River joins the Atlantic.

The map was a handsome thing produced in 1961 by the geographical institute of the Belgian Defence Ministry. Across the Congo reached a red web indicating roads, black dashes for the railways and pale-blue streaks for navigable rivers, the whole thing studded with topographical markings for mines, churches, missions and settlements.

Adolphe bent over the map as I continued to deliver my patter. I was getting into my stride, talking about the historical importance of the trip, when it became apparent that he was not actually listening. He was tracing his forefinger up and down the middle of the map, mumbling to himself. My voice trailed away to nothing and for several minutes I watched him as he concentrated in silence.

Finally he snorted. 'There,' he said, pointing carefully with his fingernail and turning his beaming face up to mine. 'That is where I was born.'

'When were you last there?' I asked as I peered at the minuscule script next to a confluence of Congo tributaries where he was pointing.

'Maybe fifteen years ago. I cannot remember, to be honest. There is nothing there now.'

I found it very moving when he pleaded for a copy of the map. No better map had been produced since 1961, and it seemed to connect him to a lost childhood. He knew the red road system had been reclaimed by the jungle and the mission stations abandoned, but, for a moment at least, the map took him back to a cherished memory of an earlier, less chaotic Congo.

'At this time I cannot guarantee anything. The fighting is too bad and there are too many groups operating there, many of whom answer to no outside authority. But the situation can change, and so let's keep in contact.' In the circumstances, it was the best I could hope for. The leader of the Congo's largest rebel group had not ruled out my trip completely.

When I arrived in Goma six months later to cover the eruption, Adolphe had better things to worry about than my travel plans. Millions of tonnes of molten volcanic rock had glugged in a malodorous slick from the peak of Mount Nyiragongo straight through the town centre. This eruption was not of the explosive, carry-all-before-it sort. It was more sedate, just an endless flow of liquid rock creeping inexorably down the mountainside, burning and smothering everything in its path. You could walk faster than the lava flowed, so few people actually died. They simply made their way to high ground and watched as the lava stream consumed their houses and much of their town, before slopping steamily into Lake Kivu. Goma was built on the shore of the lake as a riviera-style resort for Belgian colonialists, and the lava flow passed through the remains of some of its grandest lakeside villas, with their old boathouses and sun terraces.

By now I was beginning to believe the Congo had some strange hold over bad news. It was somehow no surprise that Africa's worst volcanic eruption in decades should happen here. While the lava flow could have gone in countless other directions from the mountain top, damaging nothing but rainforest, the stream had in fact come straight down the main street of Goma, swallowing the town's Catholic cathedral and cutting the airport runway neatly in two. In July 1994 the town witnessed hellish scenes after an outbreak of cholera among hundreds of thousands of Hutu refugees, who had fled to the town from neighbouring Rwanda when the Tutsis took power. The disease killed so many that bulldozers struggled to dig mass graves quick enough to dispose of the bodies. Atrocities were committed in Goma in 1997 and 1998 when Tutsi soldiers from Rwanda tried to clear Hutu

gunmen from the town's remaining refugee camps, and yet again
this benighted town had been hit.

'I told them this would happen. I told them an eruption was
imminent and it would come through the town centre.'
Dieudonné Wafula sounded like a raving madman when I first
bumped into him among the crowds watching the lava stream. He
was holding a bundle of papers, waving them furiously, so I asked
if I could have a look.

'There it is,' he said, pointing at the top sheet. It was a letter he
had written several months earlier, accurately predicting
Nyiragongo's eruption. 'I sent it to the Americans but they did not
listen, they did not listen.'

Dieudonné was no evangelist. He was the Congo's sole
volcanologist.

I spent the next few days with Dieudonné and his story
enthralled me. He was proof that the Congo had once worked as
a country. In the 1960s and 1970s the education he enjoyed
allowed him to develop into a genuine expert on volcanoes. No
matter that today he lived in appalling conditions in Goma and
went unpaid as he slogged up and down the forested slopes of
Nyiragongo, plotting the levels of its lava lake. In Dieudonné I
saw proof of how sophisticated the Congo had once been.

One day we blagged two seats on a creaking Ukrainian-crewed
UN helicopter as it flew up to the top of the volcano. Dieudonné
peered anxiously out of the porthole windows, taking notes and
marking furiously his home-made sketch of the summit plateau,
but I was more interested in what I could see out to the west. We
were on the Congo's eastern edge and, as the helicopter climbed
higher, I could see nothing but an unbroken spread of vegetation.

I was looking at the Congo's rainforest, one of the natural
wonders of the world. Conservationists describe it as one of the
Earth's lungs, an immense expanse of oxygen-generating green,
matched in size only by the Amazonian rainforest. Explorers
recorded it as one of the most impenetrable and hostile environ-

ments on the planet – as clammy as a pressure cooker, thick with disease, capped by a tree-top canopy too solid for sunlight to penetrate. They recorded it was almost impossible to navigate through. As I peered through the porthole on the helicopter, it stretched all the way to the far horizon and, I knew, a whole lot further beyond. It was a formidable natural barrier and somehow I would have to find a way through it if I was going to cross the Congo.

I flew back to Johannesburg with the Congo squatting on my conscience, refusing to surrender to the stream of colleagues, friends and journalist contacts who said my plan to cross the Congo was doomed.

A couple of years passed. Various African crises came for me to cover, but the Congo was my constant. It reminded me of Philip Larkin's 'Toad' poems that I read as a child. He wrote that for the middle Englander, work was like a toad, sitting on his shoulder, teasing and nagging. My toad was the Congo, and wherever I went the toad was there, working away at me.

The office in my Johannesburg home took on the air of a bunker where I brooded and plotted. Jane would occasionally join me, patiently listening to me droning on about how I planned to tackle the journey, humouring what she half-suspected would always remain a fantasy. On the walls, I hung maps and pictures, trying to match place names used by Stanley with later names from the colonial era and beyond. No corner of the Internet was too remote, as I searched for clues. I visited white-supremacist websites, designed by American racists, in which the Congo was held up as proof of the black man's inferiority. I scoured the sites of missionary organisations, praying I might find a missionary with knowledge of the back roads of eastern Congo. And I discovered a mysterious American scientist who had dared to venture into remotest Congo during the war to continue research into the okapi, a peculiar forest beast that is part-antelope, part-zebra and part-giraffe. There were even websites run by former Belgian colonials forced to leave the Congo forty years ago, where rose-tinted memories of the old days were exchanged.

A stream of second-hand books arrived, ordered on the Internet from dealers all over the world. No matter how obscure, if there was a Congo connection, I was interested. I bought mining manuals with pages of data on Congo's copper production in the 1930s and 1940s; a propaganda puff for Belgian rule in the Congo that painted Leopold as a benign, benevolent force for good in Africa. Much of what I was reading belonged to an age long gone, like the missionary diatribes with the title 'Do Missions Spoil the Natives?'

I discovered I was not the first person to have the idea of following Stanley. In the 1960s an American television journalist had tried an identical crossing of the Congo, but was blocked by war, rebellion and logistical problems. His attitude to journalism was a little different from mine. At one point he described how he not only joined a band of white mercenaries, but armed himself with a rifle and went out on combat patrol. His book made me particularly gloomy. In the four decades since he had failed, every aspect of Congo travel had become harder.

There were setbacks in my research, like the day I received an email from an African explorer who had canoed the headwaters of the Congo decades ago. I approached him to help me with crossing similar territory, but the title of his email told me exactly what he thought of my plan. All it said was 'Death Wish'. Even the *Telegraph* thought the idea too dangerous, refusing to back me in case I was killed. In a formal letter from the paper's Foreign Editor I was told, 'In view of the great dangers involved in the trip, it is not one that I would endorse on behalf of the *Telegraph*.' He later added, in a more personal, hand-written note: 'For God's sake be careful.'

My dream seemed to be log-jammed. The Congo was so large

and so fractious that I could find nobody who could make sense of the entire country. The largest United Nations peacekeeping operation in the world – known by its French acronym MONUC – had been deployed there during the latest war, but it was grounded in a few barracks dotted across the country in places where there had once been towns. It was too dangerous for these peacekeepers to travel overland and they simply flew in, served their time and flew away again.

I refused to give in to the doomsters who sent me newspaper reports written during visits to aid projects in the east of the Congo. The reports were almost always rich in accounts of cannibalism and black magic, mutilation and lawlessness. One of my best friends in Johannesburg took great pleasure in arguing that crossing the Congo today would be more dangerous than when Stanley did it in the 1870s. 'At least the natives back then didn't have Kalashnikovs,' he smirked.

With the help of diplomats, mercenaries, missionaries and aid workers I managed to piece together a picture of the modern Congo. It was not pretty. The entire country had been effectively carved up by three armed factions 'mining' various natural resources, such as diamonds, gold or cobalt.

Mining might convey an image of industry or technology, but I found this was not the case in the Congo. In the so-called 'mines', a brutally primitive process was in place involving what was effectively slave labour clawing minerals from the earth so that they could be shipped to eager cash buyers in the developed world. President Kabila headed what was effectively a cobalt and diamond cartel, while two rival factions (one backed by neighbouring Uganda, the other by Rwanda) divided up the rest of the country's resources. Crudely, Uganda got gold and timber, and Rwanda got tin and coltan – a mineral used in mobile telephones.

These groups were interested in nothing but these 'mines'. They built, ran and protected facilities deep in the forest, using airstrips to export the product and banking their money overseas. Outside the perimeter fence, the rest of the Congo – its roads, towns, schools, railways, ferry boats – rotted in the tropical heat, squabbled over by warring militia. What passes for economic activity in the Congo involves uncompromising (many would say unscrupulous) businessmen paying bribes to gangster politicians in return for a slice of the mining action. I know this because a representative of one of the most uncompromising groups told me so.

'Sure, doing business in the Congo is unconventional, but try to look at it from a strictly business point of view. The fees we pay to the government are no different from taxes paid in other countries. Everything we do is legal to the extent that there is any law in this country. If the regime says we pay for this licence, we pay for the licence. It just so happens the money might be paid in a big, black plastic bag delivered at night to a politician's house.'

Clive was a white Zimbabwean. He was thickset, assured and very well connected within the Kabila regime. Cited in a United Nations report for profiteering from the war in the Congo, he had been forced to spend twelve months clearing his name, arguing (successfully) that he should not be persecuted for the lack of accountability in the Congo's own government. The argument persuaded the UN inspectors, and his name was taken off their proscribed list.

'It would be better if the money we paid in "taxes" went to the people of the Congo, rather than a few unelected members of an unelected regime. But you cannot really blame someone like me for the failings of those that run the Congo.'

I met him through a friend in Johannesburg and it was my first major lucky break. Born in what was then Rhodesia, he was an expert on African history and took great interest in my plan to cross the Congo.

'When I was a child we came up to the Belgian Congo for our holidays. Friends of mine drove all the way from Rhodesia to

Goma for their honeymoon. It was possible to do that in those days. Now things are a bit different and God knows what goes on up in the east of the country, where you want to start. But if there is anything I can do, get in touch.'

His connections to the Kabila regime would be useful if I ever made it through to Lubumbashi, the capital of Katanga province, where Clive's cobalt-mining operation was based, but my biggest problem remained the Congo's chaotic east, where no miner or peacekeeper dared venture. To follow Stanley's route, I would have to travel overland through this dangerous eastern sector for about 500 kilometres from Lake Tanganyika to the headwaters of the Congo River before heading downstream. I knew the river descent would be hard, but the thing that worried me most was this overland section. For months I emailed every aid agency and missionary group, no matter how loose their connection with the Congo, but they all said the same thing: overland travel was simply too dangerous.

In 2002 I had my next lucky break, when a peace deal was signed between the factions who had been fighting since 1998. I got back in touch with Adolphe Onusumba, my rebel contact from Goma, who, under the terms of the treaty, was invited to move to Kinshasa to take part in the transitional national government.

His response was the most encouraging news I had heard since embarking on my Congo project:

Tim,

I think now time has arrive for your trip, because looking at the way the proccess is moving even slow, we can expect something positive to come.

All the best and waiting news from you.

Dr Adolphe ONUSUMBA YEMBA

Vice-Président de l'Assemblée Nationale de la RDC.

I replied immediately, but he urged me to be patient, promising to ask his colleagues in the transitional government, on my behalf, for permission to travel in the east of the country. By the time another year had passed, I had grown tired of waiting for Adolphe to deliver.

While my work as a journalist has taken me to numerous war zones, I have always taken the most cautious route, reducing risk as much as possible. Climbing mountains has always been a passion of mine and I borrow from the language of climbing. Climbers talk of two types of danger – subjective and objective. The subjective is the danger that it is in the hands of the climber to influence – having the right equipment, maintaining the correct level of fitness or skill, gleaning as much information about a target mountain as possible. Climbers aim to reduce the subjective danger as much as they possibly can. Objective danger is different. This is danger from random storms closing in, or an unpredictable break in a piece of equipment. It is a danger over which climbers have no influence. They accept a certain amount of objective danger when they set about a potentially life-threatening route. It is regarded fatalistically. While something can be done about subjective danger, there is nothing that can be done about the second type – it is an occupational hazard.

I apply the same rules to my journalism. I will do everything I can to reduce risk, but if, finally, there is no alternative than to cross an active frontline, even with a likelihood of being shot at, then I am prepared to do it. As long as I know I have reduced all the risks that are in my power to reduce, then I am prepared to accept this secondary type of risk as an occupational hazard.

By mid-2004, I was approaching that stage with the Congo. I had done everything I could to glean advice and information about crossing the country. My notebook was full of contacts, some less savoury than others, and I had waited patiently for the longest lull in the country's fighting for a decade. But it slowly became clear that there was nothing else I could reasonably do. If

I was serious about crossing the Congo, I would have to go there and try. Realising this was a moment of personal release. For so long I had fretted and plotted. Now, all the plotting and fretting were done.

The peace treaty meant that the Congolese national airline was just starting to operate again after years of being grounded. In August 2004 I booked a flight from Johannesburg to the Congo, wrote my first will and kissed Jane goodbye.

2.

The Final Frontier

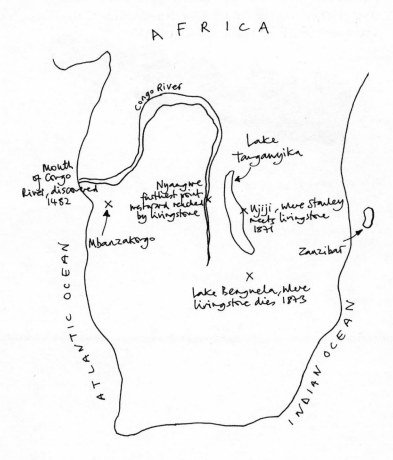

A F R I C A

Congo River

Lake tanganyika

Mouth
of Congo
River, discovered
1482

Nyangwe
furthest point
westward reached
by livingstone

Ujiji, where Stanley
meets livingstone
1871

Mbanzakongo

Zanzibar

ATLANTIC OCEAN

Lake Benguela, where
livingstone dies 1873

INDIAN OCEAN

H.M. Stanley's collapsible rowing boat, the *Lady Alice*

Mystery had swirled around the Congo River since 1482 when Diogo Cão, a Portuguese mariner, became the first white man to set eyes on it. Portugal was the dominant maritime power of the Middle Ages, and it was around Africa that many of its greatest discoveries were made in the search for a sea route to the East Indies. By the time Cão left Lisbon in 1482, previous missions had already discovered the major rivers and headlands of the upper west African coastline, the Gambia River and Sierra Leone River, where the continent bulges westwards into the Atlantic Ocean, and the swampy, mangrove-clogged delta of the Niger River. But as Cão reached further down the coast than any of his predecessors, he came across something sensational.

Shortly after crossing the Equator he watched the Atlantic turn sedgy-brown. Through his eye-glass he made out an immense river mouth, guarded by two long spits of sand reaching far out from the mainland like the mandibles of a giant insect. He knew immediately that the river was greater than any so far discovered in Africa.

Modern hydrographical surveys show the outflow of fresh water from the Congo River is so strong that it has carved out of the seabed a submarine canyon 1,000 metres deep reaching almost 200 kilometres out into the ocean. In the late fifteenth century Cão did not have the benefit of such surveying equipment. He measured the river's force more prosaically – he recorded that the outflow of fresh water was so prodigious that far out to sea from the river's mouth it was possible to drink water straight from the ocean. His discovery was later described by a Portuguese historian:

31

So violent and so powerful from the quantity of its water, and the rapidity of its current, that it enters the sea on the western side of Africa, forcing a broad and free passage, in spite of the ocean, with so much violence, that for the space of twenty leagues it preserves its fresh water unbroken by the briny billows which encompass it on every side; as if this noble river had determined to try its strength in pitched battle with the ocean itself, and alone deny it the tribute which all other rivers in the world pay without resistance.

Cão turned his small caravel towards the river mouth and cautiously nosed his way up Africa's mightiest river. A leadsman at the bow of the vessel reported an immense depth of water, and the boat struggled against the powerful eight-knot current running out to sea. After battling a few kilometres upriver from the mouth, he put ashore on the left or southern bank of the river, and his crew's landing party became the first Europeans ever to set foot on Congolese soil.

Cão's crew reported seeing a group of natives as the boat approached the river bank. One can imagine the suspicion and fear on both sides as the landing party descended over the side of the caravel and headed towards the shore. They took with them a large, stone column or *padrão*, which the Portuguese explorers routinely used as a sort of calling card. Similar *padrãos* were used to mark the extent of other journeys by Portuguese explorers, but the wording of the declaration inscribed at the top of the column left by Cão is intriguing:

In the year 6681 of the World and in that of 1482 since the birth of our Lord Jesus Christ, the most serene, the most excellent and potent prince, King John II of Portugal did order this land to be discovered and this pillar of stone to be erected by Diogo Cão, an esquire in his household.

The planting of the *padrão* was not a moment of colonisation or acquisition. The contrast between Cão's behaviour and that of the outsiders who arrived subsequently in the Congo is stark.

Some of the natives came forward to speak with Cão. Members of his crew knew dialects from further up the African coast, but they had never heard words like those spoken by these river people. Cao heard the name Kongo being repeated. Following the pattern of other African groups, they explained they were the BaKongo people and called their language KiKongo. Inland, they said, was the capital of their tribe, MbanzaKongo, where there lived a powerful leader or king, the ManiKongo.

When Cão asked them about the river, they replied that in their language it was called *nzere*, or *nzadi*, meaning 'the river that swallows all rivers'. It remains a wonderfully appropriate name. The main river reaches almost 4,500 kilometres across Africa, draining every marsh, lake and watercourse in a river basin larger than the subcontinent of India. Three of the Congo River's tributaries are longer than the Rhine, western Europe's longest river. The Congo River is fed by snow melt from the freezing summits of volcanoes in central Africa, floodwater spilling from Lake Tanganyika, Africa's oldest and deepest lake, and rainwater from the second-largest rainforest on the planet.

By the time it reaches the sea, 'the river that swallows all rivers' pumps out more fresh water into the ocean than any other river in the world except the Amazon. It has another extraordinary feature. Unlike any other major river system, the outflow of the Congo remains steady all year round. Other rivers – even mighty ones like the Nile and the Amazon – have dry and wet seasons when the flow dips and rises, but the Congo River is relentless. Its catchment straddles the Equator, meaning that all year round at least part of the river system is experiencing a wet season, so at its mouth the flow is both prodigious and permanent.

After his first encounter with Congolese people, we know that Cão explored a short distance up the river. He did not reach the impassable rapids that lie 120 kilometres from the Atlantic, but the enormous flow of water and the wide, navigable channel dotted with large, bush-covered islands convinced him he had found an artery reaching deep into Africa.

Cão decided to make contact with the ManiKongo. He chose four crew members – Africans pressed into service on his ship from coastal communities further north and baptised as Christians in Portugal – and dispatched them as emissaries to the ManiKongo. They were to be guided by tribesmen from the river mouth, who warned Cão that the round trip to the kingdom's capital would take weeks. So after dressing the four ambassadors in the finest clothes he could spare and giving them gifts to offer as tribute to the ManiKongo, he sailed back out into the Atlantic and turned his ship south.

He pushed on a further 500 kilometres, before turning north again, clearly anxious to find out what his four crew members had learned. He was disappointed to find they were not there. He waited for a few days but, growing impatient, decided on drastic action. He abducted four natives, sent a message to the ManiKongo that he would only free them in exchange for his four crew members and headed home.

It was a clumsy start to the Congo's relationship with the outside world, but not as cruel as it might at first seem. The four Congolese were treated well and when the ship reached Lisbon in 1484 the court of the Portuguese monarch, King John II, showed none of the assumed superiority of white over black that would characterise the relationship between Africa and the outside world for so many centuries. The four men were given rooms in the palace, groomed, fed and clothed as royalty and immersed in Portuguese life. They were taught the language, taken on tours around the kingdom and exposed to Christianity in its fullest pomp. Cão's discovery of a great river on the west African coast, and his account of its potentially rich African kingdom, whetted

John's appetite, but instead of using force of arms to secure a Portuguese foothold there, his strategy would be one of persuasion, not coercion. By impressing these first Congolese visitors with the wealth and sophistication of a modern European kingdom, John would forge a link with the newly discovered kingdom on the edge of the known world.

It worked well. The emissaries were shipped back to the Congo, where they made their way eagerly to the kingdom's capital, dressed in European clothes and carrying a vast stock of gifts as a gesture of goodwill for the ManiKongo. On their arrival they found that just as they had been well treated by their new patrons, so had the four crew members whom Cão had left as pro-tem diplomats. The ManiKongo wanted to take the relationship with Portugal further, so he allowed the four outsiders to leave, accompanied by four new ambassadors of his own people. This time, he would be represented not by tribesmen plucked randomly from a riverside village, but by the sons of senior members of his court, led by a prince called Nsaku.

They carried with them the finest gifts the kingdom could offer – ivory and cloth woven from raffia palms – and showed themselves willing to embrace the religion of the white man. When these newcomers reached Lisbon, John himself attended Nsaku's baptism, where the African prince was christened Lord John of the Forest. Like the earlier party of Congolese guests in Lisbon, Nsaku was treated royally and shown all the majesty Portugal could muster, before being put on a ship heading back home to forge the next bond between Portugal and the newly discovered kingdom of Congo.

He did not make it home, but was killed by an outbreak of plague that struck the flotilla shortly after leaving Lisbon. In retrospect, it seems an accurate omen for the relationship between the two peoples. The Congolese were willing to embrace the Portuguese, only to discover later they had unleashed a force that would destroy them from within.

*

The next two decades marked the Golden Age of relations between Portugal and the people of a territory that European cartographers were already calling the Congo. In 1491 the first Portuguese visitors finally reached MbanzaKongo, the capital, after the long sea journey to the river mouth and a three-week overland journey inland from the coast. The ManiKongo, who was called Nzinga a Nkuwu, staged a royal welcome that fits the most lavish stereotype of a first meeting between white and black. Surrounded by his various wives, princes and courtiers, the ManiKongo sat on a wooden throne inlaid with ivory, which had been placed on a raised platform. He was dressed in cloth woven from raffia, and the Portuguese visitors noticed that he was also wearing a piece of damask, a remnant of the tribute left for him by Cão a decade earlier. In a gesture of welcome to the leader of the Portuguese group, he bent down, picked up a handful of dust and pressed it against his chest and then against the visitor. It marked the start of a brief alliance of equals.

What we know about the kingdom of the Congo, we know from the Portuguese. With no written language, Congolese history was maintained by oral tradition, and the Portuguese used this to construct a lavish picture of a vast kingdom covering thousands of square kilometres, with a population of several million. But it is important to remember that this history was written with hindsight. The first written account of the 1491 visit was assembled a hundred years after it happened.

Drawings by early European explorers present the capital, MbanzaKongo, as any European city, with large, multi-storey buildings laid out along tidy streets, leading up to a crenellated castle atop a rocky outcrop overlooking a river. This was fanciful nonsense. If you go to the site today, it is a long way from any river and the ground is not high enough to dominate the surrounding area. No European-style castle ever existed.

Some modern historians describe the Congo of old as one of

Africa's greatest kingdoms, although there is no way this can be verified. With little historical material on rival African kingdoms in the area, it is impossible to gauge the Congo's place in comparison to other local communities. But it was the first African kingdom below the Equator discovered by the white man, and the Portuguese presumed to talk up its importance, not least because for a brief period towards the end of the fifteenth century they regarded it as Europe's most significant discovery anywhere in the world.

Something that is certain is that the kingdom of the Congo was not at peace. Raiding parties from neighbouring tribal groups were a constant menace, attacking villages, claiming outlying territory and slaughtering the king's people. And we know the king sent out expeditions of his own warriors to do the same in retaliation. It is safe to conclude that the king's willingness to welcome the Portuguese was partly due to his zeal to acquire the modern weaponry the Portuguese brought with them.

He swiftly agreed to accept the religion offered by the first Portuguese visitors in 1491. Within weeks, an elaborate ceremony of conversion was held and Nzinga a Nkuwu was christened King John. Only a short time later he dispatched his first war party, supported by armed Portuguese soldiers. They routed their enemies, forging, through war, an initially warm relationship between Europe and the Congo.

The Congo's status as Portugal's greatest discovery did not last long. Less than a decade after Cão reached the Congo River, another Portuguese mariner, Bartolomeu Dias, went ever further south to discover the first sea route from Europe to the Indies by rounding the heel of Africa. Dias encountered such rough weather that he called it the Cape of Storms, but the Portuguese authorities soon changed the name to reflect the great economic opportunity it represented. They called it the Cape of Good Hope, close to where Cape Town stands today. The Congo's output of the occasional shipment of ivory or raffia could not compete with the huge volume of silks and spices available in Asia and, in the face of commercial competition, the Portuguese soon found another asset they could take from the Congo – slaves.

Slavery was a long-established practice among African tribes. Any raiding party that successfully attacked a neighbour would expect to return with slaves. But what made the Portuguese demand for slaves different was its scale. The simultaneous discovery of the Americas by European explorers created an apparently limitless demand for labour to work on the plantations of the New World, and in Europe's African toeholds slavery was turned overnight from a cottage industry into a major, global concern.

The effect on the Congo was devastating. The plunder of people started out on a small scale in the early 1500s, with Portuguese traders paying Congolese warriors for the occasional slave they brought back with them from raids. But as the market value of slaves soared, the whole economic dynamic changed. Raiding parties would set off inland just to fill ships that were sent from Portugal to transport slaves across the Atlantic Ocean to the New World.

The ManiKongo's realm felt the impact immediately. Junior chiefs arranged deals directly with Portuguese middlemen, in exchange for arms and money, and within a short time the king's traditional power base was undermined. The Congolese royal family had done everything asked of them by the Portuguese, adopting the religion of the visitors and signing peace treaties, but suddenly they found the influence of their foreign allies was destroying their society from within. John, the first ManiKongo to be baptised a Christian, had been succeeded by a son who was even more enthusiastic about the Portuguese. He had taken the name Affonso, learned fluent Portuguese and adopted European customs with zeal, even arranging for his own son, Henrique, to travel from the Congo to Rome where he was installed as the first black bishop. It would be hundreds of years before the second.

Educated and literate, Affonso wrote letter after letter to the royal family in Lisbon begging them to bring a halt to the chaos caused by the slavers. The letters were often intercepted by slavers and not delivered. But even in the face of growing evidence of Portuguese duplicity, Affonso refused to give up his faith in the common Christian decency of the outsiders. In 1526 he wrote again to the Portuguese monarch:

> The excessive freedom given by your factors and officials to the men and merchants who are allowed to come to this Kingdom . . . is such . . . that many of our vassals do not comply. We can not reckon how great the damage is, since the above-mentioned merchants daily seize our subjects, sons of the land and sons of our noblemen and vassals and relatives . . . Thieves and men of evil conscience take them because they wish to possess the things and wares of this Kingdom . . . They grab them and cause them to be sold; and so great, Sir, is their corruption and licentiousness that our country is being utterly depopulated . . . to avoid this, we need from your Kingdoms no other than priests and people to teach in schools, and not other goods but wine and flour for the holy sacrament . . . It is our will that in these kingdoms there should not be any trader in slaves nor market for slaves.

Affonso's forlorn plea, couched in the language taught by the outsider and invoking the spiritual decency demanded by the outsider, was in vain. By the time he died in the late sixteenth century his kingdom was close to collapse, and the region around the mouth of the Congo River turned into a wasteland, plundered by slavers and their ruthless, well-armed African agents. The Portuguese had been followed by slavers from other European nations, including Britain and Holland, who roamed up and down the coastline of west Africa filling the holds of their ships with human cargo. Between the late sixteenth century when the transatlantic slave trade began and the late nineteenth century when European nations finally banned it, the best estimate is that twelve million Africans were forced on board ships and the Congo River mouth was, throughout that entire period, one of the principal sources of slaves.

Centuries after it all began, when I visited Sierra Leone, I found evidence of the dominant role played by the Congo in the slave trade. Sierra Leone lies on Africa's western coast, more than 1,000 kilometres north of the Congo River mouth. It was created in the early nineteenth century by Britain after it banned slavery, and was largely populated by slaves freed by the British after they were intercepted by the Royal Navy while being shipped across the Atlantic. In the twenty-first century the locals in Sierra Leone use only one name for the slaves who were brought to the country. They are known as the Congo people.

The secret of the 'the river that swallows all rivers' remained hidden throughout this turbulent period. In the brief Golden Age, Portugal launched a few small expeditions inland from the mouth of the river, but they all failed to make any significant progress and most were lost without being heard of again. In the era of industrial slavery, the only Europeans who reached the Congo were not interested in exploring as long as the coastal African leaders kept up the flow of slaves. To solve the mystery of the Congo, geographical science would have to wait almost four centuries, until the late nineteenth century and the wave of mainly British explorers sent from London by the African Association, the body that later became the Royal Geographical Society.

African exploration was the Final Frontier of this age, attracting chancers, heroes and eccentrics on journeys that promised fame and danger in equal measure. In 1816 an officer of the Royal Navy, Captain James Kingston Tuckey, tried to unlock the Congo by sailing up the river from the Atlantic. He hoped not just to chart the lower, navigable stretch, but to push on overland beyond the cataracts first recorded by the Portuguese. His expedition was a disaster. After mooring his two ships near the lowest reach of the rapids, he continued on foot, barely making it halfway along the 300-kilometre stretch of cataracts before disease and malnutrition ravaged his expedition. Only twenty-seven of the fifty-one-member expedition survived and the charts that the survivors brought back to London were inaccurate and confused.

The focus shifted to the other side of the continent, to the island of Zanzibar in the Indian Ocean, which lay just a few kilometres off the coast of East Africa, but which was claimed by Arabs. Originally from Oman, at the mouth of the Persian Gulf, Arab sailors had been probing down the east coast of Africa at about the same time the Portuguese had been probing down the west. Like the Portuguese, these Arab outsiders settled on slaves as the most valuable commodity offered by the African territories, so the Arabs had started to capture and trade slaves, before shipping them back to Oman and other Arab city states in the Gulf.

But there was one big difference with the Portuguese slavers – the Arabs actually went on the slaving expeditions themselves. On their safe island fortress of Zanzibar, they would assemble armed expeditions before crossing to the African mainland and heading inland. It took more than a century, but as they emptied the coastal plains of potential slaves they probed deeper and deeper, setting up a network of footpaths and trading stations that eventually reached halfway across the continent.

Stories of immense inland lakes, snow-capped mountains and huge rivers filtered back through this network to Zanzibar and from there, via visiting British seamen, to London and the Royal Geographical Society. Its members sent a series of expeditions to the island with the deliberate intention of piggybacking on the Arab network of tracks and trading stations across Africa. One by one, the mysteries of African geography were being solved by expeditions launched from Zanzibar. The source of the Nile was traced; the Great Lakes were charted; and the first contacts were made with the tribal kingdoms of central Africa. Early Victorian explorers, such as Richard Francis Burton and John Hanning Speke, turned Zanzibar into the Cape Canaveral of its day, a launch pad for numerous expeditions into the unknown heart of Africa. These explorers became so famous that when one of them, Livingstone, went missing in the late 1860s, James Gordon Bennett, editor of the populist American newspaper *The New York Herald*, spotted the potential for a journalistic coup. Stanley had worked for Bennett for several years, establishing himself as the newspaper's best foreign correspondent. Stanley later described the briefing he received from his editor:

> Draw a thousand pounds now; and when you have gone through that, draw another thousand, and when that is spent, draw another thousand, and when you have finished that, draw another thousand, and so on; but FIND LIVINGSTONE!

Born a bastard in the Welsh market town of Denbigh, Stanley was a cocky chancer. Biographies have made flamboyant claims: that he was a fantasist incapable of telling truth from fiction, or a masochistic homosexual who pleasured in the hardships of African travel, or a sadistic racist. I have come to see him in more simplistic terms, a man from a wretched background who sought wealth and status through one of the most high-profile, lucrative, but risky career paths of his time, African exploration.

He was born on 28 January 1841 and christened John Rowlands after the father he never met, an alcoholic farmhand who drank himself to death. His mother, Elizabeth Parry, was an unmarried, eighteen-year-old housemaid at the time of his birth, who left her new baby in the care of her father and fled to work in London. After a childhood being bounced between the care of relatives, foster homes and the workhouse, in the late 1850s he worked his passage across the Atlantic on board the *Windermere*, a coastal packet ship, to New Orleans, where he charmed his way into the household of a local businessman, Henry Hope Stanley. The businessman effectively adopted the Welshman, providing him with a job and home. As a tribute to his benefactor, the young man took a new name, Henry Stanley, adding the middle name Morton some years later.

Stanley fought for both sides in the American Civil War. He started as a soldier in the Confederate army from the south, but after being taken prisoner by the Yankees he did what was then quite common and promised to fight for the northern army in exchange for his freedom. With the war over, he began a career as a journalist covering the wars of the late 1860s between Native Americans and the early American pioneers pushing westwards. This was the height of the Wild West era, and Stanley contributed a key part to its mythology after he met James Hickok, a tracker and frontiersman. The profile he wrote of 'Wild Bill' Hickok added significantly to one of the iconic names of the era.

His reports earned him a place with the *Herald* as a war correspondent. His first major commission from the paper took him to Africa, as a correspondent attached to a British expeditionary force deployed to Abyssinia. En route to the frontline, his ship stopped in Suez, where he made a point of befriending the officer in charge of the city's only telegraph link to western Europe. Money changed hands in what turned out to be the most prescient of bribes. On the way back from the frontline, Stanley had a copy of his report smuggled to the officer in Suez, who duly telegraphed it back to the London offices of the *Herald*. The line then stopped working for five days, with the result that Stanley had scooped not just his colleagues, but the British Army as well. The official military dispatches had not yet been sent, meaning that the civil servants of the War Office in Whitehall first learned of the outcome of the Abyssinian campaign from Stanley's account, printed in an American newspaper.

Stanley had to show the same chutzpah on his 1871–2 expedition to find Livingstone. The Royal Geographical Society had already sent a number of unsuccessful relief missions to try to find Livingstone, but nothing had been heard from him since 1866. Stanley followed the established explorer's route to Zanzibar, but as he assembled an expedition party there he concealed the real motive of his trip. The RGS had many friends in Zanzibar and they would have sought to block any freelance attempt to track their man.

Stanley was right to be suspicious of some of the stuffier attitudes within the RGS. After finding Livingstone in November 1871 at the small settlement of Ujiji on the eastern shore of Lake Tanganyika, where the 'Doctor Livingstone, I presume?' greeting scene was played out, the two men spent four months together. But Stanley could not persuade Livingstone to return to Zanzibar. So he returned by himself, carrying a bundle of thirty letters and a journal written by Livingstone as proof that he had found the explorer. This was not enough to silence the sniping from many senior members of the RGS. They leaked stories to the press demanding that handwriting experts analyse the letters Stanley 'claimed' to have been written by Livingstone and sneered that Stanley was just a newspaperman, not a professional explorer.

'There is something of the comic,' ran a piece in *The Spectator*, 'in the newspaper correspondent who, in the regular exercise of his profession, moved neither by pity, nor love of knowledge, nor by desire of adventure, but by an order from Mr Bennett, coolly plunges into the unknown continent to interview a lost geographer.' But the thing that appeared to gall the British explorers' elite most was that Livingstone had been found not by a British rescue party, but by an American one. The nationalistic chauvinism was captured perfectly by a *Punch* cartoon from August 1872, showing Livingstone comfortably reclining over a map of Africa in a hammock made from the Stars and Stripes.

All this delighted Stanley's employers at the *Herald*. It printed every detail of Stanley's trip, crowing at the achievement of the American mission and pouring scorn on various failed attempts by rival British missions. Stanley's fame mushroomed, with British publishers Sampson Low, Marston & Company paying him an advance of £50,000 – a record sum for a travel book – for his 700-page account of the trip, and after his return to London he was summoned to a personal audience with Queen Victoria. When the book came out it broke all existing sales records and Stanley crossed the Atlantic to give a series of lectures, which exploited unashamedly all the public prejudices about Africa. One of the lecture advertisements boasted:

> Costumed, armed and equipped as he was when pursuing his arduous journey into Africa and accompanied by the little native African – Kalulu! He will also display the flags, spears and other accoutrements worn by natives of Central Africa who formed part of his expedition.

Even though Stanley was now richer and more famous than he could ever have imagined possible, the sniping of his critics unsettled him. One of the most difficult trials for a journalist is how to follow success. The pressure and expectation to match previous achievements is huge, and for Stanley there was only one possible goal that could outshine his Livingstone coup: Stanley would map the Congo.

Livingstone never returned to Britain after his famous encounter with Stanley, instead continuing to explore the malarial marshlands that straddle what is today the border between Zambia and the Congo. Years of African exploration had weakened his body's defences and in May 1873, his sixty-year-old body racked by disease and hunger, Livingstone died in an African hut on the swampy shore of Lake Bengwelu. He was laid to rest in Westminster Abbey, his coffin carried by eight pall-bearers led by Stanley. The next day, Stanley approached the editor of the *Telegraph* with his idea.

His primary employer, James Gordon Bennett at the *Herald*, had begun to show signs of jealousy at Stanley's fame after the Livingstone scoop, and commissions for work from his American employer had started to dry up. Artfully playing one paper off against another, Stanley approached the *Telegraph* with his plan to complete the map of Africa, framing it as a mission to finish Livingstone's work. He called into the paper's Fleet Street offices and asked to speak with the editor, Sir Edwin Arnold. It must have been quite a moment for the editor to have the greatest media celebrity of the age walk in off the street to suggest a story idea. I can imagine the excitement in the office as word spread among the clerks, reporters and secretaries that the man who scooped the world over Livingstone was inside the editor's office.

Stanley later described the exchange he had with Sir Edwin.

'Could you, and would you, complete the work? And what is there to do?'

'The western half of the African continent is still a white blank.'

'Do you think you can settle all this, if we commission you?'

'While I live, there will be something done. If I survive the time required to perform all the work, all shall be done.'

Livingstone had left Stanley one important clue. The Victorian explorers starting out from Zanzibar had mapped much of Africa's eastern half, but had barely touched on the western half of the continent, the catchment area for the Congo River system. Livingstone himself had come closest to solving the mystery while trekking through the bush savannah to the west of Lake Tanganyika in 1871. As with the other Western explorers, he was mainly following trails blazed by Arab slavers from Zanzibar, but unlike other Westerners who stopped at the lake, he went beyond, eventually coming across a huge river running northwards. Known by the local tribesmen as the Lualaba, it was plausible that this was connected to the Congo River, which, Livingstone knew from the Portuguese maps, joined the Atlantic thousands of kilometres away to the north and west.

Livingstone was sceptical about the Congo connection. The upper Lualaba was as far as the Arab slavers had ventured from Zanzibar in a westerly direction and they knew nothing about where the river ended up. The Arabs reported that the river tribes were particularly vicious and hostile, and various attempts by the slavers to journey down the river had failed. Livingstone was the first white man to see the Lualaba, but its northward trajectory convinced him it could not be connected to the Congo River and he concluded that it must be a previously unknown tributary of the Nile.

Livingstone had spoken at length with Stanley about the Lualaba during the four months they spent together back in 1871. As he prepared to venture into the 'white blank' west of Lake Tanganyika, Stanley knew that exploring this river would be the key to the success of his expedition and, in honour of his old patron, he started to refer to it not as the Lualaba, but as the Livingstone River.

Knowing that Bennett would not risk being outdone by a rival British newspaper, Stanley skilfully persuaded the *Telegraph* to back his venture with £6,000 and used this to leverage exactly the same amount from Bennett. He needed the money because unlike explorers such as Livingstone, who travelled light, carrying barely more than a change of clothes and a Bible, Stanley approached African travel like a military deployment. His party would be heavily armed and equipped with the best navigational technology that Victorian London could offer, including the latest surveying instruments – three chronometers that were to be carried in their own special cases packed with cotton wool –

and the most modern medicines to protect against tropical disease.

The crowning glory of the expedition's kit was Stanley's brainchild, a collapsible boat commissioned from a Thames boat-builder, James Messenger of Teddington, to be made from Spanish chestnut. Twelve metres long, the vessel would break down into five sections that could be carried by bearers through the African bush and launched on the various lakes and rivers that he knew he would encounter. He named her the *Lady Alice*, in honour of his American fiancée, Alice Pike, and then set about recruiting other members of his team.

Stanley's fame was so great that when the two newspapers announced his next African adventure, he was inundated with replies. He received a total of 1,200 letters from 'colonels, captains, midshipmen and mechanics'. Stanley was scornful of them all:

> They all knew Africa, were perfectly acclimatised, were quite sure they would please me, would do important services, save me from any number of troubles by their ingenuity and resources, take me up in balloons or by flying carriages, make us all invisible by their magic arts, or by the 'science of magnetism' would cause all savages to fall asleep while we might pass anywhere without trouble.

In the end, Stanley took just three white assistants, all men of lower social standing who would not pose any risk of challenging his authority as leader. They were Frederick Barker, a clerk at the Langham Hotel where Stanley was staying in London, and two brothers, Francis and Edward Pocock, who worked as crew on the luxury yacht owned by the editor of the *Telegraph* and moored on the River Medway near Maidstone.

As well as human companions, Stanley took two mastiffs, Castor and Captain, which had been presented to him as gifts, and three other dogs: a retriever called Nero, a bulldog called Bull and a bull terrier called Jack, which Stanley adopted from the Battersea Dogs' Home.

It took six months for Stanley to complete his preparations for the journey and to reach his starting point in Zanzibar. Finally, on the morning of 17 November 1874, the expedition column gathered on a sandy beach track on Africa's east coast and stirred to the sound of Edward Pocock's bugle. Consisting of 352 bearers, some carrying bundles of supplies and others sections of boat, it stretched for more than a kilometre and bringing up the rear came the four white men, mounted on asses, with the five dogs padding along by the side.

Stanley noted that most of the bearers smoked cannabis, which made progress slow. By the end of the first day the column had moved only a few kilometres and Castor, the bigger of the two mastiffs, had already died from heat exhaustion. It was an inauspicious start to the most ambitious expedition in the history of African exploration.

3.

Cobalt Town

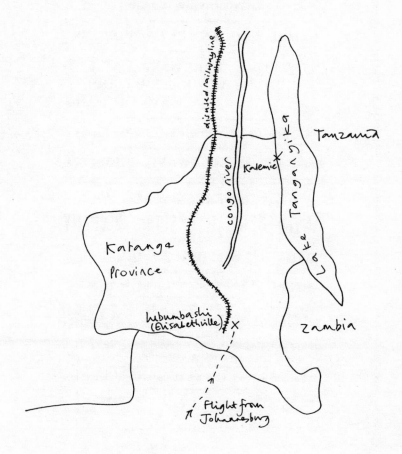

Advertisements from *The Guide to South and East Africa (for the Use of Tourists, Sportsmen, Invalids and Settlers)*, 1915

The airline that was to fly me to the Democratic Republic of Congo in August 2004 was as rickety as the country's latest peace deal. Hewa Bora had been cobbled together from the remnants of various bankrupt versions of the national carrier – Congo Airlines and Zaire Airlines – and although the flight I was waiting for was a scheduled one from Johannesburg to Lubumbashi, the Congo's second city and capital of the south-eastern province of Katanga, there was something about the behaviour of the ground crew and my fellow passengers that suggested it was anything but routine.

A middle-aged Congolese man, hoping to make it to Lubumbashi, spotted my concern as I winced at the check-in muddle. He tried to reassure me. 'I have family here in South Africa, but whenever I travel with Hewa Bora I never know for sure if the plane will take off, or even if there is a plane. It really is a Maybe Airline – Maybe You Get There, Maybe You Don't.'

I waited patiently, watching the ebb and flow of the passengers' mood. One minute they seemed happy, as a female member of staff in Hewa Bora uniform – an elegant blue cotton wrap spotted with yellow teardrops – checked the name of the person at the front of the queue against the manifest. But then the same member of staff would get up from her chair and disappear from view, prompting groans of frustration from the crowd. The flight was not full, but my fellow passengers all seemed to be carrying unfeasibly large amounts of luggage, mostly electrical goods like televisions and CD players, wrapped in the woven-plastic, tricolour bags of red, white and blue that you see all over the developing world.

Against this bulky display, my own luggage seemed rather meagre. I had a green rucksack packed with clothing, bedding and a mosquito net, and two shoulder bags for my notebooks, camera, laptop computer and satellite telephone. I wanted to keep it as light as possible so that it could be carried on foot if need be, so the only book I brought with me was Stanley's account of his journey, *Through the Dark Continent*. I had read it several times, but if my journey was successful I wanted to be able to make a direct comparison between what he found in the late nineteenth century and what I found in the early twenty-first.

My first problem was how to reach the spot where Stanley arrived in the Congo in September 1876. He had been following the established route of Arab slavers across what is now the east African country of Tanzania, before crossing Lake Tanganyika by boat and arriving in the Congo at the village of Mtowa on the lake's western shore. Under the Arabs, Mtowa developed into a large centre for the trans-shipment of slaves and ivory. Its name is not to be found on modern maps of the Congo, but I had been able to establish that it lies about thirty kilometres north of Kalemie, a once-prosperous port set up by the Belgians on the lake. Fifty years ago it was possible to reach Kalemie by rail, road and ferry, but today its only regular connection with the outside world is a weekly shuttle flight arranged by the United Nations peace-keeping mission, MONUC, to serve Kalemie's small garrison of peacekeepers. The shuttle flight leaves from Lubumbashi, capital of the Congo's Katanga province, and a UN administrator had promised that if I made it to Lubumbashi, I could take my place on a waiting list for the trip to Kalemie.

The chaos at the check-in desk in Johannesburg took hours to sort out, but I was in the wonderful position of being under no time pressure. Whenever my journalism has taken me overseas, time has always been of crucial importance, a situation made worse by twitchy foreign editors, deadlines and competitive colleagues. But this time I faced no such constraints. For my attempt to cross the Congo I was entirely on my own. It was pleasantly liberating and as time passed at the airport I was happy to people-watch, trying to guess the nationality of the one other white person on the flight, or why an Asian lady was travelling solo to the Congo.

Johannesburg International Airport is one of the great hubs of modern African travel, a first-world airport offering flights to some of the rougher third-world destinations. As I headed to the gate for the Lubumbashi flight, I looked at the well-stocked boutiques and felt the downwash from the powerful air-conditioning, and wondered when I would next experience the same.

The Hewa Bora cabin crew had laid out copies of a Kinshasa newspaper, *L'Avenir*, on the seats in business class and I snaffled one as I shoulder-barged my way to my economy seat. It was more of a samizdat newsletter than a newspaper, comprising four pages amateurishly printed on a single folded sheet of very cheap, coarse paper. The ink came off on my fingers and there were no decipherable photographs. But I could decipher the paper's tone, a tone that was rabidly anti-Rwandan. There were various articles claiming that the paper had seen documentary evidence proving Rwanda was about to attack the Congo and there were vicious denunciations of various pro-Rwandan Congolese rebels, such as my old contact, Adolphe Onusumba. Under the terms of the 2002 peace deal that was meant to have ended the Congo's war, all the major rebel groups, including the pro-Rwandan ones, had taken their place in a transitional, power-sharing government in Kinshasa. The arrangement was fragile and, as I could see from the deeply xenophobic tone of *L'Avenir*, the fault line separating Rwandans from Congolese remained explosive.

Since the 1994 genocide, Rwanda has been regarded by many outsiders as a tiny, frail country bullied by its larger neighbours. This is a grossly inaccurate generalisation. With a government now dominated by Tutsis, Rwanda punches way above its weight in regional affairs. There are clear parallels with Israel, another small country of people driven by the memory of mass murder committed against them to dominate its neighbours militarily, and the neighbour that Rwanda bosses most is the Democratic Republic of Congo. On a map, tiny Rwanda is overshadowed by the vastness of the DRC, but for the past ten years it has been Rwanda that has loomed over the DRC. In 1996 Rwanda's Tutsi-dominated forces invaded the country and orchestrated the ousting of Mobutu the following year, and in 1998 the same forces turned on Laurent Kabila, the man they had installed as Mobutu's replacement, starting the conflict that has so far cost four million lives.

For many Congolese, the Tutsis who now rule Rwanda play the role of bogeymen. Tutsis are taller and thinner than their ethnic neighbours, with finer features, and I heard many Congolese cursing them for 'not looking like us'. There were plenty of less polite insults. The Tutsi/non-Tutsi divide is one of central Africa's great social divisions and it was to have enormous impact on my attempt to cross the Congo.

Eight weeks before I flew to Lubumbashi, an ethnic Tutsi Congolese warlord broke the terms of the 2002 peace treaty when he mobilised a force and launched an attack on the Congolese town of Bukavu that sits on the border between DRC and Rwanda. His motives were unclear, but the result fitted into the depressing pattern of central African turmoil. After thirty-six hours of savagery, scores of people lay dead, thousands had fled their homes and the entire eastern sector of the country was pushed to a state close to war. The Congolese authorities were quick to blame the Tutsi-led regime across the border in Rwanda, accusing them of arming and protecting the rebels. The accusations were soon followed by retaliatory attacks from Congolese troops on groups linked to Rwanda's Tutsis. I knew that the relationship between the DRC and Rwanda was tense, but the racist bile I read in *L'Avenir* revealed the depth of enmity between the two sides. All I could do as the plane made the three-hour crossing from South Africa over Zimbabwe and Zambia en route to

Lumumbashi was pray that some sort of calm would be re-established before I reached eastern Congo.

If you look at a map of the Congo, you see that the country appears to have grown a vestigial tail around its bottom right-hand corner, known as the Katanga Panhandle. On the surface there seems no clear reason for this outcrop of Congolese territory surrounded on three sides by its southern neighbour, Zambia. It is below the soil that you find the reason why the early Belgian colonialists in the late nineteenth century staked the territory so obstinately, in defiance of British pioneers probing northwards from what was then Rhodesia. The panhandle includes some of the richest deposits of copper, cobalt and uranium on the planet, a geological quirk that the early Belgian colonialists identified more smartly than their British counterparts.

While Congo's other provinces have large diamond and gold deposits, it was mainly on Katanga's mineral wealth that the Belgian colony grew rich in the mid-twentieth century. The uranium for the atom bombs dropped by America on Hiroshima and Nagasaki came from a mine in Katanga, and it was Katanga's vast copper deposits that really powered the colony's growth when the reconstruction of Europe and Japan after the Second World War drove a surge in demand for copper. Most of the mineral profits from Katanga were taken by the Belgians, repatriated to Brussels and divided among shareholders from various private corporations, or *Sociétés*, created by the colonial authorities. But some of the profits were reinvested in Katanga, to build a number of mines, processing plants and factories, serviced by new towns built out of the virgin bush and connected by a web of roads and railways. By the mid-twentieth century Katanga was the most developed province in all of the Congo.

The blessing of Katanga's mineral wealth became its curse when Belgium granted independence to the Congo on 30 June 1960. While maintaining the illusion of handing over a single country to the black Congolese, the authorities in Brussels secretly backed the secession of Katanga from the Congo, financing, arming and protecting the pro-Belgian Katangan leader, Moise Tshombe, in return for a promise that the Belgian mining interests in Katanga would be protected. It was one of the most blatant acts of foreign manipulation in Africa's chaotic independence period, and it culminated in one of the cruellest acts of twentieth-century political assassination, when Patrice Lumumba, the first Congolese national figure to win an election, was handed over by Belgian stooges to be murdered by Tshombe's regime.

Lumumba's mistake was to hint at pro-Soviet sympathies. The mere possibility of the Congo, with its huge deposits of copper, uranium and diamonds, falling into the Soviet sphere of influence during the Cold War was too much for the Western powers. Several African nations were already moving into the Communist camp but the Congo was, in the eyes of the West, simply too important to lose so Brussels, with the connivance of Washington, engineered Lumumba's arrest, torture and transfer to the capital of Katanga, then known by its Belgian name of Elisabethville, today's Lubumbashi.

It was at the city's airport in the middle of January 1961 that Lumumba was last seen in public. Members of the UN, already deployed to Katanga to try to deal with the secession crisis, watched Lumumba being bundled out of a cargo plane by soldiers loyal to Tshombe. They said he had been so badly beaten on the flight that he barely moved when he was pushed into a waiting vehicle that whisked him away to a nearby villa owned by a Belgian colonialist. For a long time, what happened next was one of the great mysteries of modern African history, mainly because Lumumba's body was never found. There were rumours that it was cut up and fed to pigs, or even thrown into the headwaters of the Congo River that rises in mountains to the north-west of Lubumbashi. Tshombe's regime initially refused to admit he was dead, but when they finally did, they lied, claiming he had been shot dead by villagers after he escaped on foot from police custody.

It took almost forty years before the mystery was eventually solved by a Belgian academic, Ludo De Witte, piecing the history together from official documents released by Brussels in the 1990s. He discovered that various Belgian policemen and security officers – nominally under the command of Tshombe but, in reality, following orders from Brussels – had, on the night of 17 January 1961, driven Lumumba from the villa where he had been taken to rendezvous with a firing squad of local Katangan soldiers about forty-five minutes' drive from the airport. Lumumba, his face battered almost beyond recognition and his clothes spattered with blood, was made to stand against a large anthill illuminated by the headlights of two cars. He was then executed by firing squad and his body buried in a shallow grave. Fearful the grave might be discovered and turned into a shrine, the Belgians and their Katangan stooges later moved to erase all traces of the Congo's elected leader. The day after the execution, the corpse was exhumed and driven deeper into the Katangan bush, where it was reburied in another shallow grave until arrangements could be made to get rid of it once and for all.

Under cover of darkness on 22 January 1961 two Belgian brothers, with connections to the Belgian security forces, returned and exhumed the body for a second time. They used a hacksaw and an axe to dismember the decomposing corpse, before dissolving the remains in a 200-litre petrol drum filled with sulphuric acid taken from a nearby copper-processing plant. One of the brothers later admitted he used pliers to remove two of Lumumba's teeth as souvenirs.

Thoughts of assassination, acid baths and dismembered bodies were not the only dark images in my mind as the plane descended towards the tarmac at Lubumbashi. In 1997 a close friend of mine had come closer to death at this airport than at any time in his long career covering international crises as a journalist. It was during the last chaotic days of Mobutu's rule when Laurent Kabila's Rwandan-backed insurgency was about to topple the ageing dictator. Troops loyal to Mobutu were becoming increasingly desperate and had gathered at the country's few functioning airports hoping to escape. It was at Lubumbashi airport that my friend was seized by some of the Special Presidential Guard, a notoriously brutal cadre of Mobutu supporters who could expect no leniency when his regime's end came. He was stripped to his underpants and threatened at gunpoint for several terrifying hours. It did not help that he was with a fellow journalist who had a video shot some time earlier of Rwandan troops on the march towards Kinshasa. When the guards discovered the tape, they said they were going to execute the reporters as Rwandan spies. It took them hours of desperate pleading to convince the guards they were simply journalists.

Looking out of my window as the plane descended towards Lubumbashi, just before the moment when the ground blurrily rushes into one's field of vision, I caught sight of a single figure, a Congolese woman standing right on the edge of the tarmac runway. She was barefoot, dressed in rags, with a pile of firewood balanced on her head and a cold, wide-eyed expression on her face. No matter that this was one of the Congo's major international airports of considerable military importance, for her it was a place to gather firewood.

From my earlier visits to the Congo, I knew what to expect when the fuselage door finally opened. At the bottom of a set of stairs, manually wheeled into position, a crowd of people had gathered, all claiming to be an official of some sort and all demanding payment. I watched as the Asian lady I had spotted at Johannesburg airport stepped gingerly into the melee, only to be tossed and spun like a piece of flotsam, blasted by loud demands for payment. The last I saw of her was an unedifying spectacle. She was fighting back tears, bidding for her own luggage that was being auctioned back to her.

Before boarding the flight, I had played the first of my Congolese jokers. I had contacted Clive, the Zimbabwean businessman who had good connections with the Kabila regime, and asked for his help. The Kabila family originally came from Katanga and, while the regime's control of much of the country was nominal, they made sure their home capital remained in their hands. Clive's cobalt-mining operation was based in Lubumbashi and although he was not going to be in town when I arrived, he warned me the only way I would get through the airport in one piece was if his people smoothed the way. It was with relief that in the crowd down on the tarmac I spotted a man holding up a piece of paper with the name 'Kim Butcher' written across it. I caught his eye and he threw himself bravely into the muddle, before grabbing me reassuringly by the shoulders and leading me through the scrum.

'Welcome to Lubumbashi. My name is Yav,' he said in French from behind imitation Ray-Ban sunglasses. He had to shout to make himself heard above the din of jet engines and grasping officials, but there was a steadying calm about him. Turning to a large man standing next to him, he spoke again. 'Let me introduce you to the director of immigration at the airport. This is the man who helps us, when our visitors come through the airport.'

The director looked at me coldly and nodded a silent acknowledgement. I knew enough about Congolese officialdom to keep my mouth shut. Yav was clearly happy that the nod represented all the necessary formalities and he nudged me firmly past the director and up the path to the 1950s-built terminal, where some of the noisier luggage-auctioning was going on.

'There is just one fee you need to pay, an entry fee of ten dollars,' he said. I handed him a twenty-dollar note, which he then passed to an underling, who disappeared into a side-room with my passport. The man came back two minutes later and gave Yav change of a ten dollar note. Yav immediately rubbed the note between his fingers and frowned. 'This is not a real dollar note.

This is counterfeit. Get me a good one,' he said, raising his voice at the underling and sending him back inside.

It took a few minutes for my rucksack to appear. I stood in the crowd trying to look inconspicuous, yet confident. The Congo is a police state maintained by numerous security services, military units and gendarmerie, all of whom take a close interest in any outsider daring to venture into the country. I knew from my earlier visits that roving journalists in the Congo are subject to particularly close scrutiny, and I was anxious to get through the airport as quickly as possible. Journalists were routinely expected to go to Kinshasa and pay officials large amounts in bribes for 'accreditation' that took weeks to complete, before they could even think about trying to move around the country. I wanted to avoid this lengthy detour to Kinshasa and was hoping to slip into the Congo through Lubumbashi and then use the UN flight to reach the east of the country, where Kinshasa's authority did not hold. If I made it up there, I had in my rucksack a 'To Whom It May Concern' letter signed by the Congolese Ambassador to South Africa, introducing me as a writer trying to follow Stanley's historical route. This, I gambled, would at least allow me to open negotiations with what passes as officialdom in the east of the Congo before they detained me on suspicion of being a spy.

Without Yav, I would not have made it through Lubumbashi airport. I could see by the way he breezed past soldiers guarding the entrance to the baggage hall that he was a man of standing, something that I exploited unashamedly as we waited for the luggage to appear. I edged closer to him, trying to look at ease and not catch the eye of various officials whom I could see closely questioning the other white man from my flight. There was a bullet hole in the glass partition above the door leading into the baggage hall, and a rusty fan, mounted on the ceiling, hung motionless. Apart from brightly painted signs advertising mobile-phone companies, nothing seemed to have changed from the time when the airport staged the brutal finale of Lumumba's life.

Eventually I pointed to my bag and Yav barked at an official to take it outside to his waiting car.

Rather unexpectedly, he began to quiz the baggage handlers about a set of golf clubs that had been due in on the flight for one of the senior mine employees. Years earlier I had met some wealthy Zimbabweans who told me an amazing story about how the wealthy live in Lubumbashi. The city is only a few kilometres from the border with Zambia, connected by one of the Congo's few functioning roads. One of the wealthy white mine owners is so keen on show-jumping that each winter in Lubumbashi he hosts his own event, inviting Zambian, Zimbabwean and South African show-jumpers to drive their horses all the way to the Congo. Border guards are bribed and special supplies flown into Lubumbashi. No matter that the Congo is ravaged by war, poverty and corruption, this man is wealthy and eccentric enough to convene his own Horse of the Year Show in the Congo. If it is possible for Lubumbashi to have its own show-jumping competition, I suppose I should not have been that surprised that it has a golf course.

For almost a hundred years Katanga's growth had been based almost completely on copper. For a long time the province was known as Shaba, the local Swahili word for the metal. But the problem with copper is that the production process is relatively complex. Expensive mining equipment is needed, as well as skilled labour and large amounts of chemicals for processing and other supplies that have to be imported. This was all possible during the Belgian colonial era when law and order existed, but through the chaos of Mobutu's rule during the 1970s and 1980s, foreign investors saw their copper mines repeatedly flooded, supplies plundered and attempts to bring in replacement equipment blocked by corrupt and incompetent local officials.

By the time I reached Lubumbashi, copper was in decline, but the town was in the grip of a new boom, one driven by cobalt.

Cobalt had suddenly become commercially attractive because the world price had been driven upwards by a surge in demand from China's fast-growing economy. The cobalt price had grown by 300 per cent in less than year, from $8 to $24 per pound, a dramatic change that had had a dramatic effect in Katanga, home to some of the world's greatest and most accessible cobalt deposits.

Cobalt mining in Katanga does not require massive investment or expensive processing. Here, a man with a shovel can become a cobalt miner, simply by digging away the topsoil and looking for the darker, greyish or purplish rock that is rich with cobalt salts. The rock is then purified in the most primitive way, using a hammer to chip away the non-cobalt-rich rock, a process that the Congolese miners call 'cobbing', a word imported from Britain where it was first used by seventeenth-century Cornish tin miners. The demand from China is so great that middlemen in Lubumbashi, often Lebanese or Indian, are willing to pay cash for sacks of the grey rock. The sacks are then collected, packed on trucks and driven on a long and tortuous journey past grasping officials on the Congolese border with Zambia and then 2,000 kilometres south to the closest functioning port, Durban, in South Africa, before finally being shipped to China.

The whole procedure is relatively straightforward, and for a while I almost bought into the sentiment expressed on a road sign I spotted as Yav drove me into Lubumbashi. The sign said, 'Lubumbashi – City of Hope'. There were plenty of cars in the town centre, a few shops were open, and I was told a hotel near the main square had just started taking guests again for the first time in years.

But during the four days I spent in the city, staying at the guest house in the compound used by Clive's cobalt-mining operation, I learned how this sense of normality was an illusion and how regular rules of commerce simply do not apply in the Congo. For those who think Africa's problems can simply be solved by the injection of money, I would recommend a crash course in cobalt economics in the Congo.

In 2004 the cobalt boom meant there was plenty of money in Lubumbashi, but the presence of money did not guarantee that the local economy grew or even stabilised. In the town's Belgian Club, I saw Chinese traders and Lebanese middlemen splashing money around on $20 pizzas and expensive imported beer. They had plenty of cash and they wanted to spend it on raw cobalt ore. But in spite of this substantial income, the pernicious reality of Congolese commerce meant that norms of economic development did not apply.

In order for the investor to make any money he needed the necessary paperwork to drive the cobalt out of the country, and in order to arrange the necessary paperwork he needed to pay off the Ministry of Mines, not just locally in Lubumbashi, but also at the national level in Kinshasa; and if the Minister of Mines changed, which happened regularly, a whole new matrix of payments and bribes had to be put in place for the new man in the job. And once you finished with the Ministry of Mines, you would have to repeat the whole process at the Immigration Department, the Department of Customs, the local Governor's Office, and so on. So gross were the profits to be made on the cobalt that some investors were prepared to pay the web of bribes and unofficial 'taxes' demanded by the authorities, and to tolerate this commercial chaos.

At the Belgian Club I drank Simba beer and ate chips doused with mayonnaise, in the Belgian style, with one of the few Europeans bold enough to risk involvement in Lubumbashi's cobalt boom. Belgium's links remain closer with Katanga than with any other province of their old colony and a photograph of the Belgian royal family looked down on us from the wall as I listened to his mind-boggling stories about local business anarchy. On numerous occasions trucks had been loaded in Lubumbashi with sacks of cobalt ore worth $50,000, but when they arrived in South Africa the sacks were found to contain nothing but worthless soil.

'Between here and South Africa you don't just have thousands of kilometres of tarmac road,' he said. 'You have three international borders, from the Congo into Zambia, from Zambia into Zimbabwe and from Zimbabwe into South Africa. At each one, you have officials demanding handouts. Each one of them can be bribed by a rival cobalt shipper to cause you delays and other problems. And the drivers can be bought off by rivals, so when they stop to sleep at night, God knows what happens to the bags of ore on the back. Some of the buyers who come here to Lubumbashi decide it's cheaper just to set themselves up on the main road south through Zambia, say, and wait there with a gang of gunmen armed with AK-47s to help themselves to whatever comes down the road. The truck drivers are so badly paid that they are not going to risk their lives to protect the load. If you offered them a hundred-dollar bill, most drivers would pull over and let you pinch some or all of what's on the back.'

There was nothing funny about some of his other stories. The cobalt mining was, for the large part, unlicensed and chaotic, as artisanal miners – men with shovels – dug deeper and deeper pits to get at the grey, cobalt-rich rock. The stories of miners being killed by landfalls were so routine the authorities did not bother responding to them. And an attempt to restart one of the old processing plants near Lubumbashi had raised other health hazards. The processing uses local ores known to be rich in uranium. Without any meaningful local environmental standards, there were concerns that radioactive isotopes of uranium were being released by the process into the atmosphere as smoke particles.

What made it so galling to me, the outsider, was that of the large sums paid by the various mining companies, brokers and traders, only a tiny fraction ever reached the local economy. The vast bulk was lost in bribes demanded by corrupt officials at all levels.

Lubumbashi's cobalt bonanza brought home to me how money alone will not solve Africa's problems. Until the Congo's economy is underpinned by the rule of law and transparency, it will remain stagnant, chaotic and unproductive.

Those days in Lubumbashi spent waiting for the UN shuttle flight northwards to Kalemie felt rather surreal. I rarely ventured from the sanctuary of the compound, which lay behind a high perimeter wall in a relatively smart area of Lubumbashi, near the governor's residence. The view I got from there was entirely skewed. For those, like Clive, with good enough connections, it was possible to live comfortably in the Congo's second city. It was hugely expensive, as everything – from cartons of milk to the satellite television dish – had to be imported, mostly by plane from South Africa. When I got there a large box of umbrellas had just arrived in anticipation of the next rainy season. But it was clear the potential profits from cobalt were so enormous that as long as the mine kept producing and the trucks managed to get past the corrupt customs officials into Zambia, then the whole operation was cost-effective.

The problem with Lubumbashi's cobalt boom was that it was too inefficient to be of genuine economic benefit to the million or so Katangans living in the city. A mining expert I met explained one of the main inefficiencies.

'The cobalt-rich rock is simply bagged and driven out of the country,' he explained. 'That way ensures the smallest amount of benefit to the local economy – just the few dollars a day paid to each miner. If the local authorities were interested in helping the local economy, then they would have a processing plant here in Lubumbashi that converts the cobalt-rich rock into concentrated cobalt salts. It is not a complex procedure, but it multiplies the value of the cobalt product by fifty times, maybe a hundred times. It is much more efficient to transport the concentrate than the untreated rock and the profit margin is much greater. Under the system we have now, some plant in South Africa or China makes the profit on the treatment of the rock, a profit that is lost to the Congo.

'But the reality is this. The authorities in the Congo are not interested in how cobalt mining benefits the local economy. They are only interested in what they can take in bribes. And it is easier to count sacks of rock at the border and work out how many dollars you can cream off per bag. Until that fundamental attitude changes, then the cobalt boom driven by China will not benefit more than a few members of the Congo elite.'

There was one entirely personal and self-indulgent thing I needed to do while I was in Lubumbashi. I wanted to go to the town's railway station and see where my mother had caught the train that took her across the Congo in 1958.

Simon, a factotum from the mine office, agreed to take me there on a Sunday morning when, I gambled, there would be fewer police and gendarmerie in the town centre demanding to see my papers. As we drove into town, I was struck by Lubumbashi's resemblance to other southern African cities. In my mind the Congo belonged to the continent's sweaty, tropical centre, but Lubumbashi's topography and climate were much closer to those of Johannesburg or Harare. The air was dry and the land was covered not by dense rainforest, but open scrub. It was more high-veld plateau than steamy equatorial river basin. The streets were even lined with the same fast-growing jacaranda trees that I recognised from the garden at my Johannesburg home, although Lubumbashi's position closer to the Equator meant they were already putting on their bright-purple display of springtime blossom two months earlier than those in chillier South Africa.

We passed the Cathedral of St Paul and St Peter, a large red-brick structure in the centre of Lubumbashi, built in 1919, and I could see it was full of worshippers. Some of the older, wider boulevards were paved with hexagonal cobbles made from some sort of dark, possibly volcanic, rock. The work that went into laying these roads must have been enormous, but they were in much better condition than the potholed modern roads.

Apart from being tatty, Lubumbashi's town centre is largely unchanged since the Belgian colonial period. There is a 1950s post office fronting a main square from which various roads radiate between some fine Art Deco buildings. There are a few modest general stores selling imported goods, although fresh bread is available from a Greek-owned patisserie. We walked the last few hundred metres to the railway station. I had heard that a two-year work programme by foreign aid groups had recently enabled the station to reopen for the first time since the war, connecting Lubumbashi with Kindu, a port on the upper Congo, and I wanted to see if this was really true.

Simon and I approached a man in dark glasses standing guard at the gate that led onto the platform.

'Please can you tell me about the train to Kindu.'

'Who are you? What is your business here at the station? This is a military installation, who gave you permission to come here?'

The man was not just drunk, he was aggressively drunk. I recoiled and let Simon deal with him. Simon edged forward, took the guard's hand in his hand and started speaking in Swahili, his voice dropping almost to a whisper. I made to look away as Simon slipped the guard a folded-up bank note. The gate opened.

I walked out onto an open platform. Unlike British railways where the platform stands much higher than the track level, this station was of a more continental European design, the tracks only a few centimetres below the platform. I looked around and saw a blackboard with a message chalked across it referring to the train to Kindu. It said that it leaves every first of the month. Simon assured me this was nonsense as no train had left in the first two weeks of August. But the thing that was oddest about Lubumbashi station was the complete lack of trains. There was no rolling stock, no carriages, nothing. The whole place was silent and empty.

*

The longer I spent in Lubumbashi, the more nervous and sick I felt. The powerful anti-malaria tablets I was taking caused the nausea, but the nervousness came from the growing sense that my whole trip now depended on the next few days. I knew my attempt to cross the Congo would have to begin in Kalemie, but I also knew it might end there. During my months of research at home in Johannesburg, I had trawled the small number of aid workers and missionaries based in the town, but none of them had ever heard of an outsider travelling overland from Kalemie deeper into the Congo.

My most positive lead had come from Michel Bonnardeaux, a civilian UN employee from Canada who had been based in Kalemie, on and off, for more than two years. When he arrived, the war was raging in the eastern Congo and Kalemie was filled with refugees, but since the 2002 peace treaty Michel had seen a small but steady improvement in the security situation. While most of my e-correspondents had dismissed my plan to follow Stanley's route as being either impossible or insane, Michel was one of the few who did not reject it out of hand. It might have been his contagious enthusiasm for local Congolese history or just his upbeat positive nature, but like a drowning man to a piece of flotsam, I latched firmly onto Michel and his advice.

According to Michel, the 500-kilometre route overland from Kalemie to the upper Congo passed through the land belonging to the Banga-Banga tribe. From the many Banga-Banga refugees living in Kalemie, he knew the security situation in the area had improved enough to allow a trickle of people to arrive in town by foot. Many came pushing old bicycles laden with produce, which was then traded at the port for salt, soap and other commodities. The distances were immense and the tracks tiny, but if you could get a bicycle along them, Michel reckoned, you could also get a small motorbike along them.

The security situation remained the great unknown. The peace treaty had technically ended the war, but gangs of armed militia still roamed the forest and savannah west of Kalemie. Many of the bicycle bearers arrived in town with stories of atrocities in the anarchic region between Lake Tanganyika and the upper Congo. Cannibalism was common, and rape was a ghastly routine for villagers populating this vast swathe of territory.

The one thing I had going for me was the scale of the place. After Kalemie, the next UN base was 700 kilometres away on the upper Congo River, at the town of Kindu. The distances were so enormous that if I could move quickly by motorbike, and not advertise my plans in advance to anyone minded to arrange an ambush, I gambled that I could get through safely. But whether I would manage to find a lift on a motorbike, let alone someone prepared to act as guide and interpreter, were great unknowns. Language would definitely be a problem, as my French would only be of use in the Congo's larger settlements, where I could be sure to find village elders with the remnants of a school education. In the rural areas I would need someone who spoke Swahili to ask for help and directions from villagers we met. There were no reliable maps of the area I wanted to cross, so I would have to rely on local directions.

Peacekeepers from MONUC would not be able to help because they had a policy of only going to places that could be reached by jeep – in the case of Kalemie, this meant that they operated within a few kilometres of the town centre. The MONUC bases at Kalemie and Kindu were linked only by air, so I turned my attention to the few aid groups operating in the eastern Congo to beg for help. The problem was not one of expense – I could afford the few thousand dollars cost of a bike and wages for a guide. The problem was more simple – finding anyone who was prepared to travel overland through such hazardous terrain. One by one the aid groups turned me down. They had, after all, their own important work to do, and helping out an adventurous hack did not fit readily into their schedules.

In the months leading up to my trip I had finally made contact with a group that offered me a glimmer of hope. Care International had been developing its network of contacts around Kindu and I heard that its country director, Brian Larson, had personally organised a convoy of motorbikes that ventured 200 kilometres south of Kindu, to see how viable it was to move supplies down jungle tracks to people who had received no humanitarian aid for years. For me, this was precisely what I was looking for: someone who was prepared to take a calculated risk to open up areas viewed for a generation as impassable.

We exchanged emails. Brian jokingly dismissed his motorbike adventure as an 'interesting way to get a sore backside' and I eventually summoned the courage to ask him directly if I could borrow a motorbike and a guide from his Care International staff. The fact that he did not turn me down flat meant I was in with a chance. He promised to mention my idea to his staff around Kindu and urge them to see if they could coincide one of their reconnaissance trips with part of my itinerary.

These half-chances suggested by Michel and Brian had been the grounds for my decision to fly to Kalemie but they were not enough to convince Jean-Claude ('Call me J-C') – a third-generation Belgian colonialist who worked for Clive's mine operations. He seemed to take a mawkish pleasure in telling me my trip was doomed.

When I told him that all I had with me was my 'To Whom It May Concern' letter introducing me as a writer following Stanley's route, he snorted dismissively. 'That won't be enough. You will need written authorisation from the local intelligence service. They are very strict here and without their permission you won't get anywhere,' he said. And when I told him I had a satellite telephone, he snorted even more loudly. 'You won't get far with that unless you get permission from the military police. They will take it away from you the moment they find it.

It will cost you a lot of money if you try to get it back.'

I was beginning to take against J-C.

'I've got a map here. Come and show me where you want to go,' J-C said on my first day in Lubumbashi, unfolding an out-of-date map of the Democratic Republic of Congo.

I stood over it and pointed to Kalemie, the port on Lake Tanganyika. Technically it is in the same province as Lubumbashi, Katanga, but it lies 1,000 kilometres to the north. As I described the major sections of the trip, overland from the lake to the headwaters of the Congo River, J-C rather irritatingly sucked in his breath and shook his head, uttering something like 'not possible' or 'cannot be done'.

After I finished he launched into a hugely pessimistic declamation.

'I know all this area really well from when I was younger. This area is not a cobalt area like down here in the south of Katanga, but a gold area. Not big-scale stuff, but artisanal, small-scale gold mines. So with the presence of these mines, you are going to get people with guns wanting the gold action. And I am sure you know what happened up here recently.' He was pointing at Bukavu, the scene of the attack by pro-Rwandan rebels just a few months earlier.

'Well, all the government troops have now gone into the town to punish the rebels. And so those rebels have fled into the bush about here.' He was now pointing to an area close to Kalemie.

'And that means the militia who were already living in the bush have been pushed further south, to where you want to go.'

He shook his head and, with a final flourish, pronounced his judgement. 'You don't stand a chance.'

I had had enough of J-C and took solace in the house's South African satellite television. I turned on the news and could not believe what I heard. The anchorman told me that 156 ethnic Tutsis from the Congo had just been murdered at a refugee camp across the border in Burundi where they had sought sanctuary from the turmoil caused by June's events in Bukavu. I tried to follow what the anchor was saying about who might be responsible. His version was muddled and confusing, but one thing was perfectly clear to me. My journey had just got a whole lot more complicated.

4.

The Pearl of Tanganyika

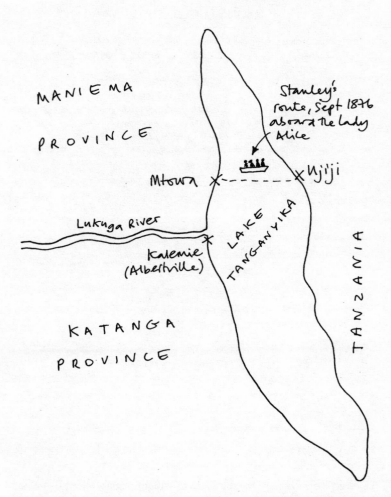

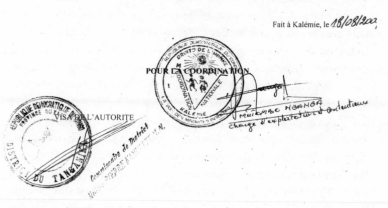

DROITS DE L'HOMME
LA VOIX DES MINORITES INDIGÈNES
V.M.I. / O.N.G.D
KELEMIE

FEUILLE DE ROUTE N° 172/VMI/MG/COORD/2004

DE MONSIEUR : GEORGES MBUYU BUTU-KU-MAHA

GRADE : PRÉSIDENT DU CONSEIL D'ADMINISTRATION

MATRICULE :

FONCTION : COORDONNATEUR

SERVICE DE : DROITS HUMAINS

ACCOMPAGNE DE : BUTCHER TIMOTHIR, BENOÎT BANGANA, NGENDA OMBA

SE REND DE : KALEMIE - KABAMBARE

MOTIF DU VOYAGE : VISITE SANTE DROITS HUMAINS

DEPART PREVU LE : 19 / AOÛT / 2004

RETOUR PROBABLE : 02 / SEPT / 2004

MODE DE TRANSPORT : L'ÉLO, MOTO, VÉHICULE, PIROGUE

MENTIONS SPECIALES :

N.B.: Les autorités tant civiles que militaires sont priées de lui venir en aide en cas de besoin.

Fait à Kalémie, le 18/08/200

POUR LA COORDINATION

VISA DE L'AUTORITE

Laissez-passer issued to the author, August 2004, by Congolese authorities in the province of Katanga

The Belgians called the port of Kalemie the 'Pearl of Tanganyika' and I was hoping it would gleam for me as I approached on the UN flight from Lubumbashi. The light aircraft bucked and yawed as the pilots slalomed between skyscraper storm clouds, but my face stayed firmly glued to the tiny porthole, anxious for my first glimpse.

Lake Tanganyika is a scientific oddity. Scientists believe it to be the oldest and deepest lake in Africa, with many of its own unique species of water micro-organisms and creatures. And unlike the other Great Lakes of Africa, it is drained not by a large, permanent river but by a more modest stream, the Lukuga, which acts like an overflow in a bath. For much of the year the river is stagnant and silted up, only surging into life during the rainy season when the lake level rises.

Folklore among the tribes who live on the lake's edge says it was created as a punishment. The tradition goes that a family, living on the sweltering savannah of central Africa, had enjoyed their own private spring for generations, drawing from an unlimited supply of cool, fresh water and feasting on the sweet-tasting fish that lived in the pond formed where the water issued from the ground. The family was sworn to secrecy about the source of the water and the fish, and was issued with a dire warning that all would be lost if the secret was betrayed. One day, the family's matriarch began an affair while her husband was away. The lover was treated to a feast of fish, his thirst slaked with the cool, fresh spring water. He became so enraptured with the sweet taste of the water and fish that he insisted on knowing where they came from. The woman was initially reluctant, but finally gave in to temptation and the spell was broken. At that moment the earth was rent and a great flood welled up from below, drowning the lovers and creating the lake we see today.

When I first read this fable, I was struck by how good an analogy it is for the entire Congo. Local tribesmen had survived in peace for generations before outsiders – Arab slavers and white colonials – turned up and beguiled them into giving up first slaves, then ivory, then rubber and mineral wealth, before the traditional Congolese way of life was overwhelmed by the outsiders.

Five hundred kilometres or so east of my flight path, on the other side of Lake Tanganyika, was the air space of Tanzania. Light aircraft would be a common sight there, ferrying tourists between Africa's biggest mountain, Kilimanjaro, and the country's world-famous safari parks. But on my side of the lake, visitors to the Congo were rare and light aircraft rarer still. It had taken a month to negotiate my way onto the plane, but I had no other option. Like all UN missions, MONUC can be criticised for being bureaucratic and inefficient, but in the absence of any meaningful government in the Democratic Republic of Congo, MONUC was the closest the country came to a genuinely national organisation and, for me, it provided the only way to reach Kalemie.

Sadly, the 'Pearl of Tanganyika' did not glimmer for me that day. The cloud cover was too thick and all I saw of the lake was a slab of grey in the distance as the aircraft made its final, frantic lunge for Kalemie before bouncing to a halt on the bumpy strip.

The airstrip might technically be described as a UN military installation, but such a term would be an overstatement. The runway was unfenced, crowded on all sides by unkempt scrub, and the old grey tarmac of the strip was pitted with divots and splodged with dark repair patches. The only military structure was a white, wooden watch tower, with a platform just three metres off the ground, where I could see a UN infantryman. His tin helmet was painted UN blue, crammed low on his head, while his shoulders were bulked up by a flak jacket, also blue. The gap between helmet and body armour was tiny and his anxious, beady eyes looked like those behind the prickles of a balled-up hedgehog summoning forlorn defiance at an approaching lorry.

Our plane was the sort in which the pilot has to inch his way, bent double, back through the tiny cabin to free the passengers. I followed, slowly unfolding myself from my boxed-in sitting position, relieved to be able to stretch, as I went down the three-step ladder onto the ground. I might not have been able to see the lake but I could smell it now – a rich, sedgy aroma in the still, steamy atmosphere. Although Kalemie is in Katanga, the same province as Lubumbashi, the eco-system is radically different. The city lies on a dry plateau or veld, but the lakeside port is surrounded by lusher, more tropical forest. By the time I finished stretching, I could feel the first drops of sweat pasting my long-sleeved shirt to my back.

There was not a single building in sight, although the MONUC soldiers had set up a bunch of prefabricated containers to act as an arrivals hall. These white, box-like units are a common feature of any UN operation around the world. If connected to an elec-trical generator and a water tank, they can provide an anodyne, air-conditioned living space, no matter whether you are up a snowy mountain in Afghanistan or in the deserts of the western Sahara. They ensure each UN mission operates in its own little bubble. There might be a war going on outside, but UN peacekeepers can expect to have one of these little white boxes in which to work, sleep, eat or even connect to the Internet .

'Please follow me,' said a white girl wearing a crisp uniform of blue and grey. Her English had a Slavic accent and her name tag bore the flag of her homeland, Croatia. The outside atmosphere was hot and cloying, but she was wearing several layers of clothing – her workspace was heavily air-conditioned. After following her inside to have my name ticked off the passenger manifest, I shivered. I hurried back outside to wait for Michel Bonnardeaux, the UN worker whose optimism had brought me here in the first place. He had promised to meet me off the plane, but as I stood there with the sedgy smell of Lake Tanganyika in my nostrils and my shirt increasingly sodden with sweat, there was no sign of him.

Kalemie was one of the first settlements developed by Belgian colonial agents in the Congo after Stanley's journey of discovery. When the explorer finally reached Britain in 1878 with proof the Congo River was navigable for thousands of kilometres halfway across Africa, he first tried to persuade London to claim the territory as a British colony. He failed. At the time the British colonial authorities were not impressed with the returns offered by Britain's relatively modest African holdings. Vast fortunes were being made in India and the Far East, but Africa, in the age before its large gold and diamond deposits had been discovered, was not nearly as attractive. Maintaining the Cape Colony around Cape Town at the foot of Africa was costing Britain a great deal. British troops were being lost in a series of frontier wars with the Xhosa and battles with the Zulu that would lead, within a year, to the disaster of Isandlwana and the defence of Rorke's Drift. The timing of Stanley's approach was not good and his suggestion that Britain should colonise the Congo River basin was firmly rejected by Whitehall.

In Brussels, Leopold proved more receptive. He had been dreaming for years of establishing his own colonial empire, but he had failed to locate the right piece of territory. When he learned of Stanley's success in charting the river, he invited the explorer to his palace in Brussels and made sure Stanley was treated lavishly. Within a few weeks the pair had hatched an ambitious plot. The ruler of one of Europe's smallest and youngest nations (Belgium was founded in 1830) commissioned the Welsh-born, naturalised American to stake the entire Congo River basin as the private property of the king. Stanley would be paid handsomely and Leopold would have the foundation for his empire.

Just two years after he crossed the Congo as an explorer, Stanley returned as a coloniser. This time he came by ship to the mouth of the river, before heading inland with a party of road-builders, determined to construct an access route through the Crystal Mountains that guard the impassable lower reaches of the river. It took two years and cost the lives of hundreds of African labourers, who were literally worked to death, but slowly some of the most inhospitable terrain in Africa was tamed. It was this display of indefatigability, as much as any of his other actions during his African expeditions, that earned Stanley the soubri-quet *Bula Matari*, or Breaker of Rocks.

In keeping with the prevailing attitude of racial superiority assumed by almost all white visitors to Africa, Stanley paid little heed to the millions of native Congolese. There were times where he went through the motions of arranging 'treaties' with local chiefs, drawing up documents that effectively ceded the rights over the land to the 'king over the water'. It was hardly a negotiation between two equals, as the chiefs knew perfectly well what would happen if they did not sign. They would be overrun by the motley gang of well-armed colonial pioneers and camp followers accompanying Stanley. And just like the European slave traders of 400 years earlier, Stanley was adept at playing the tribes off against each other, providing arms, clothing and alcohol to one group so that it could conquer its local rival. Like dominoes the Congolese tribes fell, one after the other, to Stanley and the early colonial agents of the Belgian king as the white man's influence crept steadily inland across the immense river basin.

Leopold's colonising coup in the Congo led the other European powers to reconsider Africa. France, Germany, Spain, Portugal and Britain had largely ignored the African interior until now, but the acquisitiveness of the Belgian king forced them to think again and in the early winter of 1884 the great European powers gathered at a grand conference convened in Berlin to carve up what remained unclaimed in Africa. Leopold was able to present his colonial claim over the Congo as a fait accompli and, when the conference ended in February 1885, the Act of Berlin gave its legal recognition to the Congo Free State. With a surface area of more than three million square kilometres, it was claimed not by Belgium, but by the king himself. Never in history, neither before nor since, has a single person claimed ownership of a larger tract of land.

The territory was mostly virgin rainforest and savannah, criss-crossed by the Congo River and its countless tributaries, inhabited by millions of Congolese, but in those first years of colonial rule it was not the natives who posed the greatest threat to Leopold's interests. Arab slavers in the east of the country – the ones whose stories of a mighty river in the centre of Africa first attracted Livingstone and Stanley in the 1860s and 1870s – were a much greater concern for Leopold. Many of these Arabs had already lived for decades in the east of the country, organising raiding parties to plunder slaves and ivory, which would then be transported by caravan back to the large Arab trading centres around Zanzibar. But the Berlin Conference had been a white man's meeting. The Arabs of east Africa had not been invited.

Various half-hearted attempts were made to forge peace treaties between the early Belgian colonists and the Arab slavers, but an increase in tension was inevitable as the Europeans grew steadily more avaricious. The rising tension culminated in a brief but bloody war that began in 1892. Both sides used Congolese tribes-men as foot soldiers and both sides committed atrocities, but modern European weapons meant that the Belgians prevailed, mopping up Arab resistance in a series of battles and skirmishes, as the white colonialists sought to purge the Congo of its Arab population and to draw up a clear frontier once and for all for the territory claimed solely by Leopold.

Lake Tanganyika was a convenient boundary marker. It is only seventy kilometres across at its widest point, but from north to south it runs for 650 kilometres, and the Belgian pioneers quickly focused on it as a natural border for the easternmost limit of the Congo Free State. First, they had to deal with the large local Arab population on the lake's shore. Ever since they first reached the Congo in the early nineteenth century, the Arab slavers had arrived on boats crossing the lake. A large settlement had grown at their principal landing site on the western shore of the lake, Mtowa, a short distance north of the mouth of the only river that drains the lake, the Lukuga.

On 5 April 1892 a Belgian sergeant called Alexis Vrithoff clashed with an Arab raiding party on high ground next to the river mouth. He was killed, but after the Belgians eventually crushed the Arabs, the site around the estuary was developed into the Congo's most important inland port, serviced by a railway, completed in 1915, that brought goods from the Congolese interior, and by ferries and steamers that crossed the lake to ports in what is now Zambia, Tanzania and Burundi. In honour of Albert I, the Belgian king who succeeded Leopold, the town was named Albertville – its name was changed to Kalemie in the late 1960s – and, according to my 1951 *Travel Guide to the Belgian Congo*, the construction of this great transport hub meant the port was 'destined to have a great future'.

I saw little evidence of this 'great future' once Michel finally picked me up at the airstrip. From a distance Kalemie looked regular enough, and as we approached, bumping along on a sandy track contouring round the edge of Lake Tanganyika, I could see the town's main church, a white building with a rather elegant bell-tower standing proud on a headland, against a knobbly horizon of tree-covered hills, commanding a fine view over the lake. In the foreground, among the green of coconut palms and banana trees, there were two distinct columns of rust-red, corrugated-iron roofs flanking what appeared to be a main thoroughfare. And in the distance there was a small harbour tucked in the lee of a graceful breakwater, next to a railway terminus and marshalling yard.

But as the jeep laboured around the lake and we got closer to Kalemie, the most extraordinary thing happened. The fabric of the town grew flimsier until it seemed to vanish altogether.

What I had taken to be an estate of factories, damaged in the recent war in the Congo, turned out to be a ruin dating from a much earlier age. Faded advertisements could just be made out on the walls, although the logos dated not from the 1990s or the 1980s, but from half a century ago. Grass grew long and untroubled through the railway sleepers on the approaches to the disused station, and the sandy soil on either side of the tracks was drummed hard by generations of feet that had turned the old carriageway into a simple, arrow-straight footpath, walled on both sides by reedy grass swaying way above head height. An old railway carriage – built decades ago in South Africa and still bearing instructions in Afrikaans forbidding smoking – stood rusting in the tropical heat. In one of its compartments someone had made a small cooking fire on the floor, now surrounded by various dirty pots, and the carriage had the smell and stains of a doss-house.

Instead of a functioning high street, what I found was a dusty space filled by gaggles of meandering locals. A few hawkers sat behind small piles of stale biscuits or flat bottles of orange soda smuggled into Kalemie by boat from Tanzania on the other side of the lake. The more ambitious traders offered things like batteries and radios, but while the names on the Chinese-made packets sounded familiar, the misspellings of Philipps or Pannasonic suggested that nothing was genuine. Pedestrians could peruse at their leisure. They had no reason to worry about being run over as in the entire town there was only a handful of vehicles, mainly UN jeeps and one venerable Land Rover owned by some missionaries. And even when I saw one of these vehicles actually moving, they could only manage a walking pace, to avoid bucking and rearing uncontrollably over various potholes, uncovered drainage ditches and other obstacles in the town centre.

There were bicycles, old-fashioned things with solid frames painted black and primitive lever brakes, manufactured in China, propped up in the shade of the roadside trees, as their owners waited to offer them as taxis for customers willing to pay twenty Congolese francs, or four pence, to be taken from one end of the dusty strip to the other. I watched as women, wrapped in printed cotton cloth, some clutching salted fish bundled up in banana leaves, took up genteel side-saddle positions on the padded cushions attached to the racks above the bicycles' rear wheel, while the taxi boys heaved in the heat against the pedals. I could hear the soft chiming of Swahili as two women passengers chatted to each other while they were being slowly pedalled in parallel along the roadway.

Of the buildings themselves, there was little left beyond the fronts. Rust had not just coloured the roofs, but eaten out huge holes, through which tropical rain had flooded for countless rainy seasons. Damp, seasonal flooding from the nearby lake and collapsed foundations meant the interior rooms were mostly empty. Pipes that once brought mains water to each building lay broken and there was not one working light bulb. The town's main terrace of shops looked like one of those Hollywood filmsets, which from the front has the appearance of solidity, but from the back is nothing but a few beams propping up a façade.

Without cobalt or diamonds or gold to draw outsiders' interest here, Kalemie had been hollowed out by the years. Where once there had been a substantial settlement, nothing but the husk remained.

As we drove into Kalemie, Michel quizzed me on my motives. He was extremely knowledgeable about the local history, and seemed delighted to have found in me someone to share his interest.

'So you are the man crazy enough to want to follow Stanley's route. The history of this place is extraordinary – the slavers and their ivory, the Belgians who fought battles right here where the town now stands, and the wars since independence – but I have never met anyone who comes here just for history's sake. History is a luxury people cannot afford around here, where the more pressing things are where the next meal is coming from or the next drink of clean water.'

He spoke slowly, concentrating hard on steering the jeep along the bouncy road into town, sitting forward in the drivers' seat, anxiously trying to see over the bonnet to anticipate the next pothole.

'It's not the worst town in the country I have been to, but things are pretty basic here. The town is meant to get its electricity from a hydroelectric plant in the mountains north of here, built back in the 1950s – it's the one that Che Guevara attacked – but it's pretty intermittent these days. Some places are lucky enough to get a day of power, now and then, but we've had nothing for weeks now.'

I had read Guevara's diary about his time in the Congo. It was 1965 and he arrived here fired with revolutionary zeal, willing to risk his life in the fight against the Mobutu regime that America was in the process of installing. It was an era when the Cold War was being fought in numerous proxy wars all over Africa, and Guevara flew from Cuba to communist-controlled Tanzania to stage his insurgency across Lake Tanganyika. During a brief stopover in Tanzania he spent time with Laurent Kabila, then a young Congolese dissident and opponent of Mobutu. It would be more than thirty years before Kabila eventually replaced Mobutu, but at his first meeting Guevara was not overly impressed with Kabila's revolutionary credentials. He described him as a drunken womaniser rather than a true freedom fighter.

With heavy historic irony Guevara, the anti-colonialist par

excellence, arrived in the Congo just as Stanley, the colonial pioneer, had done – by small boat. Guevara came under cover of darkness with a raiding party made up of trusted Cuban revolutionaries and a few anti-Mobutu Congolese rebels. Their landing place could only have been a short distance from the spot where Stanley made landfall in his British-built, collapsible boat, the *Lady Alice*, and after landing Guevara's team slipped into the heavily forested hills to the west of Lake Tanganyika, where they spent a few weeks trying to strike a blow against the Mobutu regime. Guevara sounds increasingly miserable in his diaries. His zeal for revolution steadily diminished as his fellow African revolutionaries proved incapable of organising basic supplies or communications.

It all ended in a chaotic attack on the hydroelectric plant at Bendera, about 150 kilometres north of Kalemie. The plant was one of the last construction projects completed by the Belgians, in the late 1950s, and involved an ambitious plan to dam a river in a steep-sided gorge halfway up a mountain, before piping the water through turbines. The terrain meant the project was difficult to complete, but it also meant it was difficult for Guevara to attack. When the assault failed, he blamed poor communication among his fellow fighters and the tone of his diary suggests the fiasco made him lose faith in his Congolese collaborators. He simply thought they were not up to the task of running a revolution. Within a few days Guevara was back on Lake Tanganyika, this time heading to Tanzania under cover of darkness. He never returned to the Congo.

Michel asked me in detail about the route I hoped to follow, from Kalemie all the way to the upper Congo River.

'I would love to go through that area. I have read about it and flown over it, but I would love to see what is happening there, on the ground, after all this chaos.'

'So why don't you come with me?' I asked. 'It would be great to have some company.'

Michel shook his head. 'My bosses would never let me. Our security rules would never allow it. Especially now, after the latest news from Burundi. I assume you have heard what happened?'

I nodded.

'Well, the very latest is that the leadership of the pro-Rwandan rebels have left Kinshasa in protest at the killings. And one of the rebel leaders has been quoted as saying the whole peace treaty is off and the transitional government suspended. If that is true, then I guess we can expect the war to be back on in a couple of days.'

For two years Michel had worked at the UN mission in Kalemie as a sort of combat disc jockey, learning Swahili and immersing himself in the traditions and lore of the local Congolese tribes. He ran the local office of Radio Okapi, a UN hearts-and-minds operation broadcasting to the 200,000 Congolese crowded into the town. Kalemie might be one of the biggest towns in the Congo, but it has no state radio or television, no newspapers, no landline telephones and no Internet access. I arrived the day after the opening ceremony for the 2004 Olympics in Athens but, were it not for Michel's radio station, the event would have passed unnoticed in Kalemie.

We passed the ruins of the old airport, a single-storey 1950s building perforated with bullet holes and surrounded, on all sides, by puddles of shattered, red roof tiles. It had been shot up so many times that I was sure even the bullet holes had bullet holes. On top of one of the piles of broken masonry sat a Congolese militiaman, who seemed to scowl directly at me, idly waving his assault rifle, as our jeep crawled past.

Michel noticed me wince and tried to sound reassuring. 'In town itself, things have been pretty quiet since the peace treaty. As you probably know there was some pretty bad fighting back here during the war and air raids by pro-government war planes, but the rebels, the mai-mai, and the government troops now seem to be getting on.'

I was only half-listening as I watched a group of charcoal-burners struggling to bring the produce of their day's work into town. Large chunks of charcoal had been crammed into floppy cages woven from thin strips of brown bark. The cages were then flung across the handlebars and frame of old bicycles, with more cages piled on top. The crazy, tottering loads were on the final leg of their journey, heaved through the sand into town by the bare-chested men, whose already dark bodies were streaked with smears of sweat-congealed, jet-black charcoal powder.

But then Michel said something that brought my attention straight back to him.

'As you probably know, like all of the eastern DRC, we had a bit of a wobble a few months back. If you look over there you will see what I mean.'

Kalemie was just a few hundred kilometres south of Bukavu, the scene of the June attack by pro-Rwandan rebels. It had prompted a backlash by the Congolese authorities against anyone linked with Rwanda, especially the Banyamulenge, a tribal group from eastern Congo who trace their ancestry back a few hundred years to the Tutsi tribes of Rwanda. No matter that the Banyamulenge have been in the Congo for generations, their association with Rwanda was enough to see them murdered and persecuted today by the Congolese.

'There you can see our local Banyamulenge,' Michel said as we passed in through the gate of the UN base in Kalemie. He was pointing at a 200-strong crowd, mainly of children, gathered around a standpipe where they were messily filling bright-yellow, plastic water containers. 'They arrived at the gate one day in one big group and said they feared for their lives. They have been here, living right there under plastic sheets out in the open for the last few months. We don't know quite what to do with them, but for the moment we are happy for them to camp at our gate.'

*

Evelyn Waugh was not overly impressed with Albertville when he passed through here in 1930. He arrived by ferry, spent two nights in the town and then headed west into the Congo proper by train. He wrote a travel book about his journey called *Remote People*, in which the Congolese section of the trip was described in unflattering terms. The relevant chapter is entitled 'Second Nightmare' and in it Waugh grizzles at length about the petty bureaucrats responsible for immigration at the port and the lack of anything for the visitor to do in Albertville, although he is fairly complimentary about the service he enjoyed at the port's principal hotel. He describes how he took out his portable typewriter and wrote some of the early chapters of the travel book as he was dive-bombed by mosquitoes, before he got into a steaming row with an irksome ferry-boat captain, who marooned him on the Congo River.

Michel told me it was not possible for me to stay at the UN base, so we went in search of the hotel Waugh described as offering 'fairly good food'. What we found was a two-storey ruin on the main street with flaking paint and broken windows. A spacious first-floor balcony was supported by a number of elegant, fluted columns, but they were all pock-marked with what appeared to be bullet holes, and when I looked further up the front wall I could see why. The hotel had been converted, years after Waugh passed through, into an officers' club for the Congolese army, and the name still painted on the front wall, *Mess Des Officiers*, made it suitable for target practice during any of the town's subsequent periods of instability.

'Try the Hotel Du Lac along the road,' a man shouted from the balcony when I asked if I could have a look around. 'This is a military building now. You cannot come in.'

A larger three-storey structure, a short distance away, bore the hotel's name. Its construction in the 1950s came during Albertville's *belle époque*, the period when the town was booming, and at the time it must have been an impressive place, the largest hotel for hundreds of kilometres. I stood back on the other side of the road and tried to picture it with cars parked outside, music coming out of the dining room, fans spinning in the rooms to keep down the heat and the mosquitoes. It took quite a leap of imagination. Fifty years after it was built, the hotel had no electricity or water and the rooms were mostly empty shells. Some people sat on chairs on what was once a terrace in front of the hotel, but when I asked about rooms they shook their heads.

I cursed silently. The American journalist who had tried to follow Stanley's route in the mid-1960s had passed through Albertville. The civil war was already five years old when he arrived in Albertville, and he described his euphoria at making it safely to the port. After all my own troubles reaching this spot, I recognised the same sense of euphoria in myself, but what I did not recognise was the town he portrayed, with its comfortable, functioning hotel offering hot water in every room.

I had one other option for accommodation. During my research I had made contact with the International Rescue Committee, an American aid group, which kept an office in Kalemie during the war. I had tried to contact the office manager, Tommy Lee, by email, but he was using a fairly intermittent system that relied on a satellite telex that only worked a few hours each week, so I was not entirely sure if my messages had got through.

'The IRC house is just down the road, but before I take you there, I want to show you something you might find interesting.' Michel was really getting into his role of Kalemie Tour Guide.

He drove me back along the main road, past the bicycle taxis and the derelict terrace. The awful road surface meant we only managed a walking pace and Michel was forever greeting people in Swahili, joshing and waving out of the jeep window, before he steered the vehicle up a steep hill, bouncing violently over some exposed tree roots and parked in front of what looked like a pair of giant, brown beetles.

'What on earth are those?' I asked.

'Go see for yourself,' answered Michel.

It was as I got out of the car that I spotted the gun barrels emerging from under the scarab-like metal covers that looked like overturned, oversized woks.

'First World War naval guns,' said Michel. 'The Belgians brought them here when Albertville was worth defending. I guess they remind you that once upon a time Europe thought this town worth fighting over.'

In 1915 Kalemie was strategically important enough to stage one of Africa's most peculiar episodes from the First World War. Two British motor launches were smuggled here by the Royal Navy for a surprise attack on a flotilla of German warships, which was enjoying unchallenged control over Africa's deepest lake. The railway might be a ruin today, but almost a century ago it was so well established that British naval planners used it to bring their attack boats here by train, after an overland journey from Cape Town, almost 5,000 kilometres to the south. The subsequent successful raid on the German ships became part of British naval lore, and a bowdlerised version of the story formed the basis for C.S. Forester's novel *The African Queen*, which was made into a 1951 Hollywood film starring Katharine Hepburn and Humphrey Bogart.

Michel dropped me outside the IRC house in Kalemie, a rather sinister-looking building built from dark, volcanic stone, made even more imposing by its formidable iron gate. As his jeep pulled away, I heaved my rucksack onto my back and knocked loudly. A small shutter, the size of a letterbox, clunked open in the gate at eye level and a pair of eyes looked me up and down. Before I said anything, the gate swung open. Being white was clearly enough to gain entry.

'Please come in, we were expecting you, Mr Tim.'

It took me a moment to work out what had happened. My emails must have got through and my name must have been passed to a gatekeeper who was not exactly overwhelmed with white visitors.

'Please go inside the house. You will find Monsieur Tommy there.'

I put my luggage down on the steps leading up to the house and made my way inside. In the front room, a black man lay dozing on a tired-looking sofa, and so, treading gingerly, I entered a large, dusty sitting room with a television at one end and a dining table at the other. The room was crammed with the furniture and kit I associated with itinerant aid workers – piles of food sacks, rucksacks and an array of electrical equipment like computers, satellite phones and cables – all covered in a filigree of dust and all connected to the same overworked power point.

'Mr Lee, Mr Lee,' I called faintly. Kalemie's position just south of the Equator meant twilight would last only a few minutes. Darkness was already gathering, so I flicked a light switch. Nothing happened, so back outside I went, trying not to wake the man I assumed to be the housekeeper.

I failed, and in a blather of blinking and yawning, the figure sat upright and spoke to me in the strongest American accent I had ever heard.

'Hi. You must be Tim. Welcome to Kalemie. I am Tommy Lee, a pleasure to meet you.'

I sat with him for a while on the sagging sofa as he came round. Night had fallen and, without any lights in the town, the darkness was complete. Tommy stirred, saying something about this being the worst time for mosquitoes, and he checked that all the screened doors and windows were fully closed. He asked me about my plans and raised two heavy, querulous eyebrows when I said that I had come to Kalemie to try to travel to the river.

'Folks don't move around much overland here.' He spoke slowly and deliberately. 'Some of our staff use our motorbikes to visit our projects out in the bush, but they don't go far.'

I could not let the mention of motorbikes pass, so I plunged in.

'Would there be any chance I could pay you to use two of your bikes?'

'Son, I would love to be able to help you. But those bikes are about the most valuable thing we have around here, and my bosses would never let me give them up to you. You are talking about a long distance to the river, seven hundred kilometres or more. I could not be sure the bikes would ever make it back.'

I was disappointed, but at least I now knew that it was possible to get motorbikes along some of the bush tracks.

It was now very dark, but inside the main room I could make out a shadowy figure moving around, skilfully managing to avoid bumping into the furniture. I peered harder and Tommy spotted my curiosity.

'That's our cook. We eat early round here and that's dinner she is laying out. We have a generator, but we don't have much fuel so we don't turn it on until we really need it. Come on in, it's time to eat.'

He shouted over his shoulder for one of the security guards to turn on the generator and, after a distant mechanical roar, the house lights flickered into life and for the first time I could have a good look around. On the simple dining table two places had been set and between them sat a large, battered cooking pot and I could see the red blinking lights of various pieces of valuable communication equipment as they greedily took their nightly recharge from the power.

Tommy saw me staring at the plug. Keeping the batteries of my camera, satellite phone and laptop topped up required careful husbandry and I did not know when I would next have a chance to recharge.

'I am lucky because we are just about the only house in town with power right now, but it takes a lot of effort to get the right fuel, make sure it's clean and keep the generator running. Sure, you can recharge, but we only run it for a few hours so you better sort it out now.'

The tour of the house continued as we turned down a single, dark corridor.

'At the end there, that's the bathroom. It's not much, but the water is clean enough to wash with, and here is your room.'

The room was more passed through than lived in. Without many alternatives for accommodation in Kalemie, this house would have been visited not just by the IRC staff, but by all sorts of hangers-on like me, and the room reflected this. A large bed, as saggy as the sofa outside, filled the middle of the room, boxed in by a cavernous mosquito net, and around the edge of the room were various old bits of luggage and clothing abandoned by previous visitors.

Back at the dinner table, Tommy was already serving me rice and chicken, before offering me a glass of water. A few hours earlier Michel had pointed at a crowd of women washing in the stagnant water of the Lukuga River and told me about Kalemie's recent cholera outbreak, so I paused before accepting the offer. Tommy tried to reassure me. 'We boil all our water and then we filter it – it's routine.'

After dinner, the generator was turned off and I sat in the darkness listening as Tommy told me about himself. I could make out the shadows of his hands tweaking the whiskers on his chin as he described a career spent largely doing aid work in Africa. He had served most of his time in francophone west Africa, which explained his excellent French and Nigerian wife, and had only arrived in the Congo relatively recently. But in the short time he had been here, he had already had a grim experience.

'I was in Bukavu in June, when those rebel soldiers came into town. It was a bad scene, man, a really bad scene.'

I asked him to explain.

'As you may know, Bukavu is like the capital for the aid community working in that region of the eastern Congo. Every group is there. And for the sake of security, all the groups are on the same radio net, so we all know what is going on. When the rebels arrived, we all just hit the deck, staying in our houses and listening in on the radio to try and work out what was happening. Well, there was this small aid group with a compound, where a young Irish girl was working with an older woman – from Denmark or Sweden, I think. Anyway, the rebels got in there somehow and we all lay there on the ground, listening on the radio, as this young woman was raped.

'It was horrible. But the older woman, who had been shot but was still alive, kept telling us what was happening. She was a nurse and somehow she kept her voice under control the whole way through, describing things clearly and factually. It was awful, man. We had a running commentary. She hoped the message would get out to the UN troops up there from South Africa, but they were fucking hopeless, man – it took them more than a day before they eventually came into town.

'That was my welcome to the Congo. Scary, eh?'

With that Tommy got up and left me, muttering something about needing to check his messages from the United States. I sat in silence, thinking about the story he had just told, before heading to the sanctuary of my net-shrouded bed. The last I saw of Tommy that night was through the window of his small office. It was dark apart from the glow of his laptop reflected on his whiskery face, as he tapped out messages for relay via satellite phone and swatted insects attracted to the only light source for kilometres around. It made me think of the mosquito-plagued Evelyn Waugh, tapping away on his portable typewriter as he worked on his first draft of *Remote People*, in this same town seventy years earlier.

The following morning I was woken by a voice asking, insistently, for Monsieur Tim. Dawn had broken, but it was still early and there was no sign of Tommy. I hauled on my trousers and shirt and emerged blinking to find a smartly dressed Congolese man sitting on my favourite saggy sofa.

'Good morning. My name is Benoit Bangana. I work for Care International and have been told you need help with motorbikes.'

'Yes, that's right.' I was not yet fully awake and was struggling to take this in. Brian Larson, the boss of Care International based thousands of kilometres away on the other side of the country, had delivered on his half-promise of help.

'Well, I am here with one other colleague. We have two motorbikes and, if you are prepared to take the risk, we will take you some of the way.'

Still half-asleep, I was not sure I could believe what I was hearing. It just did not compute with everything I had been told about this place. A series of questions came blathering out from me, as my sleepy head cleared. Where had this man come from? How had he got here? Was he serious about heading overland to the Congo River?

'I am based in the town of Kasongo, a little over halfway between here and Kindu on the river. Kasongo is about five hundred kilometres from here, and Care International is the only aid group based there. Normally we come and go by plane, but recently we have been trying to extend our area of operation and for the past few months we have been preparing to go overland from Kasongo to the town of Kabambarre, about three hundred kilometres from here. Motorbikes are the only way to travel. When we got the message that you needed help, I was already planning a trip to Kabambarre, so my boss asked me if I would come all the way here and take you back.'

I was thrilled.

'How far can you take me? Do you know the way?'

Benoit smiled and tried to sound reassuring.

'I reckon I can get you to Kasongo. Our bikes are good and I think we can buy enough petrol here in Kalemie. Out there, there is nothing, so we will have to take everything we need for the journey from here, all the food, all the water, everything.'

That was progress, but my main concern was the security

situation. 'Is it safe? What about the rebels and the mai-mai?'

At this Benoit stopped smiling and looked more sombre.

'For the security situation, well, that would be your own risk – I cannot guarantee your security. You can meet mai-mai anywhere out there and if you are lucky, and they are not drunk, then you can get through. I am not so sure about a white man, though. I have never travelled here with a white man. I am sorry, but I cannot guarantee anything out there.'

Those words stayed with me long after he stopped speaking. 'I cannot guarantee anything out there.' They tempered the excitement I felt about securing a motorbike. When I conceived this trip, I hoped to slip round the rebel soldiers, but Benoit seemed adamant this was not possible.

We took two cups of black tea from the cook, who had returned to her cooking station – a charcoal burner on the back step of the house – and discussed options. I wanted to know more about Benoit and why he was prepared to risk his life in the badlands of Katanga.

'I am an engineer by training, but there is no work in the Congo apart from with aid groups like Care International. Now the war has ended we can hope again for an improvement in our lives, but the improvement will only come if there is normality, and there will only be normality if you can, once again, travel safely across our country. Someone has to be the first to go along these roads after the war, and as long as I make all the right preparations, then I am happy to be the first person.'

'But aren't you scared when you travel in these sorts of areas?'

'I am afraid a little, but then I think about the good that will come to the people of Katanga if the roads are made safe again and life can go back to normal. Every village we reach, every stream we cross, is another small movement towards normality again in the Congo.'

'What about travelling with a white man? Won't that be even more risky for you?'

'I always ride with my colleague, Odimba, and we have developed our own little strategy when we think it looks dangerous – we try not to stop. Out in the forest the rebels are not expecting bikes, so if we are lucky we hurry past them and the first they see of us is our backs, disappearing into the forest. If we keep going they have no idea if we are black, white, Congolese or foreign.'

I looked at Benoit very closely. I was not just asking him to risk his life on my behalf. I was considering trusting him with my own. It was a big call, but the thing that swung it was the way he answered my question about how much I should pay him for his help.

'I am paid by Care International, who have asked me to extend our range around Kasongo. Travelling with you is part of my job, so you don't have to pay me anything. If we get to Kasongo, you can talk to the senior man there about the cost of hiring the bikes. But as for me, I don't expect any payment.'

That was the moment I decided Benoit Bangana was a man I could trust, but before I made any more decisions about the security situation, I thought it wise to ask Michel's advice.

I found Michel at work in his radio station, a standard-issue UN container at the garrison headquarters built in the ruin of a Belgian-era cotton factory on the outskirts of town. Thousands of workers had once processed raw cotton grown in the sweaty Congolese interior and shipped here by lorry and train. Terraces of brick houses had been erected for hundreds of workers, but most of them lay in ruins now outside the razor-wire perimeter of the UN base.

Michel was deep in thought, trying to work out how the local UN commander should deal with an imminent public-relations crisis. Peacekeepers in Kalemie and elsewhere across the Congo had been caught paying local girls, under age of consent, for sex. Almost all UN missions suffer from the same problem, with bored, well-paid young men deployed to places where poverty is so acute that girls are willing to sell themselves. Michel had just come from a meeting where the large scale of the problem in Kalemie had been revealed. He seemed happy for the distraction I provided when I introduced Benoit and explained about the motorbikes. Michel was impressed.

'You move fast. Having a motorbike is great news. Well done.'

'But I am still worried about security. Benoit says there are mai-mai all along these tracks. Do you know anyone local they might listen to, who could help me get through?'

'There is one person I know about from Kalemie who dares to travel regularly through the bush. He is a pygmy and he runs a small aid group here in town that tries to protect the rights of pygmies. The group's name is *La Voix des Minorités*, Minorities' Voice, and the man's name is Georges Mbuyu. I have interviewed him many times.'

The name sounded familiar. I looked back at my research notes and saw that an Anglican missionary from Uganda had once told me of Georges Mbuyu and his pygmy rights group. I had read a report about the role Georges played in negotiating the release of four local villagers arrested during the war by the pro-Rwandan rebels, who were then in control of Kalemie, but the missionary had told me that getting in touch with Georges was impossible from outside the Congo. Now that I was in Kalemie, Michel assured me that finding Georges could not be simpler.

Benoit and I piled into Michel's jeep and drove back through town, past the bicycle taxis and the hawkers. We followed the road up past the church on the headland and, just as we came level with a derelict Belgian villa, Michel stopped. The façade was cracked, standing on half-collapsed foundations left exposed by numerous seasonal rains. A small man, a tad under five foot in height, wearing a T-shirt, dark trousers and plastic flip-flops, emerged from inside. When he saw Michel, he grinned.

The pair greeted each other warmly in Swahili and then Michel broke into French, introducing me as a writer. Georges raised his eyebrows in astonishment and then seemed to remember his manners.

'Please come into my office,' he said, leading me over the broken verandah and into a bare room where most of the plaster had either fallen off the wall or was about to. He proffered me a rickety chair and asked me my business.

'I want to go overland from here all the way to the Congo River. I want to follow the same route used by the explorer, Stanley, when he became the first white man to cross the Congo. But I am worried about security. Can you help?'

He thought for a moment.

'I cannot remember the last time a white man went through that area. It has been many, many years. But I know some of the mai-mai near town. It is not just the pygmies that my group represents. We represent all minorities, and sometimes that includes mai-mai. Some of the mai-mai are not rebels, they are just villagers who want to protect themselves. These are good people and I can talk to them. The problem is the outsiders who come down here into our province of Katanga – they are the ones who are out of control.'

'Would you be prepared to accompany me, by motorbike, towards the river?' I tried not to sound too desperate as I asked the question.

For a moment, Georges was quiet. He looked at his colleague, a much taller man, Mutombo Nganga; they had a brief exchange in Swahili and then he turned to me.

'I cannot go with you all the way, but I am prepared to take the risk along the roads close to Kalemie. I think you will be safe if I go with you. I know these mai-mai well. I grew up in the bush and I know their families and their villages, so I could try to help you.'

There was something reassuringly trustworthy about Georges. Like Benoit, he did not mention money, but when I asked him if I could pay him, he mumbled something about me making a donation to *La Voix des Minorités*.

'But have you been there recently, along the road between here and Kindu?'

'No-one has been all the way along that road recently. It is a long way, more than seven hundred kilometres. But in our province, Katanga, closer to here, I have walked along some of the roads in recent years. The mai-mai are not all out of control, you know. I have been with many of them and they will listen to me. But once you leave Katanga and enter into the next province of Maniema, then that will be different. I do not know that place at all.'

When Stanley passed through here, the name Maniema itself was enough to cause many of his bearers to run away. It had terrible associations with cannibalism and sorcery. I was more sanguine about it. Maniema was a problem for another day some time in the future. For the moment, I had a much bigger problem to deal with. If Georges was going to come with us, I needed to find another motorbike.

It was Benoit who immediately spotted the problem.

'We have only two bikes. You will ride with Odimba on one bike and I will ride on the other with all our luggage. There is no space for Georges, and how would he get back here to Kalemie? I have been in this town for a few days now and I have not seen any other suitable bikes we could use.'

I asked Michel and he was more optimistic. He took us into the centre of town and stopped near a small office run by the World Food Programme, the UN agency responsible for feeding refugees, left us in the jeep and walked over to the security guard. After two minutes' conversation he came back.

'My friend here knows a man with a motorbike, who might be prepared to rent it for Georges as long as he only goes a short distance out of town. He will try to find the man, but it will take half an hour or so.'

Michel had to leave, so Benoit, Georges and I all jumped out of the jeep and killed time in the centre of Kalemie until the guard came back. The heat was getting to me and I needed to drink something. Some bottles of sugary orangeade were the only thing available, so I bought three from a hawker and we all stood in the shade of a coconut tree drinking them. On the other side of the road was the relic of a building that looked like a restaurant or café. There was a fenced-in garden and an old sign that said '*Cercle des Cheminots*' or 'Railwaymen's Club'. I remembered seeing photographs of this place from the 1940s and 1950s when it was full of Belgian railway employees, seated at small wooden tables draped with chequered table cloths and laden with plates of food and bottles of wine. For years the railway company – *La Compagnie des Chemins de Fer des Grands Lacs*, or CFL – had been the biggest employer in the town, and this was where the employees drank, ate and socialised.

I walked inside to find a wreck. A wooden bar ran along one wall and a tall Congolese lady stood behind it.

'Do you have anything I could drink?'

'No.'

'Do you have anything I could eat?'

'No.'

Before I left, I spotted a pile of crockery on a table. The top one caught my eye. It was marked with the livery of CFL, a swirling red-and-white pennant, a relic of an age when customers and staff would have eaten off company crockery.

Back on the main street, we returned to our rendezvous to find a grubby-looking man talking to Michel's security guard. His eyes were bloodshot and his breath smelled of alcohol.

'If you want a motorbike, I am your man.' He could barely stand he was so drunk.

My response was a bit tetchy and impatient.

'If I am going to allow my guide to ride with you on your bike, I need to see it.'

'I have thought of that. Follow me.'

The man, Fiston Kasongo, then led us down a track away from Kalemie's high street to the abandoned railway, where he had hidden a bike in some long grass.

'There is my bike. It is a great bike.'

I could see Benoit was not convinced. Benoit had a pair of Yamaha off-road bikes. They were only 100cc, much smaller than the 900cc bike I used to ride in London, but Benoit assured me they were the best bikes for Congolese tracks; light enough to lift over obstacles and strong enough to cope with the huge distances and awful trails. The bike Fiston was offering had a brand name – TVS Max – that I did not recognise, and was much less sturdy.

Benoit tapped me on the shoulder and took me off to a safe distance so that he could raise his concerns.

'I have never seen that make of bike before. It does not look good enough to me.'

I was beginning to feel sceptical, but Georges then joined in.

'The bike looks okay for me. I am only going to come with you for a day or so, not the whole journey. In the past I have walked this same distance, so if we have any problems I can always walk.'

If Georges was game, that was enough for me. Benoit nodded slowly and I returned to the swaying Fiston. A price was then settled upon. I asked Fiston how much he wanted per day. He hesitated for a moment and said $125. Benoit's eyes flickered disapprovingly, so I offered $50. Fiston did not hesitate for a second, agreeing enthusiastically to the price. He shook my hand, promised to meet me at the IRC house and, before leaving on his bike, asked for a down payment to allow him to buy some fuel. I gave him $20 and he disappeared, weaving along a footpath through the high grass in a cloud of blue exhaust smoke that spoke of an engine in distress.

I spent the next three days preparing for the journey. First, I had to get permission from both the local district commissioner and military commander. Even in a large town like Kalemie where the state fails to provide any teachers, doctors or policemen, it still insists on pieces of paper to authorise the toings and froings of foreigners. I was wary about making too many introductions as I feared the authorities would whip up greater problems, but Michel assured me that the commissioner, Pierre Kamulete, would not cause trouble. Michel volunteered to make the introductions, so on my second morning in Kalemie he drove me and my team – Benoit the biker, and Georges the pygmy – up past the main church and along to the ruins of the old colonial governor's house, which now served as the commissioner's office.

We sat on an old school bench in the hall outside the commissioner's office, along with a few other supplicants waiting for an audience with the commissioner. When our turn came we all trooped into a large room, at the end of which stood a big desk with M. Kamulete sitting behind it. The desk was bare apart from a piece of paper torn from a school textbook, covered in handwriting. At the other end of the room sat two military men, one a large man in khaki fatigues and the other smaller, also wearing uniform, but with naval insignia on his epaulettes.

'Look at this, Michel, what do you make of this?' The commissioner knew Michel well and wanted his opinion on the handwritten page. He handed it to Michel, who read it slowly. It was a public attack on the commissioner, an anonymous Swahili denunciation of the inefficiency and corruption of his administration. Written in capital letters using a blue biro, it had been discovered that morning pinned to a coconut tree in the town centre. It accused the commissioner and his staff of deliberately cutting the power line connecting the town with the Bendera hydroelectric power station for sinister, political reasons. The pair of them discussed it earnestly for a few minutes and I quietly shook my head. While the rest of the world drowned in information provided by broadband Internet connections and live satellite television, the political debate here in Kalemie revolved around a rude message, written on a child's notepad and nailed to a tree.

Once the issue had been dealt with to the satisfaction of the commissioner, Michel thought it was time to introduce me. He emphasised my interest in the explorer Stanley and my historical connection through the *Telegraph*, before I was allowed to thank the commissioner for his time and ask if he would grant me the necessary authority to head on my way though Katanga.

The trouble I was expecting did not materialise. The commissioner listened to my plans and made a few remarks about how difficult it was to travel safely through the Congo. He gave the impression of finding my plan trifling, not suspicious, humouring me like someone on a fool's errand, confident I would be back in Kalemie in a few days after failing to get through Katanga. At no stage did he ask for money. He simply checked my passport, looked at the identity documents of Georges and Benoit, and barked an instruction at his secretary to prepare the necessary stamps. It was then that he pointed to the larger of the two military men in the room, telling me I would also need the permission of the local commander, Lieutenant Colonel Albert Abiti Mamulay. The colonel squirmed in his seat as the commissioner pointed at him and said we must come up to his headquarters for the relevant stamp.

We followed the colonel outside to his waiting staff car. It was an old Peugeot, which looked too fragile to take any more crashes or bumps. I was wrong. As we watched, the colonel's driver jammed the car into reverse and rammed it firmly into a rocky bank, before over-revving and charging off up the hill towards the barracks, bumping over exposed tree roots and rivulets scoured into the roadway by rain.

I remembered the description by the American journalist Blaine Littell of the same military barracks in the 1960s. He had reached Albertville just after the town had been recaptured by government troops, and when he got to the barracks he was given his own display of torture tactics. A hapless rebel, accused by the government troops of involvement in Albertville's uprising, was paraded and humiliated for Mr Littell at gunpoint.

There were no rebels to torture when I arrived at the same building forty years after Mr Littell. I saw the colonel disappear into a tatty old house and we tried to follow. A squat man, a pygmy the same size as Georges but without his charm, barred our way and told us firmly to wait outside. I handed over the piece of paper already stamped by the commissioner and stood under a mango tree with another group of men. Some of their clothing was khaki, so I assumed they were soldiers. The oldest then did something peculiar. From the lower branches of the tree he plucked a silver bugle. It was buckled and pitted, but he solemnly set about polishing with his sleeve.

I walked across and asked him who he was.

'I am the bugler. It is my job to sound the bugle at dawn, midday and sunset.'

'Have you always been in the army?'

'No, I was only just brought into the army this year. I was a musician in the railway band before the Belgians left and I am the only person left in Kalemie with any musical knowledge.'

With the necessary stamps on my travel pass, all that was left was to arrange the fuel, food and water for our trip. But before that I wanted to test the bikes, so I suggested a run to Mtowa, the lakeside village at the spot where Stanley first reached the Congo.

Georges said he knew Mtowa well and would guide me, so off we headed for my first taste of Congolese motorbiking. Benoit rode his bike with Georges riding pillion, and I rode Benoit's second bike. The route took us out over the bridge across the Lukuga River, a cast-iron structure built by the Belgians with a single carriageway. It was swarming with pedestrians and cyclists as Benoit led the way, tooting on the bike's horn to clear a path, before we headed north from the town past the UN base. When Michel had picked me up from the airport the road had felt sandy, and on the bike it was downright dangerous. The sand made the tyres slew extravagantly from side to side and one particularly deep trough pitched me heavily down on my side. Breaking an ankle now would not be a good idea, I thought, as I dusted myself down and set off more cautiously.

The road took us round the back of the UN base and for the first time I could see the scale of the old cotton factory that the Belgians had built here. As well as the large warehouses for processing the cotton, there were dozens of houses for the employees, covering a huge campus. The cotton was not grown here on the lakeside as the climate was not quite right. To grow, the cotton plants needed the greater heat and humidity of the Congo River valley, and under the Belgians the raw material was then transported hundreds of kilometres by rail and road to this factory, where it was spun into fibre and then woven into cloth. By its size alone, I could tell the plant must have been an impressive sight when operational, but all lay in ruins as we buzzed by on the bikes.

The going was slow. We were following what had once been a road, but we were forever slowing to pick our route over streams that had carved their way across the carriageway, or patches of mud that had dried in wavy ridges. For several kilometres the terrain was low and flat before the track started to climb a series of hills. Just as the road began to rise, we passed through several villages, where the sound of the bikes was enough to draw crowds of children. In one village I saw Georges tapping Benoit on the shoulder, asking him to stop. He hopped off the bike and began to talk with a group of villagers. There was something slightly odd about the scene, but it took me a few moments to work out what I found curious – Georges no longer appeared short.

'This is a village of pygmies,' he explained. 'I come here from time to time to hear about what is happening to these people. Throughout the history of the Congo the pygmies have suffered, and it continues today. That is one of the largest parts of our job, to fight for the rights of these people.'

A lopsided sign was tied to a tree. It was a piece of bark that had been flattened and a name had been written using ash in crude, uneven letters on its pale underside. It reminded me of illustrations from A.A. Milne books and it read '*La Voix des Minorités*', the name of the group run by Georges. The village was composed of tiny grass huts arranged around an area of dirt beaten flat by shoeless feet. As Georges spoke to the village elder, a group of children wearing rags played a rather hazardous game, which involved the player trying to pick up as many sticks as possible that had been scattered on the ground while dodging a coconut thrown at her by rival players.

Back on the bikes, the road climbed and the bush got thinner until finally I got the view of the lake I had been hoping for. I stopped my bike and climbed up a bank. The lake stretched away to the east as far as I could see, but just below me was the village of Mtowa and a headland, the first piece of Congolese land Stanley touched when he arrived here by boat across the lake in September 1876.

'I know everything about Stanley.' The words of the village chief, Idi Kavunja, grabbed my attention. It had taken me a week to get here from Johannesburg, but I was finally on the trail of the explorer. Hearing his name, pronounced in the French style of 'Stan-lay', threw me. I was talking to a chief whose forebears could have met the explorer, but the magic of the moment was lost when it became clear he was talking rubbish.

'He is buried here. If you pay me money, I will show you the grave.' I looked into a pair of eyes that had an oily, unfocused sheen. The chief was now craning forward, the sinews on his scrawny neck as tight as guitar-strings, and his breath was pungently high. 'You are a white man, you have a phone. I am a chief, I need a phone. You must give me your phone.'

There was nothing threatening about the chief. He was a slight man, wearing the remnants of a pin-striped suit that was several sizes too big for him. Inside a wide and grubby shirt collar, his neck rattled around like a turtle's, giving him the impression of a child dressed up in his parents' clothes. But there was nothing child-like about his next outburst.

'You white men only ever come here to profit from the Congo. Stanley was the first. Then came the Belgians. How do I know you have not come here to profit?'

Georges looked embarrassed and I made a polite but firm apology and returned to our bikes. We rode down to the water's edge, following a track through the reed beds that was used by fishermen. When it got too muddy for the bikes, I parked and walked down to a break in the reeds where the fishermen had pulled up their dugouts. A boy was standing ankle-deep in the jet-black mud, hunting for worms. I shouted a question, asking if he knew the name of this place.

He nodded and shouted back. 'Mtowa.'

I wanted to see if any of Mtowa's history still lingered about the place, asking, 'Do you know the old name? It used to be called Arab's Crossing. This was where the slavers used to arrive from the other side of the lake.'

The boy thought for a moment, shook his head blankly and continued worming. Suddenly he shouted something in Swahili, something that made Georges become visibly more tense.

'He said there are land mines all around here, left by Ugandan troops when they occupied this area during the war.' Georges was now peering into the reedy undergrowth.

'Look there,' he shouted, pointing at a red warning sign. In large black letters it said: 'Beware! Mines!'

Very slowly, we followed our footprints back to the bikes for the return trip to Kalemie.

As a trial run, the trip to Mtowa was a success. The bikes stood up well to the shocking conditions of the track and we had managed about ten kilometres an hour. I had not hurt myself, and both Benoit and Georges had been helpful companions. But the words of the chief stayed with me, as my first hint of the residual bitterness felt by Congolese for centuries of suffering at the hands of outsiders.

The old man might have been drunk, but he was right. Outsiders have robbed and exploited the people of the Congo ever since the days of the first European and Arab slavers. The territory that Stanley staked in the name of Leopold witnessed what many regard as the first genocide of the modern era, when millions of Congolese were effectively worked to death trying to meet the colonialists' almost insatiable demand for resources, most notably rubber. And since independence, foreign powers have toyed with the Congo, stripping its mineral assets and exploiting its strategic position, never mindful of the suffering inflicted on its people. And that really was the point. At every stage of its bloody history, outsiders have tended to treat Congolese as somehow sub-human, not worthy of the consideration they would expect for themselves. For progress to be made, outsiders must treat Congolese as equals and they could do worse than follow the example of an amazing white woman I discovered after we got back to Kalemie.

It took some time to track down the town's last white, Belgian resident. Michel had lived there for two years, but he had only ever heard mention of the mysterious woman, who kept herself to herself, living in an old villa on the hill behind the main church.

Geneviève Nagant's house was tucked some way off the main road. It took some finding, and I had to clamber through rough bush before I finally found the front door and knocked. From inside, I could hear various locks being undone before it was opened by the smiling seventy-seven-year-old. The door opened into a hall and ground-floor room that were musty and full of books. The humidity had caused most to swell and lose their bindings. Many had been rewrapped in unmarked, brown-paper wrappers. It looked like the study of an eccentric Oxford don, an image Mlle Nagant reinforced as she fussed about, apologising for the mess, thrusting books and pamphlets at me, before shooing me upstairs to a much fresher, first-floor living room, which opened out onto a balcony.

On entering the room, something immediately caught my eye. On the wall there were two pictures. They were crayon drawings of tribal figures, paddling a canoe against a backdrop of thatched huts and bush. It was a hot afternoon, but the pictures gave me goosebumps. They were exactly the same as the ones my mother bought when she passed through this town in 1958.

'Do you like these pictures?' Mlle Nagant had noticed my reaction.

'They remind me of my home in England. My mother bought some pictures just like these when she travelled through the Congo before I was born. Seeing them makes me think of the stories she told about her journey.'

Mlle Nagant smiled and for a moment we looked at the pictures together. 'In the late 1950s, Albertville was the best it ever got. The trains would arrive at the station and the passengers could connect with the liners. I remember you could hear the whistles of the ships as they left the port, and sometimes you could even hear the band playing on the top deck in first class.'

We went to sit outside on her balcony. The house stood on the headland near the church and from up there I got a fine view of the lake. The sky was clear and the bright sun made the water sparkle for the first time during my visit to Kalemie. At last I could see why the Belgians knew it as the 'Pearl of Tanganyika'.

'I was born near Liège, but arrived here in 1951. I was in my twenties and my job was as a teacher of social science. My duties were to teach Congolese ladies who came from villages about life in towns such as this one. We had classes in water hygiene, cooking, baby care and that sort of thing. People remember the Belgian colonial rule as a time for cruelty, but towards the end progress was being made across all of society. I used to live with a nurse who worked on a health programme that was successful in ending leprosy in the area and much of the malaria. Can you imagine that? Today, leprosy and malaria are killing thousands of people all over the Congo.'

In 1960, within days of independence being granted to the Congo, the first violence broke out. In Albertville, almost the entire Belgian community left within a matter of weeks. Why had Mlle Nagant stayed?

Her elegant reply revealed that she was a rare breed of Belgian colonial, one who genuinely cared for the local Congolese people. 'Because when you plant a seed you must tend it before it will blossom.'

Since independence, she had lived through four decades of chaos. Her tiny Belgian civil-service pension used to be sent here through the post office, but when the postal service collapsed in the 1970s she began relying on the kindness of Belgian missionaries, who would courier the small amount of money back when returning from leave.

And how does the situation today compare with what Mlle Nagant has witnessed since 1951?

'I am sorry to say that today is worse than ever before. I have got used to the lack of water. I have got used to the lack of power. I have got used to the lack of supplies in town. But the thing that makes today so bad is the lack of the rule of law. There was a time when at least there were some police who could keep some sort of order, or even soldiers you could go to, but today there is nothing. Everything is upside down. Today, a driver for the UN here is paid ten times more than the provincial governor from the government. How can you run a government in circumstances like that? As I said, everything is upside down.'

She went inside and emerged a few moments later with a clinking tray. On it was a recycled wine bottle and two glasses. We watched as the blue of the lake steadily darkened with the dipping of the sun, and she toasted my health with her home-made white wine.

I asked her how she filled her days and she explained that she was writing an anthropological thesis on the early Congolese tribes discovered by the first Albertville residents in the last years of the nineteenth century. She was particularly interested in a local man, Stephano Kaoze, a priest who became the first black abbot of the Congo. It had become her life's work to record the thoughts and writings of Abbot Kaoze.

When I told her about my plan to travel overland to the river, she thought for a moment and went to get something from the chaos of her study downstairs.

'Here it is – this is one of the sayings of Abbot Kaoze, which might be of value to you.'

I took the flimsy notebook she offered me and read what she was pointing at. In the late 1890s Abbot Kaoze had this to say about travel. 'When going on a journey it is not just the strength of a man's legs, but the provisions he prepares for the trip.'

I walked back through the derelict ruin of Kalemie thinking about my own provisions and preparations. My mind was working as I tried to decide what I should do in the aftermath of the killings in Burundi and the resulting threat by the pro-Rwandan rebel group to rip up the peace treaty.

If the war restarted, there was no way I would take the risk of trying to cross the Congo. Michel said the UN alert state had already been raised as a result of the killing, but the UN was waiting to see the next move by the various rebel groups before it began the subsequent stage of its security plan – withdrawing all civilian staff, like Michel, from the Congo.

I had until 5 a.m. the following day to make up my mind. Benoit and Odimba had been away from their Care International base for more than a week and, with the security situation deteriorating, they were anxious to get themselves and their precious motorbikes back to base as soon as possible. They told me they would be leaving at 5 a.m., with or without me.

The sun had set and the town was deathly quiet as I walked down the hill past the empty plinth, where a statue of the Belgian king, Albert I, had once stood before an angry crowd had ripped it down in the aftermath of independence. I continued past the silent railway station, where my mother had arrived in the 1950s, and the ruins of the hotel, where Evelyn Waugh stayed in the 1930s.

It had taken me four years of research and patience to get to this point. If I did not take my chance tomorrow, there was a risk it would be years before the next opportunity would come round.

5.

Walked to Death

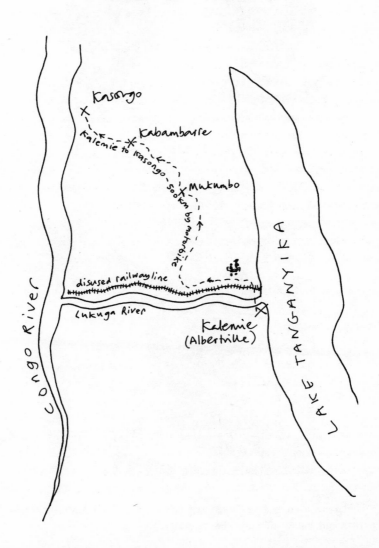

UBUJWÉ AND UGUHA HEAD-DRESS.

UGUHA HEAD-DRESS.

Hairstyles from eastern Congo as recorded, above, by H.M. Stanley in 1878 and, below, by the author in 2004

As I emerged from the house on the morning we were to leave Kalemie, Benoit appeared to be wrestling with eels. It was still dark, and with my head torch all I could make out was his shape, leaning over the back of one of the motorbikes, struggling with various long, black things with a springy and clearly disobedient life of their own. The eel image was reinforced by Benoit's outfit. He was wearing a bright-yellow plastic raincoat, with heavy gloves, kneepads, goggles and black, shiny wellington boots. He looked like a ninja North Sea trawlerman.

'Can I help?' I asked without much conviction.

He ignored me and, in between the grunts and curses, I worked out what was going on. He was using old bicycle inner tubes as luggage straps to attach my kit to the back of his motorbike. Knowing the balance of his bike and how it depended on the loading, he insisted on doing it by himself. Eventually, after much stretching, snapping, knotting and restretching, he stood back, let out a sigh and pronounced himself satisfied everything was secure. To me, it looked anything but. The 100cc motorbike was now sitting heavily on its rear wheel, with my rucksack, a jerry-can and various other pieces of gear bulkily taking up most of the rider's seat. Above the handlebars was another hulking arrangement of fuel bottles, water canisters and other bundles, trapped in its own web of straining inner tubes. And on top of it all, Benoit was wriggling into two rucksacks – one on his back, the other slung in reverse across his chest.

He could see I was sceptical. 'It's okay; these bikes are amazingly strong.'

I found him reassuring. The same cannot be said for Fiston. My 'local hire' motorbike-man had turned up stinking of booze, swaying extravagantly and mumbling something about needing more petrol. The day before I had impressed upon him the importance of having a full tank when we set out, and had paid him part of his fee in advance so that he could make sure it was full. In retrospect, this was a stupid thing to have done. He had clearly spent the cash on getting wasted. I grimaced, but, yet again, Benoit was the one who dealt with the problem.

'I thought this might happen,' he said. 'Last night I bought another few litres of petrol for emergencies.'

In a town like Kalemie where there are no petrol stations, fuel is sold on an ad hoc basis. It is of dodgy provenance, having been smuggled here by boat from Tanzania, and of even dodgier quality, 'watered down' with palm oil or any other suitable solvent. It is sold in old bottles, jars or cans and nobody cares too much about making sure they are clean. By torchlight I watched Benoit filling Fiston's tank from a plastic bottle. Instead of throwing it away, once he finished pouring he carefully crushed it flat, screwed the top back on and tucked it under one of his tame eels.

'Never know when you might need that,' he said quietly.

A frantic footfall announced the arrival of Georges. He barged through the gate, panting an apology for being late. As he caught his breath, there was a brief conflab about who would ride where. Benoit would ride alone with his unfeasibly large luggage load; Odimba, Benoit's colleague from Care International, also dressed like a ninja trawlerman, would follow with Georges as a passenger; and I would sit behind the sozzled Fiston and pray for him to sober up.

The engines of the three bikes stirred into life. It would be an exaggeration to say they roared. But in silent Kalemie even these puny machines sounded pretty impressive and we made quite a din as we swept out of town. In eastern Congo, a land of pedestrians and bicycles, the 100cc motorbike is king.

In our headlights I could see we were approaching the iron

bridge across the Lukuga River on the northern edge of town. A Royal Navy officer, Commander Verney Lovett Cameron, had been the first European to explore the river. Cameron was one of the great 'what if' figures of African exploration, an adventurer of no less ambition than Stanley, but who somehow never quite staked his own place in the public's imagination. He never came up with a soundbite as memorable as 'Dr Livingstone, I presume?' Cameron actually beat Stanley to this spot by two years. He, too, had heard tales from the Arab slavers about an immense river somewhere out there to the west. And he, too, was willing to trek through the bush for week after week to check if it were true.

But, unlike Stanley, he failed to make the river descent. Once he reached the upper Congo River he tried to persuade local villagers to take him downriver in their canoes, but they refused. He spent several weeks camped on the swampy river banks becoming more and more frustrated with the intransigence of the river tribes, and more and more sick from malaria. Eventually he abandoned the plan to follow the river, setting off overland due west instead, ending up on the coast of what is now Angola. Cameron's journey was an amazing achievement, one of the earliest and most significant trans-African treks, but his failure to solve the riddle of the river has seen history pass him by. What if Cameron had descended the Congo River? What if Cameron, more of a British establishment figure than his parvenu rival (Cameron dedicated his book, *Across Africa*, to Her Majesty Queen Victoria, while Stanley dedicated his to the newspapermen who commissioned him), had returned to London having charted a navigable river reaching across Africa and had successfully persuaded Britain to stake the land as a colony? How different would African history be, had a British Congo, not a Belgian Congo, dominated the centre of the continent?

No so different, is my conclusion. I have met British colonial types in Africa who scorn what Belgium did in the Congo and try to draw a distinction between the colonial system imposed by

Brussels and that imposed by London. So much crueller than any British colony, they say, so much more brutal towards the local Africans, so much more manipulative after begrudgingly granting independence. But the history of British colonialism in Africa, from Sierra Leone to Zimbabwe, Kenya to Botswana and elsewhere, is not fundamentally different from what Belgium did in the Congo. You can argue about degree, but both systems were predicated on the same assumption: that white outsiders knew best and Africans were to be treated not as partners, but as underlings. What the British did in Kenya to suppress the pro-independence mau-mau uprising in the 1950s, using murder, torture and mass imprisonment, was no more excusable than the mass arrests and political assassinations committed by Belgium when it was trying to cling on to the Congo. And the outside world's tolerance of a dictator in the Congo like Mobutu, whose corruption and venality were overlooked for strategic expediency, was no different from what happened in Zimbabwe, where the dictator Robert Mugabe was allowed to run his country and its people into the ground because Western powers gullibly accepted the way he presented himself as the only leader able to guarantee stability and an end to civil strife.

Those sniffy British colonial types might not like to admit it, but the Congo represents the quintessence of the entire continent's colonial experience. It might be extreme and it might be shocking, but what happened in the Congo is nothing but colonialism in its purest, basest form.

I thought of Cameron as our bikes clattered over the loose planks on the river bridge, because his first attempt to reach the Congo River had begun right beneath us, on the Lukuga. It is the only river that drains Lake Tanganyika and the young naval officer was convinced he could descend it by boat, all the way to its confluence with the much bigger, then-unknown river somewhere out there to the west of Lake Tanganyika. What he had not understood is that the Lukuga is impassable by boat because of the odd geographical feature that it only moves when the lake level rises during the rainy season. Cameron managed to get his small boat just a short distance down the Lukuga before he hit an immense and impenetrable barrier of silt and reed beds. He struggled for days, trying to hack his way through. He described how his heart sank as the channels he cut were immediately filled by matter floating up from below. It must have been wretched work – sweaty, insect-plagued and, ultimately, doomed.

Within minutes of crossing the bridge we left behind the sticky atmosphere that tormented Cameron. The air began to cool nicely as we followed a track climbing up and away from the lakeside still. Nightjars roosted on the path. I would pick them up in our headlights and watch as they sat frozen to the spot, exploding at the last second from underneath the lead motorbike, peeling up and away into the darkness. Although Kalemie had appeared asleep as we left, for the first few kilometres I kept spotting ghostly figures on the roadside. They were women, with baskets and tools perched on their heads, making their way out to the bush to tend plots of cassava and other crops. From a distance I would make out their dark shapes against the lightening sky and then, for an instant, they would be caught in the headlights, the colours of their cotton wraps bright and their wide eyes frozen in surprise.

I love starting a journey very early in the day. It offers the comforting sense that if something goes wrong, there is still the whole day to sort it out. As we left Kalemie before dawn that August morning, I felt a strong sense of well-being. The track was overhung with dew-drenched branches and twigs, and within a few minutes my wet clothes showed why Benoit and Odimba were wearing waterproofs. But the fact that I was soaked did not dim my spirits. After all the planning and worry, I was finally on the track of Stanley in the Congo, picking my way from Lake Tanganyika across ridges and through valleys that he had traversed in 1876. I can remember feeling excitement. And I can remember just how the euphoria began to ebb a few kilometres down the track when we had our first flat tyre.

I was bouncing happily along the track, tucked up behind Fiston. The fresh air had sobered him up and although the track was appalling, he was riding well, anticipating the divots, holes and obstacles, slowing down with his gears and using just the right amount of power to manoeuvre round them. For the first hour or so everything seemed perfect. August was the last month of the dry season and the rising sun had quickly dried the dew from my clothes. In spite of the track, we were skipping along at a healthy speed, peaking sometimes as high as 30 kph. But all of a sudden I saw Odimba, the rider ahead of us, slowing, peering down at his rear wheel and stopping.

The tiny form of Georges slipped off the back of Odimba's bike. Within a few minutes Odimba had undone the wheel, slipped off the tyre and begun searching for the leak in the inner tube. It reminded me of repairing punctures on my bicycle as a child.

Dawn had now broken and the low sun lit the feathery heads of the long grass on either side of the track. Without the sound of the bike engines, it was a scene of still beauty. We were within a few degrees of the Equator, but the early morning temperature was comfortable and the bush was still relatively open savannah, not the dark, claustrophobic hothouse of true rainforest. With good rivers, heavy dew and rich soil, no wonder the early Belgian colonialists here believed they had found an Eden.

Behind me I heard murmuring. I turned to see Odimba hand Benoit something. It was a rusty, bent nail about three centimetres long. Since we had left Kalemie an hour back we had seen nothing modern or man-made and yet we had managed to find an old nail.

Benoit and Odimba were clearly a team. While Odimba dried and prepared the inner-tube hole, Benoit cut an appropriately sized patch from his store of old, recycled tubes, the same ones he used as luggage straps. Having cut the right shape, he used a file to scour the surface of the patch so that it would grip glue.

'It will take twelve minutes for the glue to be ready,' Benoit announced with typical exactness.

I turned back to the feathery grasslands and listened for the sound of any birdlife. There was almost none. Georges explained that hunger drove local villagers to trap and kill birds as a source of meat. Exactly on cue, twelve minutes after administering the glue, Benoit and Odimba replaced the tyre and we were off again. And exactly twenty minutes later we had our first encounter with the mai-mai.

The track had narrowed to a thin file between dense undergrowth and I saw Benoit slow to negotiate a tricky bit of ground. All of a sudden he braked and flung his weight to the left, desperate to avoid something. Slowly from the bush on the right side of the track emerged two gun barrels – rusting Kalashnikovs – held in the bony, dirty hands of two anxious-looking people, a teenage girl and a man old enough to be her grandfather.

I swallowed drily. Meekly dropping my gaze to the ground, all I could see were Georges's feet as he slipped off his bike and walked forward, talking all the time in a reassuring tone. He spoke in a blend of Swahili and a tribal language. Calmly, Georges turned back towards me and asked me quietly for cigarettes. I had a couple of packets on me, but they were crushed in the pocket of my trousers. This did not bother the mai-mai. I handed over two particularly mangled-looking specimens and watched as they delicately stroked them back into shape, licked one side to slow the burn rate and lit them. I had stolen a better look as I handed them over. What I saw were the modern descendants of the African tribesmen met by both Stanley and Cameron. They were wearing the same necklaces of feathers, bones, and fetishes described by the two nineteenth-century explorers, but their clothes were more modern – unmatching khaki trousers and ragged T-shirts – and they had nothing on their feet.

I watched Georges rummage in his shoulder bag and produce a wad of pamphlets. I recognised them as publications from the MONUC base back in Kalemie, a sort of local newsletter with photographs of UN-sponsored events and good-news stories about the peacekeeping mission. These seemed to have a magical effect on our two armed interrogators and they immediately lowered their weapons and began to laugh and relax. With colour photographs and print, these magazines were evidence of a modern world and here in the Congolese bush they clearly had some status.

Through Georges's smiles, he calmly told me what was going on. 'They are guarding their village. It's just a few hundred metres over there in the bush, but they know that if trouble comes, it comes along this track. They told me there is a bigger mai-mai group in the area, and they have heard of villages being attacked and people killed. But as far as they know, this other mai-mai group is around the village of Mulolwa up ahead on this track. There is no problem with these guys, but we must be aware of the other group. They will definitely give us more trouble.'

Growing in confidence, I asked the old man his name. 'Mikejo,' he said, pulling heavily on a second cigarette I had given him. He had red-rimmed eyes from a night's guard duty and his skin was pale from the thinnest coating of dust and fissured with age. He was the same small, pygmy build as Georges. Mixing between pygmies, central Africa's oldest indigenous people, who lived in the central region's forests as hunter-gatherers for thousands of years, and Bantu tribes, who arrived here about 1,000 years ago before persecuting and subjugating the pygmies, blurred what had once been a clear distinction. I could not tell if Mikejo was a pygmy proper, or the offspring of some ancient merging of central Africa's oldest and newest bloodlines.

The mai-mai of eastern Congo are known for their cruelty, violence, even cannibalism, but in this old man defending his village I saw something less threatening. With his venerable gun – it was highly unlikely he actually had any live rounds – he was simply defending his bush home. He belonged to mai-mai who act like a Congolese version of Dad's Army, trying to protect their villages from armed attack by the many outsiders who have run amok here for the last forty years. These local mai-mai do not cause major problems because they rarely move far from their home villages. It is the ones who wander who cause the chaos. The nomads survive by plundering whatever they can find. It is these mai-mai marauders who are responsible for the lawless cycle of murder and reprisal that has paralysed this region for so long.

Benoit was anxious to get on and, with a nod from Georges that indicated the danger had passed, he restarted his bike and careered off down the track. We followed, but we had not got far when we had our second flat tyre, this time on Fiston's bike where I was riding pillion. I felt the rear go soggy, causing us to slew to one side, and then we were down to the hard rim, bumping to a halt.

After the calm of the first repair, this second one was much more tense. Fiston showed no knowledge about how to repair his bike and had no tools or repair kit. Benoit and Odimba took control. But when they opened up the rear wheel of Fiston's bike, they lost their cool.

'Look at this inner tube, Fiston,' Benoit said sharply.

'There are more patches on this tube than the original tube. It must have been mended twenty times. And look here at the side of the tyre. It is worn away from being pulled on and off the wheel. It's almost useless.'

As Benoit tried to work out how to stick a patch on an existing patch, Fiston stood in glum silence. It was clear he did not really care. All he wanted to do was get back safely to Kalemie, and a flat tyre was no bad thing as it would bring about his return journey quicker.

I found the whole situation bewildering. I had been planning this journey in my head for years, trying to anticipate and deal with every conceivable problem. I had never thought that the success of the whole trip might turn on a perforated inner tube.

It was the first time I had heard a tone of anger in Benoit's voice. It was contagious and I began to fret. My early morning excitement had long gone and I was trying to calculate the impact of these delays on our journey. After Kalemie, my next safe haven was in the town of Kasongo, where Benoit's Care International colleagues were based, but that was still almost 500 kilometres away. With marauding mai-mai in the area, Benoit knew that to dawdle was dangerous. He had hoped that if we got away early enough we could possibly reach a ruined mining town called Kabambarre, 300 kilometres from Kalemie, tonight. Benoit was confident he could find somewhere safe there to spend the night. With these breakdowns, it was looking increasingly likely we would have to overnight in the bush.

There was now one other thing to consider. Georges said the news about the mai-mai group at Mulolwa chimed with what he had already heard on the rumour mill back in Kalemie. This group had some ruthless, godless gunmen and he was anxious that if we were to get through safely, it would be important to catch them at the right time of day.

'These guys get drunk and stoned by the afternoon, and you don't want to be negotiating with them in that state. We must get there as early in the morning as possible for the best chance of getting through,' was his advice.

Staring at Odimba as he mended the second puncture, I started doing the mental calculation. We could only make Kabambarre in one day if we averaged 20–25 kph and so far we had covered about thirty kilometres in more than two hours. And the precious protection of morning from the mai-mai of Mulolwa was fast disappearing.

By the time we got going for the third time, my stomach was knotted and my knees were beginning to ache again.

Five kilometres later we had our third flat tyre. The rear on Fiston's bike had gone down again.

Benoit was getting agitated. He discussed options with Odimba and decided what we needed was some water to check out exactly how bad Fiston's troublesome inner tube was. After botching an emergency repair and pumping up Fiston's rear, we scooted on a kilometre or so until we reached a village, where Benoit stopped and started talking to a group of children. Like the pygmy community I had seen on the track up to Mtowa a few days earlier, this village was a collection of small huts, made with materials from the bush – frames of branches covered with grass. The only remotely modern thing in the entire village was an old, rusting wheel hub, a relic of the days when normal road traffic passed this way. Benoit decided this was a suitable receptacle to carry out the repair and while he filled it with dirty stream water and began working on Fiston's lacerated inner tube, Georges beckoned me over to a small boy wearing rags.

'He says this village is called Ngenzeka and that there was fighting here a few years back. He asked if you want to see the bones.'

The boy had the expression of an old man on his ten-year-old face. It was care-worn, cold and unsmiling. The arrival of our small convoy must have been the most interesting thing to happen in Ngenzeka for months, but there was no sparkle of excitement in his expression. I soon found out why.

He took me a few paces off the track. The bush was thick, but he skilfully slipped through the branches. He was wearing nothing but some grubby brown shorts, several sizes too big for him, but he twisted and shimmied without getting snagged on thorns that teased out my hair and scratched my skin. After a few minutes I emerged from a thicket to find him standing over a human skull, bleached on the ground. There was no lower jaw, the front teeth were missing and I could see a web of cracks in the cranium. The boy spoke quietly.

'There was fighting here one day. We do not know who was fighting who. We just ran away into the bush. But when we came back there were too many bodies for us to bury. Some of them were left out in the sun like this.' The boy's description was as matter-of-fact as a news reporter. As we walked back to the track he pointed to other human bones lying white among the green undergrowth.

Benoit was not interested in old bones. Shaking his head he announced that the inner tube on Fiston's rear wheel was, basically, ruined. He said he had repaired it properly for the second time, but could not guarantee it would work and suggested that as we were already way behind our safe schedule, Georges should set off back towards Kalemie with Fiston, leaving Odimba and him to carry on with me.

This prompted an animated discussion with Georges. Georges insisted that we all continue together, as he could walk back to Kalemie if necessary. It boiled down to this: Georges felt as if he had not done his job; he had not talked us past the Mulolwa rebels; and he was reluctant to head home before he had earned his fee. It was an astonishing display of duty.

Benoit finally issued an ultimatum. 'Okay, we will carry on, but if the tyre goes down again, that will be it.'

We did not have to wait long to face the ultimatum. Less then five kilometres from skull village, Fiston's rear wheel was flat again. The morning had been wasted and we were not even halfway to Mulolwa, the village rumoured to be a mai-mai stronghold.

Benoit was angry, I was jumpy and Georges was apologetic.

'I want to help you, but I know you have a long way to go and you cannot keep stopping like this.' Georges tried to sound positive.

I was sad to say goodbye, but I gave him the donation I had promised for his pygmy group and posed for a photograph. It shows me lowering over his tiny form. I am wearing grubby trousers and a polo shirt with a faded sunhat crammed on my head. Georges is much smarter with a fresh-looking long-sleeved shirt, belt and pleated trousers. Pygmies have been stigmatised over the centuries for being primitive and backward. I know who looks more backward in that photograph.

'The parting of good friends,' Georges said shaking my hand and smiling, after Benoit had fixed Fiston's wheel for a final time. Georges jumped up behind Fiston and the pair set off back in the direction we had just come from. I feared they would have a grim trip home. The tyre on Fiston's bike would most probably go down again, and they had no tools to repair it.

Georges had behaved impeccably towards me. He had been willing to risk his life for a stranger, and there was genuine regret that we could not complete our journey together. His behaviour contrasted with Stanley's account of the unreliability of his expedition members during his trip through this same territory in September 1876:

> Unless the traveller in Africa exerts himself to keep his force intact, he cannot hope to perform satisfactory service. If he relaxes his watchfulness, it is instantly taken advantage of by the weak-minded and the indolent ... their general infidelity and instability arises, in great part, from their weak minds becoming prey to terror of imaginary dangers . . . my runaways fled from the danger of being eaten.

I did not have to worry about Benoit and Odimba's 'infidelity and instability'. After the departure of Georges, they were desperate to get on with the journey. Benoit did not waste another second. He rejigged the luggage, ordered me to ride pillion behind Odimba and jumped back on his bike.

Without Fiston and his faulty bike, our progress improved and my spirits picked up. The kilometres began to slip by and within an hour we had covered as much ground as in the first five hours of the day. Benoit seemed to be almost enjoying himself, attacking the track with his bike, flicking branches out of the way and jumping over divots. Behind him the emotionless Odimba just quietly got on with the task in hand.

Since leaving Kalemie, we had been running due west, following a ridge line above the north bank of the Lukuga River. I had been told we would turn due north near the village of Niemba, a tiny place memorable only because it was the site of an important bridge on the old railway – the one used, at various times through the twentieth century, by my mother, Evelyn Waugh and the swashbuckling gunboat crews from the Royal Navy. Come the twenty-first century and the railway has been forgotten as a means of travel, mainly because the bridge at Niemba had been washed away by floods. But it was still strategic enough to attract the attention of warring factions and for two years, around 2001, there had been a great deal of fighting in the area.

This explained why, when we arrived at a fork in the track – the first junction we had seen in eighty kilometres since Kalemie – we found a soldier in the uniform of the Congolese army sitting under a tree. I have no idea how long he had been there, how he was resupplied or how he protected himself. The Congolese army has no aircraft or helicopters, and so he must have made his way there on foot along the same awful track we had used. I did not get the chance to find out, because Benoit clearly saw in the uniformed soldier the potential for problems. Gunning the engine on his bike, he swept past the soldier before he could gather his wits and try to stop us. Benoit was sticking to the tactic of only stopping to explain yourself if you really have to. He chose the right-hand, northward track and accelerated. Odimba stuck close enough behind to be whipped in the face by branches dislodged by Benoit. I looked over my shoulder just as the bush enveloped us once more, to see the soldier hopping up and down shouting and waving his gun.

Grinning like a naughty schoolchild who has got away with a prank, I began to feel more comfortable. Bumping along on the back of Odimba's bike, I noticed the landscape begin to change. After the ups and downs of the earlier ridge track, we were now crossing flatter savannah. The track was just wide enough for people to walk single file, but the ground was beaten hard and flat, so we scooted along faster than at any stage during the journey so far.

For tens of kilometres we saw no villages or signs of life, slowing only when the track crossed a stream or river. These crossings became the curse of the journey because no sooner had we picked up speed than we had to slow, stop and pick our route over the waterway. There were scores of them. In some places branches had been felled to form a primitive bridge, but each crossing was hazardous, and countless times I had to jump off the back of the bike and help drag the two bikes across. I saw why any bike bigger than 100cc would be too cumbersome and heavy to manhandle through the eastern Congo.

The journey settled into this routine, allowing me to think about the next hazard, Mulolwa and its mai-mai. I kept looking over Odimba's shoulder to anticipate the moment when we reached the village and had to start negotiations.

Suddenly, I saw Benoit slow as he rode into a clearing in the bush. His helmeted head swung from side to side as he took in the scene. We were up alongside him in an instant and I could see what he was looking at. There were the burned remains of dozens and dozens of huts. The outline of each dwelling was marked in a ring of black ash and charred thatch around soil beaten hard and flat. In between the ruins there was nothing – no furniture, no pots, no possessions, nothing.

It would be an exaggeration to say the ruins were still smouldering, but the air still had a tang of acrid smoke. Whatever happened here had not happened a very long time ago. I looked at Benoit and saw his eyes stretched wide-open behind his goggles. He was in shock.

'Let's not wait around here. Let's go,' he said.

The village was huge, running alongside the track for at least a kilometre. Stanley had described villages in this area as big as British towns, made up of scores of simple huts arranged around the brown, beaten-earth version of an English town square. Mulolwa was one of the largest bush settlements I had seen, but there was not a soul around. We hurried past as fast as we could, through a forest void now occupied by nothing but ash circles. Finally we plunged back into the bush on the far side of the village. It felt like sanctuary.

For several hours we continued to make good time. The bush level was steadily being raised by taller and taller trees as we approached the northern edge of Katanga province and prepared to enter Maniema province. Maniema's reputation for cannibalism, which Stanley noted repeatedly in his writings, continued to the modern era. In the 1960s it was in Maniema that thirteen Italian airmen of the United Nations were killed and eaten, their body parts smoked and made available at local markets for weeks after the slaughter. Benoit assured me that we would be safe, if we made it in one piece to Maniema. It was Katanga that scared Benoit.

I was watching the slowly changing forest when Odimba's bike suddenly coughed and died on us. There was something horrible and ominous about the sudden silence. Out here in remotest Katanga, silence meant no engine, no bike, no chance of getting out.

Odimba remained unperturbed. Together we heaved the bike to a flat section of track and by the time Benoit had come back to find out what the problem was, Odimba had unpacked an oily rag wrapped around his tool collection. It might not have passed muster in an engineering support vehicle on the Paris–Dakar rally, but his battered pliers and rusty spanners were up to our needs. He undid the fuel line running out of the petrol tank, skilfully placing the empty plastic bottle, which Benoit had been so careful to keep this morning, underneath to catch the sprinkle of petrol as it leaked from the bottom. He handed it to Benoit, who delicately poured the teaspoonful back into the tank. With no chance of any fuel supplies until Kasongo, 400 kilometres away, we could not afford to lose a drop.

Odimba continued to fiddle with the guts of the bike. I heard him say something about the carburettor and the fuel line, but in essence the problem was this: the petrol sellers in Kalemie had given us dirty fuel. At one point Odimba put his lips to a pipe and blew. Chunks of grit flew out the other end. Benoit smiled.

'The fuel line was blocked. That will have cleared it,' he said.

As the pair put away their tools I felt a sense of being watched. Turning round, I was shocked to see that we were not alone. A man in rags was watching us, leaning heavily on an old bicycle laden with large plastic containers. He asked if I had any water. I handed over my bottle and he raised his lean face upwards. The sun gleamed on cheeks taught from hunger. He skilfully poured in a mouthful without actually touching the bottle to his lips. He thanked me and prepared to continue on his way, but I asked him where he was heading.

'I am walking to Kalemie. I am a palm-oil trader. My name is Muke Nguy.'

I was stunned. He still had well over 100 kilometres to walk before reaching Kalemie.

'I have already walked two hundred kilometres. It has taken me sixteen days.'

I found his words difficult to take in. He was on a 600-kilometre round trip through heavy bush in the equatorial heat, with no food and no water. His bicycle was so heavily laden with palm oil that it had long stopped functioning as a means of personal travel. He could not even get to the seat and, even if he had, I noticed the pedals were missing. His bicycle was a beast of burden, a way to haul goods through the jungle. If the thin, snaking bush tracks were the veins of the Congo's failed economy, Muke and his heavy burden were just one, solitary blood vessel. He could not afford to bring along food or water when every possible corner of carrying space was used to maximise the load. The only things on the bike I could see that were not tradable were a battered silver bicycle pump, a roll of woven grass matting and a coil of ivy.

'I drink when the pass crosses streams, and at night I eat what I can find in the bush. I have my mat to sleep on, but sometimes the insects are very strong and they eat me at night. If I get sick, I have no medicine.'

He smiled when I asked him what the loop of ivy was for. 'That is from a rubber tree. If I have a flat, I break the ivy and a glue comes out that will mend the puncture. It is the repair kit of the forest.' For the first time his gaunt face softened to a smile.

I have always fancied myself as a long-distance athlete. I am large and slow, but at least I have stamina. After that conversation with Muke, I no longer have any illusions about the extent of my stamina. I could not conceive of the strength – physical and mental – needed on a forty- or fifty-day round trip through disease-ridden tropical forest. And it was not as if the rewards were huge.

'I carry eighty, maybe a hundred litres of oil. Maybe I can make ten or fifteen dollars profit when I get to Kalemie. So I spend my money there on things we do not have at home, like salt or lake-fish. When I get home, I will see my family for the first time in months and sell some of the salt for another ten or fifteen dollars profit.'

All this effort for $30 and a fish supper. I was stunned.

Congolese like Muke are out there now, as I write this, sleeping in the bush, swatting insects, kneading blisters on unshod feet, toiling along a Ho Chi Minh trail of survival that shows just how willing many Africans are to work their way out of poverty.

Muke then asked me something.

'Did you see any soldiers? Any gunmen on the road from Kalemie? Because if they see me they will take what they call "tax". Maybe a litre of oil, or maybe what is in my pockets, or maybe even more. Sometimes I can lose all of my profit in a second because in the Congo there is no law.'

Muke was only one of many bicycle hauliers that I saw. Some carried canisters of palm oil, a few carried meat – antelope or monkey, sometimes still bloody, but often smoked – and there was even one with thirty or so African grey parrots in home-made cages. The haulier proudly said he was going to make the long and perilous journey from eastern Congo all the way to Zanzibar, more than 1,000 kilometres to the east, where he might get $50 a bird from tourists. It echoed the slave era, when Stanley saw Arab slavers in this region driving chain gangs of prisoners for the same long march to Zanzibar to be sold.

By late afternoon we were making much better progress. Benoit had given up on making Kabambarre by nightfall, but he was confident we could get out of Katanga and deep into Maniema before stopping. His confidence untied the knot in my stomach and for the first time all day I began to feel hungry. Since 4.30 a.m. none of us had eaten anything, although I had been nursing on my precious bottles of filtered water, gulping every so often and sharing with Odimba.

The track continued across flat ground, but the savannah began to blend with greater numbers of high-canopy trees. Stanley noted that while Swahili had just one word for forest, the tribal language of Maniema had four special words – *Mohuru*, *Mwitu*, *Mtambani* and *Msitu* – for jungle of increasing impenetrability. I

137

had brought a pocket-sized Global Positioning System machine to record my exact route. Every so often I took it out and read the display. It told me were tracking almost due north, but were still a few degrees south of the Equator and the true rainforest.

My backside was beginning to ache and I began to daydream of a comfortable car seat, instead of the sliver of hard plastic I was perched on, bracing my buttocks each and every time Odimba swerved. I thought of *Talatala*, a raunchy short story published about the Congo in the 1940s by Georges Simenon, the Belgian author and creator of Maigret. Simenon's contempt for the Congolese colonialists was clear. He satirised the small-minded bureaucrats, who insisted on wearing a stiff collar and tie at remote stations deep in the bush, and the double standards of colonials who slept with their Congolese maids, but expected their European wives to remain faithful. The thing that came back to me as we made our way through the bush was Simenon's description of road travel. In *Talatala* an eccentric retired British army officer keeps a racing car at his elephant-training farm in eastern Congo, driving at high speeds down jungle roads. And the other characters all move freely around the place, driving long distances between coffee plantations and border posts and colonial offices. That part of Simenon's work was entirely plausible half a century ago, but today it would be pure fiction.

When Kalemie's cotton factory was working, it was supplied with raw cotton from the area I was now entering. Warmer and wetter than the lakeside, this region was perfect for cotton growing. The raw material would be collected by lorry and driven from here to Kalemie. The tracks I travelled along were about as lorry-unfriendly as it is possible to be. During the colonial era, the Belgian administration set up an army of *cantonniers* or work-men, who were responsible for every kilometre of the colony's road network. Paid a small monthly retainer, thousands of *cantonniers* across the country would keep the roads free from the advancing jungle, the culverts clear of debris and the bridges in sound working order. By 1949 the colonial authorities boasted 111,971 kilometres of road across the Congo. By 2004 I doubt if there were more than 1,000 kilometres left in the entire country.

The hours dragged. My backside got more and more numb, and adrenalin struggled to contain my hunger. After darkness fell, Benoit started to look for somewhere to spend the night. He turned on his bike's headlight and I watched it sweep the dark forest, searching for a friendly village. After a couple of false leads, where he announced the village was too big or too spread out, he pronounced himself satisfied with a settlement called Mukumbo. I checked the distance on the bike's odometer and my GPS. After sixteen hours of travel we had covered just 211 kilometres from Kalemie, and were not yet halfway to Kasongo.

I will never know what Mukumbo looks like because we arrived there after sunset and left before dawn. As I got off the bike and regained my land legs, Benoit said he must show the correct courtesy to the village headman by asking permission to stay. He disappeared into a thicket, following a small child wearing rags who offered to lead the way. With no moon, it took some minutes for my eyes to get used to the dark, but when they did I found that Odimba and I were now surrounded by a crowd of silent children. They led us past a hut and there on the ground I could see the faintest glow of a wood fire. It was arranged in exactly the same way I had seen used by the Bushmen of southern Africa, with four or five long branches radiating out from a small, hot core. Only the tips of the branch actually burned and once the tips had fallen into the fire and turned into embers, the fire appeared to have gone out. But a prod of one of the branches, sliding the tinder-dry unburned tip over the embers, had the effect of turning the knob on a gas stove. Almost instantly flames began to dance and the fire was ready for cooking. After a few words from Odimba, someone slid one of the spokes over the embers and within minutes a pot of water was beginning to simmer.

As the flames grew, light caught the eyes of the children, who were all staring at me with the same cheerless expression of the boy at the skull village. Like most bush children in the Congo, they have learned that outsiders rarely bring anything but trouble.

By the time Benoit returned with the chief, an old man by the name of Luamba Mukumbo, a large pan of sweet tea had been prepared by Odimba. I poured some into my mug and sipped slowly. After a day of gulping tepid water from plastic bottles, it tasted like ambrosia. I could almost feel the sugar leaching into my drained system. The interaction between Benoit and the chief was intriguing. The old man wore rags and had no signs of authority or wealth, but the young outsider was polite and deferential. I heard a few references to *muzungu*, Swahili for 'white man', and a small boy was sent running off into the dark with some whispered instructions from the chief.

'The chief welcomes us and is sorry, but there is no food to offer,' Benoit was now acting as translator. 'He said the mai-mai passed through here a few days ago and they took all the food before they left in the direction of an old gold mine, the Lunga mine, down the track. He said his village is still nervous and all his people have been gathered in for the night, but he said there is a hut you can sleep in. I will go and check everything is okay.'

I returned to the puddle of firelight and began a piecemeal conversation with the chief. He said he thought he was sixty years old, but he could not be sure. I asked him what he remembered about his country's history.

'When I was a child I went to school in Kalemie. It was a great honour for one from our village to go to the big town and I was chosen because I was the son of the chief. My family walked with me through the forest to the place not far from here where the bus passed. I will never forget that first bus journey.' He fell silent for a moment, staring into the fire.

'I was still at school when independence came in 1960, and in Kalemie I remember almost all the white families fled across the lake because they were scared. I came home and since then I think I have been to Kalemie maybe two times.

'Our village here, the one you are sitting in, used to have cars come through it every few days. Just a few kilometres away is one of those guest houses the Belgians built. They called them *gîtes* and they were always open for travellers coming through by car. But all of that went with the fighting.

'Now when we hear the fighting coming our way, my people and I just flee into the bush. We have learned it is the safest place for us. We know how to survive there. And when we come back, our village is almost always destroyed and we have to build it again.

'Over the years, things have got worse and worse. We have lost the things we once had. Apart from what we can carry into the bush, we have nothing. I think the last time I saw a vehicle near here was 1985, but I cannot be sure. All these children you see around you now are staring because I have told them about cars and motorbikes that I saw as a child, but they have never seen one before you arrived.'

He carried on talking, but I was still computing what he had just said. The normal laws of development are inverted here in the Congo. The forest, not the town, offers the safest sanctuary and it is grandfathers who have been more exposed to modernity than their grandchildren. I can think of nowhere else on the planet where the same can be true.

Benoit returned to lead me to the hut that the chief had had prepared for me. It had walls of dried mud on wattle, a roof of heavy thatch and a door panel made of reeds woven across a wooden frame. Without a hinge, it worked by being heaved across the doorway, which I soon found had been cut for people quite a bit shorter than me. There was nothing modern in the room whatsoever. On the beaten-earth floor stood a bed – a frame of branches, still in their bark, lashed together with some sort of vine. The springs of the bed were made of lengths of split bamboo anchored at only one point halfway along the bed, so that when I put my hand down on them they bent horribly and appeared close to collapse. But the design was ingenious because, when my weight was spread across the entire structure, the bamboo screen supported it easily, giving and moving with the contour of my shoulders and hips. It was a Fred Flintstone orthopaedic bed and I found it amazingly comfortable.

I slipped outside to see Odimba and Benoit heaving the bikes through the small doorway into their hut next door. 'We don't want to leave anything outside to say we are here,' Benoit explained. 'The sort of people who move around at dark are the sort we don't want to meet.'

As I walked to the village latrine I stumbled over something soft on the ground. I turned on my torch and there, below me, lying on the earth wrapped in a tattered piece of cotton, was a baby. As the beam of the torch moved I spotted another child, and another, and then another. The soil was still warm from the day's sun and the mothers had left their children outside to enjoy the last traces of heat.

Back on my reedy bed, I struggled to hang up my mosquito net. Predictably enough, the picture on the bag of the elegant square shape, airily and comfortably arranged over a sleeping figure, was beyond me. After much vain wafting of the delicate cloth and careful spreading around the four corners of the bed, I ended up tightly bundled in it like a shroud. To be honest, I had stopped caring. I was done in and after one last sweep of the room with the head torch, when I spotted a russet antelope skin with white spots, creased up in the corner covered in congealed blood, I fell asleep to the buzz of mosquitoes in my ear and the scrunch of much bigger insects apparently ransacking my rucksack.

My watch said 3 a.m. when I heard Benoit's voice. 'Let's go, our journey is a long one today.'

I escaped from my mosquito-net-cum-sleeping-bag-cum-shroud and shivered. Even though the heat soars during the day in this region, a temperature inversion at night means that the small hours get amazingly cold. Most of the outsiders who have written about travelling here remark on the unexpected chill. Che Guevara described how he needed extra blankets while plotting his attacks in the hills of eastern Congo, and Stanley often referred to the additional clothing he donned at night even though he spent the day bathed in sweat.

I wrapped myself in my fleece, packed my gear and heaved everything outside. Again, Benoit used his eel-taming trick to load the bikes, and again he and Odimba dressed themselves like combat trawlermen. The noise of the bike engines starting sounded loud enough to wake the gods. I noticed that the babies who had been left outside to sleep had been gathered in. Nothing stirred as we left Mukumbo and rejoined the track.

In the pitch dark there was little for me to look at and so, after a few minutes of bumping and grinding behind Odimba, my mind started to work. We were about 100 kilometres from Kabambarre and needed to travel another 200 kilometres beyond to reach Kasongo. I had planned to be able to refill my water bottles with boiled, clean water overnight, but we had got there too late and left too early. I was sure I could get clean water in Kasongo, so that meant I had to eke out the remaining three bottles of water for 300 kilometres. Okay, I thought, that meant one bottle per 100 kilometres, and I can always ration further myself if things are getting tighter later on.

Those 100 kilometres to Kabambarre felt painfully long. I was by then aching with hunger. The only food I had with me were energy sweets, given to me as a bit of a joke by an old running partner in Johannesburg. 'In case of emergencies,' he said when handing them over. He will never know how important they turned out to be. To keep my luggage down I had gambled that the villages we passed through would provide food, but I had not taken the pillaging habits of the mai-mai into consideration. The sweets were the only things I had to eat. I devoured them greedily, but they were still not enough.

Maybe it was my empty stomach that got to me. Or maybe it was because the first few hours were in complete darkness and I had nothing to focus my mind on. Either way, I felt increasingly irritated and ratty. The river stops felt more irksome. I burned my hand badly on the exhaust as we dragged the bikes over one of the stream beds. Then we started to reach some hilly sections too steep for the heavily laden bikes to cope with, so I kept having to jump off the bike and heave myself and various pieces of luggage to the top of the slope. And then an overhanging branch caught me on the forehead, drawing blood and leaving a painful sore. As I got weaker, Benoit and Odimba carried on as if this was quite normal. They had drunk and eaten just as little as I, but they coped much better.

We had been going for two hours before the sun finally rose. Where the track opened out into less overgrown sections, I watched the long shadow of the bike, Odimba and me dancing across the red earth. The heat began to grow, so I shed my fleece, but not the feeling of torpor.

I knew what the problem was – dehydration. The bottles I had drunk the day before were simply not enough, and I had not had a drop of water overnight, leaving me with a whopping headache and a pain behind my eyes. In this failing mental half-light, Kabambarre had become the focus of all my faculties. I clung on to the bike, looking over Odimba's shoulder counting down on the odometer the 100 kilometres until we reached the old mining town. As I stared, the track seemed to get ever more difficult, the rotation of the meter numbers slowing as if in glue.

The sudden appearance of Kabambarre took me by surprise. I got no sense that I was approaching a place of human habitation until we actually reached it. It was the same with all the other settlements in the eastern Congo: the bush was just as thick, the track just as frail, yet all of a sudden you turn a corner and there is a place where large numbers of people live. In Kabambarre the population is measured in thousands, but still there was nothing to indicate we were approaching a town until, at the top of a particularly steep valley up which I had plodded behind the two bikes, Benoit pointed to something next to a tree. It was an old road sign, indicating the way we had just come and describing it as the National Highway. I could not even manage a wry smile. The sign was rotten and lopsided, much like the entire town.

Kabambarre was a major crossroads of nineteenth-century exploration. David Livingstone stayed here for months in early 1871, recovering from a fever caught on the upper Congo River. He was the first white man to discover its headwaters, although the achievement was slightly diminished because he got his rivers muddled up. He thought he was looking at a tributary of the upper Nile and did not make the connection with the Congo River that the Portuguese had discovered 400 years earlier, flowing into the Atlantic 1,000 or so kilometres to the west. Livingstone failed to persuade the locals to let him descend the river, so he began trekking eastwards, towards Lake Tanganyika, before collapsing from illness here in Kabambarre.

The Scotsman had been left frail and weak after twenty years of tramping across southern and central Africa, but it was not just the fever that troubled him in Kabambarre. His soul was wounded by what he had seen of the Arab slaving methods. He watched them descend mercilessly on Congolese villages, shooting anyone who put up resistance, pillaging anything that could be carried and pinning able-bodied Africans together with vast wooden collars for the slow, often fatal, route march all the way to the Indian Ocean and the slave markets of Zanzibar. It was around Kabambarre that Livingstone's loathing of slavery hardened into his life's work and led to this plea against slavery inscribed on his tomb in London's Westminster Abbey:

*

All I can add in my solitude, is, may heaven's rich blessing come down on every one, American, English or Turk, who will help to heal this open sore of the world.

When Cameron passed through here in 1874 he met village elders who spoke warmly of the Scottish explorer. I doubt if they said the same of Cameron. In his writings he shows little of the humanity that was Livingstone's hallmark. The two appeared to belong to totally different exploring worlds. While Livingstone travelled armed only with his Bible, Cameron insisted on more elaborate luxuries:

And it was also needful for me to keep in rear of the caravan in order to prevent my men from straggling. With all my care they often eluded me and lay hidden in the jungle till I had passed in order to indulge in skulking. The men carrying my tent and bath were especially prone to this habit although their loads were light, and I frequently waited long after camp was reached for these necessary appliances to come to the front.

When Cameron reached Kabambarre, he was, like Livingstone and me, feeling terrible. He was exhausted by the sudden gain in altitude and the endless series of ridges and dips that had to be negotiated. And when he arrived, the villagers of Maniema did not let him down, providing him with an image that fits snugly into the Victorian era's patronising view of Africa. He was serenaded by village minstrels on the delights of eating human flesh:

I was entertained with a song setting forth the delights of cannibalism, in which the flesh of the men was said to be good but that of women was bad and only eaten in time of scarcity; nevertheless, it was not to be despised when man meat was unobtainable.

When Stanley passed through Kabambarre, he too met locals who spoke highly of the 'old white man', Livingstone. This was the tribute to Livingstone from the village chief recorded by Stanley:

He was good to me, and he saved me from Arabs many a time. The Arabs are hard men, and often he would step between them and me when they were hard on me. He was a good man, and my children were fond of him.

The Kabambarre I discovered was an eerie place. For 300 kilometres since Kalemie I had seen nothing but grass-roofed mud huts, but here, at last, were some traces of a more modern world – buildings of cement and brick. But even more so than in Kalemie, they were in ruins. All of the sharp edges associated with modern towns had been eaten away by corrosion or smudged by layers of vegetation. The entire roofline of a terrace of buildings was askew, with tiles dislodged by thigh-thick ivy and gaping holes caused by collapsed beams. In front of the terrace I could just make out the trace of an old road junction, around a triangle on which had once stood a memorial to Belgian colonialists. The bronze plaque had been ripped off the concrete plinth and the roads had been reduced to footpaths meandering through thick undergrowth.

At least in Kalemie there was the UN presence and the occasional vehicle to keep the main roads open. Here in Kabambarre there were pedestrians and a few bicycles that had made it here only after being pushed through the bush for hundreds of kilometres.

My 1951 travel guide to the Congo records Kabambarre as one of the oldest Belgian settlements from the 'heroic period', meaning it was one of the places secured by Belgian gunmen in their war for supremacy against Arab slavers in the 1890s. They built a fortified storehouse and, while my travel book has a photograph of the old stockade, I saw no trace of it. Benoit was not interested in looking. He was much more focused on retrieving a plastic jerrycan of petrol that he had had the foresight to leave here on his trip to Kalemie and on getting back on the road. He drove straight into the overgrown garden of an old house and parked under a large mango tree. Odimba followed, but when I got off the bike I struggled to find my land legs. I lurched up against the tree's trunk, panted loudly and began to lose all peripheral vision.

Benoit could see something was wrong. Behind me I heard scurrying as he barked orders at someone.

'Bring a chair, bring a chair.'

Slowly I turned round and, instead of just Benoit and Odimba, there was now a forty-strong crowd of villagers who must have come running after hearing the sound of our bike engines. I was too weak to have heard them approach. From within the group a wooden chair – home-made with a woven grass seat – appeared not a moment too soon. I collapsed into it. Benoit did not stop. I watched him retrieve the jerrycan, fill both fuel tanks, rearrange the luggage and check over an engine problem spotted by Odimba. It was all a blur and I don't remember very much about Kabambarre, apart from stuffing myself on bananas that appeared out of the crowd, and the moment when the villagers insisted we take a photograph. The result is one of my most haunting images from the Congo, showing me crumpled and empty-eyed from dehydration, surrounded by a mass of earnest, unsmiling faces. Strip away my digital watch and the threadbare Chelsea soccer top worn by the man sitting on the arm of my chair, and the image could be straight out of the nineteenth century – the white man, offered the best seat in the house, surrounded by curious but watchful natives.

Time and again during my journey with Benoit and Odimba, I was struck by just how much tougher and more resilient than me they were. Travelling so close together, I had watched how rarely they drank and ate, but somehow they had a strength and stamina that were lacking in me. It gave me an enormous respect for them. I was lucky to have them on my side.

There was little time to talk or take notes. Benoit knew we still had 200 kilometres to go to Kasongo and we had spent almost half the day reaching Kabambarre. He was fretting to leave, but I did take down the name of one English speaker, a man who described himself as an English teacher, Kabinga Sabiti, and a few notes.

'Thank you for coming. Since the war came we have not seen many outsiders. The UN came here once, but only by helicopter and they touched down and left in just a few minutes. Please help us find peace.'

His plea was almost lost in the sound of Benoit gunning his engine. There was nothing I could do to help Kabinga. I felt ashamed.

We mounted up and sped through town. I could see Kabambarre had been a big settlement, built on top of a plateau with views over tree-covered countryside. A line of single-storey buildings faced onto what must have been a common back in the Belgian era, but the open ground was now badly overgrown. There were no market traders or hawkers. The only people I saw were standing around the ruins of the buildings staring at us. In the tropics concrete can actually rot. It goes black and begins to flake. I have seen it in a number of places, but here in Kabambarre on the façade of one of the blackest, darkest, most manky-looking ruins I could just make out the outline of some words painted in metre-high letters: Post Office.

The next 200-kilometre-long stretch was grim. It began well enough with a relatively fast track out of Kabambarre along a well-forested ridge. This was the main access road into the town and I spotted a group of soldiers guarding the entrance to the town. They were gathered around a cooking fire in the ruins of a building, but Benoit repeated his old trick of speeding up, and though the soldiers jumped up, grabbed their weapons and shouted after us, we had already slipped by.

The track then became strikingly beautiful. It was following what had clearly once been a carriageway wide enough for cars, lined on both sides by high banks. Huge trees grew on these raised earthworks and their canopies spread and met, creating a shady, green tunnel effect. Some of the trees were giant palms with huge, elegant fronds, plaited by the breeze into a natural roof of thatch.

Our next landmark was the Luama River. All the nineteenth-century explorers referred to wading and paddling across the Luama, one of the Congo's larger tributaries, although Benoit assured me that an old Belgian road bridge was still standing and we had no need to look for canoes. Again, the bridge did not announce itself in any way. After several hours of bouncing down an earthy track, through villages identical to those we had seen in Katanga with not a single trace of modernity, we emerged from a thicket onto a huge, iron girder bridge, spanning the brown waters of the Luama.

Benoit shouted to take care as he picked his way past holes in the planking on the bridge, but I wanted to stop and walk around. The girders were brown with rust but, to my layman's eye, they seemed sound and functional. The bridge stood ten metres above the water, so was clear of the threat of being washed away by floodwaters. But what struck me was the folly it represented. A solid bridge capable of carrying heavy trucks and traffic had been designed, built, brought here and eventually assembled on the assumption that heavy trucks and traffic would be able to reach it. Since the Belgians left the Congo, that assumption had collapsed, so there the bridge stands, a memorial deep in the jungle to the folly of planners who never dreamed that the Congo would spiral backwards as much as it has.

The rest of that day was pure purgatory. My backside had stopped being numb and had moved into a painful phase, each buttock screaming to be relieved of the pressure of being squashed against the plastic of Odimba's motorbike seat. I learned to lean on one side and then the other to alleviate the pressure, but it was agony.

Much worse was my thirst. With only two bottles of drinking water left, I rationed myself to a gulp every fifteen minutes, so, instead of watching the landscape, I started to examine my watch, urging the hands to sweep round to the quarter-hour so that I could take the next gulp. I thought of one of the nastier episodes of the early Belgian colonial period that took place around here. The Belgians may like to refer to the early years of their Congolese colony as the 'heroic period', but there was not much heroism in the way they treated Gustav Maria Rabinek, an Austrian adventurer who set himself up as an African explorer and trader in these eastern forests of the new colony towards the end of the 1890s.

The early years of the Congo's colonisation were all about control. Leopold's agents fought the Arabs of eastern Congo for control in the mid-1890s. After they defeated the Arabs, they turned their attention to monopolising all trade emanating from the territory, setting up agencies and companies claiming exclusive rights on all merchandise. Rabinek bought all the necessary licences needed to trade in eastern Congo, but the Belgian authorities took against him. He was arrested early in 1901 on trumped-up charges alleging smuggling and was sentenced by a military tribunal in Kalemie to a year in jail. When Rabinek demanded the right to appeal, he was told his appeal would indeed be heard, but that the only court senior enough to deal with the case was in Boma, the trading post at the mouth of the Congo River, then the capital of Leopold's colony. The problem for Rabinek was that Boma lies 3,000 kilometres west of Kalemie and he was told that he would have to walk all the way.

It must have been around June 1901 when Rabinek passed through the area where I now found myself. The Scottish skipper of a steamer on Lake Tanganyika had described the parlous state of the prisoner when he set out from Kalemie. By the time he got here he was close to death. He made it to the Congo River, but died on board a steamer heading downstream on 1 September 1901. The Belgians had walked him to death.

Images of Rabinek staggering through the jungle, starving, riddled with disease as he slogged his way to the Congo River, filled my muddled mind as the journey went on. My trip from Kalemie had started out exciting and become exhausting, but now it was a mess. If we ran into trouble, I no longer had the wits to deal with anything. By the time darkness came I was slumped half-asleep against Odimba's back. Every so often, I would lean over and stare at the odometer trying to count down the kilometres until Kasongo. There were times when, as I stared at the little numbers on the meter, my mind played tricks, convincing myself they were going backwards.

Night fell. We had been on the go since before dawn, but our journey was not over. The darkness was complete apart from the headlights of our two bikes. Every so often I saw huts on either side of the track and knew we were passing through villages, but the only light I saw was the occasional glow of a cooking fire.

I had lost all sense of time when I suddenly spotted a much brighter light up ahead. We were still moving, and it kept disappearing and reappearing between trees and bushes. Finally, I convinced myself it was something other than a cooking flame. It was an electric light, the first for 535 kilometres. We had reached Kasongo and the modest house maintained by Benoit's aid-worker colleagues from Care International. I remember little about the arrival, apart from the vast jug of filtered water that I gulped down and the smell of the previous night's hut on my mosquito net, in which I wrapped myself before collapsing.

6.

The Jungle Books

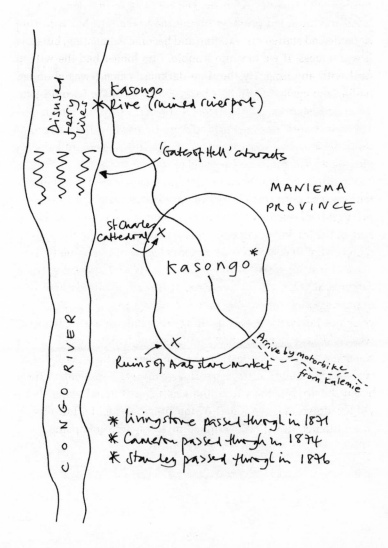

Kasongo Rive (ruined riverport)

Disused ferry Lines

'Gates of Hell' cataracts

MANIEMA PROVINCE

St Charles Cathedral

Kasongo

CONGO RIVER

Ruins of Arab slave market

Arrive by motorbike from Kalemie

* Livingstone passed through in 1871
* Cameron passed through in 1874
* Stanley passed through in 1876

European explorer crossing eastern Congo, circa 1913

Author crossing eastern Congo, August 2004

The sound of singing woke me on my first morning in Kasongo. There was not a breath of wind, but the toffee-thick drone of the male voices seemed to stir the tropical air as I slowly came round. Dawn had broken and I could see my surroundings fully for the first time. I was in a room of a cement and brick building, maybe fifty years old, lying on a sagging mattress surrounded by old bits of clothing and luggage. The room was modern enough to have a window complete with glass pane, and a door, although this was kept shut by a bent nail. A patina of dust and grime covered everything. It was a replica of the room where I stayed in Kalemie, a staging post for itinerant aid workers.

Walking out onto the front porch I found Tom Nyamwaya, the head of the Care International operation in Kasongo, sitting on a home-made wooden chair. The success of my trip so far was entirely down to Tom and his willingness to risk two of his staff and two motorbikes. I started to thank him, but he silenced me with his hand and I could see he was straining to listen to the singing. He only spoke after the voices finally fell silent.

'Those voices you hear are the voices of soldiers. I don't like it when they start singing. The last time they did that was in June after the Bukavu crisis. I have sent someone to try to find out what is going on.' Tom's English was clear with a heavy accent from east Africa. He was Kenyan, employed by Care International to run this outpost deep in francophone Africa, and he was clearly happy to have someone to speak to in English.

'It's a problem when I have to speak French. I only just started lessons and I am not finding it that easy.'

Over breakfast I explained more about my trip. Tom and I had only had a brief email exchange and he seemed interested to learn he was living in a place that once played a central part in the colonial history of the region. But what he wanted to know, more than anything else, was how I had managed to dodge the mai-mai.

'We were lucky,' I said stuffing my mouth with a hunk of sticky, browning banana. 'The only ones we saw were friendly enough and we somehow avoided all the others.'

Tom shook his head.

'Well, you must be as crazy as Stanley. God knows what they would have done to you if they caught you. What makes you do this sort of thing? I would not travel anywhere in this country except by plane. You would have to be mad to go out there into the bush. This place is like nowhere else I have ever worked. You never know when trouble is going to start. At the time of the Bukavu crisis, we were under pressure from our head office to evacuate. I was in two minds, because we are the only aid group in Kasongo. Hundreds of thousands of people rely on us – and only us. So when we went to the airstrip, the guys who call themselves the authorities and police, the same ones we have been working with for months, turned on us. One of my staff was pistol-whipped. We were all threatened. It blew up in a second and all of a sudden things were out of control.'

I was curious. 'How do you feel about living out here? There are no UN peacekeepers here, no other aid groups. You are as exposed as the first Belgians slaughtered here in the 1890s.'

'Well, it's not the best feeling. The uncertainty. The instability. The volatility. I don't think I can stand more than a few months and I will leave as soon as I can. There are some jobs like this in the aid world, which you have to do to get on. It's just the way it is.'

He explained more about the conditions he lived in. His was the only home in the old 'white' suburb of Kasongo that was still inhabited, and this was because his aid-group employer was able to maintain supplies using aircraft. But the air bridge was fragile, with irregular flights made haphazard by tropical weather conditions and non-existent facilities at Kasongo's airstrip. Across that rickety bridge came everything for his work and home life: food, fuel, communications equipment and work supplies. Everything had to be flown in.

I wanted to know how I could reach Kindu, the port on the upper reach of the Congo river, 200 kilometres further north.

'You look tired and ill, so maybe you should rest for a while here. The journey to Kindu is a tough track, which takes a few days by motorbike. Two of our bikes are due to head that way some time next week, but first you must drink more water. You look terrible.'

It was only three days since I had left Kalemie, but already I was feeling groggy and feverish. I began to worry. I still had thousands of kilometres ahead of me. Maybe I was not strong enough to cope physically with a Congo crossing. My anti-malaria pills did not help. They made me feel even more nauseous after I took them each morning.

But after a day of rest in Tom's house, I began to feel stronger and convince myself the sickness was down to my stupid miscalculation over water. I had made a huge mistake assuming we would have time to boil water as we travelled through Katanga and had not anticipated the urgent need to move as quickly as possible. Next time I would prepare adequate water supplies before I set out. I would not make the same mistake again.

The town of Kasongo is an Atlantis of central Africa, a once major city now swamped by the advancing jungle. The scale of its decay was breathtaking, but what made it so intriguing for me was how it reeked of the worst excesses of Belgium's involvement with the Congo.

Kasongo was the epicentre for the 1892 war between Belgium and Arab slavers. The Arabs had developed it into the capital of their slave state. It was near here that Livingstone witnessed the raids that made him such an ardent opponent of slavery. In

Kasongo the Arabs built slave markets where tribesmen, caught by raiding parties, were traded; prisons where slaves had their necks wedged into timber yokes, so heavy and cumbersome they made escape impossible; storehouses where elephant tusks and other booty pillaged from the local villages were collected before being hauled back to Zanzibar by chain-gangs of slaves. These early Arab invaders of the Congo were not bootleggers looking for a quick profit. They took the long view, happily staying 'up country' for years, taking native girls as wives, merging and mixing bloodlines to create a complex social structure of Arabic overlords, Arabic-African mulatto foremen and African vassals.

The most notorious of them all was Tippu-Tip, a bear of a man described by Stanley as 'tall, black-bearded, of negroid complexion, in the prime of life, straight and quick in his movements, a picture of energy and strength'. Tippu-Tip moved his base a great deal, but he lived in Kasongo for many years. It was his son, Sefu, who was involved in the incident that gave the town its notoriety.

What the Indian Mutiny was to Britain, the 1892 Kasongo incident was to Belgium, a moment of anti-foreigner brutality used to justify decades of colonial control. It took place during the war between Leopold's colonial agents and the Arabs. Ever since Stanley came back to the Congo in the early 1880s to set up Leopold's colony, Belgian officers and agents had spread across the Congo River basin staking the land exclusively for the Belgian monarch. The size and importance of Kasongo made it an obvious target, so two Belgian soldiers, Lieutenant Lippens and Sergeant de Bruyne, arrived here as early ambassadors to Sefu in the early 1890s. By the time they reached Kasongo they were riddled with fever and exhausted, but the Arabs began by looking after them well, offering them a comfortable villa next to Sefu's.

But when the first skirmishes of the Belgian-Arab war broke out, the position of the two men became precarious. There is some dispute about whether Sefu was directly involved in what happened next. What is without dispute is that both men were murdered by a mob. One version has it that de Bruyne was dragged from his writing desk by the killers. Both were disembowelled and had their hands and feet cut off and sent to a nearby Arab leader as proof of their murder.

The Belgian response was ruthless. After coercing as allies one of central Congo's fiercest tribes, the Batetele, who enjoyed a bloody and entirely justified reputation for cannibalism, a Belgian-led expeditionary force descended on Kasongo. With modern European weapons they routed the Arabs, storming the city on 22 April 1893, plundering the villas abandoned by the Arabs and allowing the Batetele to indulge in some gruesome revictualling.

Kasongo's association with blood did not end there. It was in remote centres like Kasongo that early Belgian colonialists committed unspeakable cruelty at the end of the nineteenth century on behalf of Leopold. When he persuaded the European powers at the Berlin Conference to recognise his claim to the Congo Free State, he presented it as an exercise in using free trade to bring civilisation to backward African tribes. This was a sham. From the very beginning, the Congo Free State was an exercise not in trade, but in plunder. It began with ivory in the 1880s, then the most valuable commodity found in the Congo, but moved on to rubber in the 1890s as demand for tyres surged with the mass production of cars. One of Congo's many natural resources is a thick, fast-growing ivy that occurs naturally in the rainforest and produces a sap from which top-quality rubber can be produced.

Belgian colonial officers in backwaters like Kasongo were told to do whatever it took to maintain the flow of ivory and rubber. They did not pay for what they took, devising ever more violent ways to acquire it. Playing tribe off against tribe, they gave guns to some of the people and unleashed them on their neighbours, uninterested in what methods were used to bring in the ivory and rubber. *Pour encourager les autres*, whole villages would be slaughtered, women raped and children taken as slaves. The

Belgians developed their own particular way of spreading fear among tribesmen by ordering their henchmen to cut off the hands of their victims, spreading terror across a wide area and ensuring obedience. This did not just happen once or twice. It became such common practice that early human-rights campaigners travelled all the way to the Congolese jungle to gather evidence of these atrocities. A black-and-white photograph taken by one such campaigner around the end of the nineteenth century shows Congolese tribesmen staring impassively at the camera. Only at second glance do you notice they are holding human hands, trophies from one of these raids.

The Congolese forest is so impenetrable, so laden with hazards, that even today places like Kasongo have a terrifying sense of isolation, a feeling that the normal rules of human decency might break down here. I felt it strongly as I explored the decaying ruins of the once-sizeable town, troubled by images in my mind of African villagers fleeing from wanton violence unleashed by Belgian colonials, smug in the knowledge that places like Kasongo were too remote for them ever to be held to account.

These images played on my mind as I followed footpaths snaking through the undergrowth, deviating round large trees that had grown in the middle of what had once been wide boulevards, occasionally tripping over an old fence post, broken pipe or other remnant of the old order. I was trying to picture what it must have been like back in the days of white rule. I could tell where the colonial properties had stood because through the native undergrowth pushed huge flamboyants, a tree with a distinctive red blossom, originating in Madagascar and non-indigenous to central Africa. It was a standard ornament for colonial gardens across all parts of Africa, a botanical calling card left by white outsiders.

In Kasongo, I saw many flamboyants. They would once have stood in the front gardens of the city's smarter houses but, while the trees remained, the buildings had rotted to nothing.

Walking through a section of open grassland, next to what might once have been an avenue, I was amazed to find the mayor's office still standing. I was even more amazed to find there was a mayor inside.

Verond Ali Matongo was born two years after the Belgians gave Congo independence in 1960. His story summed up perfectly what had gone wrong in Kasongo ever since.

'I was two years old when the uprising against white rule came to Kasongo. It was started by Pierre Mulele, a leader from north-east Congo, whom no-one in the town had ever heard of before. All of a sudden we were told his followers, the Mulele Mai, were coming and we must leave. They attacked anything they associated with the outside world, they killed white people or anyone they believed to be with Belgium. It was chaos. Of course, I was too small to remember anything, but I have been told the reason my life was saved was because I was lucky – the deputy commander of the rebel force took pity on me and made me his godson and I was taken to the bush. It was years before I came back here again, when Mobutu had taken control of the country. I have no idea what happened to my real family.'

He was speaking in the old chief administrator's office. Outside I could just make out a decaying sign carrying the old slogan from the 1970s Mobutu period. It said 'Peace, Justice, Work' – three of the things one would least associate with Mobutu's bloody, criminal, indolent dictatorship.

Mayor Matongo's office looked as if it had not been touched since the 1970s. There was a desk, a table, some chairs and an old bookshelf, teetering under the weight of some large, dusty books. His entire authority resided in a circular, plastic stamp and well-stamped ink pad, the sort of thing that can be purchased at a stationery shop in Britain for a pound or two, which sat on his desk. He wielded it on the rare occasions when he actually had pieces of paper to deal with.

'What do you actually do now?' I asked looking around. 'What powers do you have?'

'I am the mayor, appointed by the transitional government in Kinshasa. But I have no contact with them because we have no phone, and I can pay no civil servants because I have no money and there is no bank or post office where money could be received, and we have no civil servants because all the schools and hospitals and everything do not work. I would say I am just waiting, waiting for things to get back to normal.'

'And when was the last time things were normal?' His smiling face suggested he did not find my question overly rude.

'The 1950s. From what I hear, that is when this town was last normal.'

I walked across to the bookshelf and picked up one of the thick books. The spine was bound with canvas and the A4 pages had a line printed down the middle, with a Flemish text on one side and French on the other. I picked up another and found it was arranged in exactly the same way. They were an almost complete set of official gazettes from the Belgian colonial period, one for each year from the early twentieth century right up to the late 1950s.

Some were in an advanced state of decomposition, flaking to my touch as I thumbed the pages. Others were more solid and the print was clearly legible, listing that year's inventory of ordinances, regulations and bylaws imposed by the colonial authorities in Leopoldville, the colonial name for today's Kinshasa. They covered topics as arcane as traffic-light distribution and the construction of what were euphemistically called *cités*, but were in fact the slums occupied by black Congolese. There were long lists of how much each province, city, town and village produced in terms of agriculture or mining. And there were detailed accounts of tax revenue and income. Like so many other colonial powers, Belgium clearly believed in bookkeeping. Handling the tomes made me think of the pettifogging Belgian bureaucrats so savagely satirised by Evelyn Waugh and Georges Simenon, the pompous buffoons who lived deep in the African bush, thousands of miles from Belgium, nitpicking over bylaws.

'Why to do you keep these?' I asked.

'For reference. One day we will need these jungle books for reference' was the reply.

The first I saw of Jumaine Mungereza was his fez bobbing through the shoulder-high grass in the centre of town. He had heard there was a person passing through Kasongo who was interested in the nineteenth-century period of Arab slavery and British explorers, and he identified in me a clear commercial opportunity.

'I am the expert on all these matters of slavery and Mr Stanley,' he said.

His appearance was not entirely convincing. Seventy-two years old with grubby spectacles and a wrinkled face covered in a whiskery fuzz, Mr Mungereza did not appear at first glance to be an expert on anything. He was also dressed up like a pantomime Arab, complete with fez and a one-piece cotton gown. I later saw him wearing tattered trousers and T-shirt, so I reckoned his Arab costume had been donned solely for my benefit.

'I used to be an author of books. In 1979 I wrote the best book on Islam in Kasongo, with the help of one of the local missionaries, Father Luigi Lazzarato. If you want to, I can sell you a copy.'

This sounded intriguing. This was the first person I had met in the eastern Congo with an interest in nineteenth-century history, so I asked him to show me his work. It turned out to be a booklet of crudely photocopied pages, stapled together inside a green card cover. I flicked through to see references to Stanley, Livingstone and Cameron.

He wanted $50 for a copy, a huge sum in a place as backward as Kasongo. When I hesitated for a second, he dropped the price to $10. He was delighted when I bought his only copy, but before he disappeared I wanted to know more.

'My tribe, the Mamba, were one of the first to be fully Arabised at the beginning of the period of slavery. It was a case of survival. If we had not taken on the Arab customs, we would have been taken with the other tribes as slaves. We adopted Islam, spoke Swahili as fluently as our mother language, KinyaMamba, and for a long time we were the elite of this community. Then the Belgians came and the Muslims were pushed down.'

He was speaking as we walked through the *cité* of Kasongo, the crowded African community a world apart from the abandoned cement buildings of the 'white' suburb. The *cité* was a place of subsistence living, but it was still densely populated, with shoals of children swirling between terraces of thatched mud huts, pointing and giggling at me, the stranger. I asked Jumaine if he would show me a mosque.

Rounding the corner of a thatched hut, we came to an open space of beaten brown earth and Jumaine announced with clear pride in his voice, 'There it is. The Grand Mosque of Kasongo.'

Less imposing than the town's Catholic cathedral of Saint Charles, it was impressive all the same. A rectangular structure, the roof must have reached ten metres from the ground, and the windows and door frames were finished in rather delicate brick-work. The whole thing was the same brown tone as the earth, but as I peered through one of the windows I expected to see a splash of colour – an old Arab carpet, perhaps, or a prayer niche. There was nothing. The floor was beaten earth and the walls were muddy brown.

'There used to be many thousands of Muslims in Kasongo who worshipped every day,' Jumaine was reminiscing as we walked back through the *cité*. 'But something happened and the numbers became less. I don't know what it was. Maybe the old religions of the forest came back.'

With that, Jumaine, a living relic of the Arab slaving empire of

Kasongo, wandered off, his fez the last thing I saw disappearing behind the thatch of a hut's roof.

The next piece of headgear I saw made me laugh out loud and feel homesick, all at the same time. It was a cap made of Scottish tweed, the sort of thing I would expect my father to be wearing, black with rain on the banks of a salmon river. It did not look like the most appropriate hat for the sweaty tropical African bush, but that did not seem to bother its owner, an energetic eighty-two-year-old called Vermond Makungu.

He was one of many elderly characters I met in the Congo who conveyed to me such a vivid picture of a country in decline, a backward community that was not just undeveloped, but undeveloping. They all had stories about how life used to be relatively normal, sophisticated even, but how the modern reality was so much worse.

'I used to work for the big tropical hospital here in Kasongo back in the 1960s and 1970s.' Vermond seemed happy to have someone with whom to discuss what he called the Good Old Days. 'I was responsible for buying equipment for the hospital, so I would fly all over the world to buy X-ray machines, respirators and that sort of thing. I went to Kinshasa often. It was there that I bought this hat, from a trade fair. You can see it was exported to the francophone world, because the label here has the French for "Made in Scotland". But I flew to Japan, to Rome, to Brussels, all over Europe. Now look what has happened. Look at where I live.'

We were standing in an old shop in what one day had been a terrace close to the Belgian monument in Kasongo. Part of the roof was missing and the damp floor was cluttered with rather second-rate bric-a-brac – broken furniture, stained clothing, dirty cooking pots. Vermond clearly had a thing about hats because among his possessions I spotted a classic icon of Belgian colonial rule, a cream-coloured sun helmet, the sort of topi Tintin wore throughout his *Tintin Au Congo* adventures. Seeing it made me think of all the black-and-white photographs I had seen during my research of Congolese colonials carrying out the business of colonialism – stalking past railway stations or peering from road bridges or surveying copper mines – and always doing it while wearing one of these topis.

When I explained my ambition to follow Stanley's original route across the Congo and my interest in the local history, Vermond listened carefully and then started thinking. He turned out to be very dynamic for his age.

'When we were children in the 1930s and 1940s tourists used to come to Kasongo to see the old sites from the days of the Arab wars. Would you like to see?'

As he led me past the cathedral, I heard something that threw me for a second. It was the sound of a motorbike, the first engine noise I had heard since arriving in Kasongo several days back with Benoit and Odimba. Round the corner came an odd-looking priest. He looked odd not just because he was wearing a trilby and ski gloves in spite of the sweaty heat of the day. He looked odd because, although he was black, he did not look even remotely African. But after introducing himself as Simone Ngogo, he explained that he was very much a local, born just after the Second World War in a nearby village. I could not stop looking at his very Caucasian features and yet African skin. It was intriguing. Perhaps he was proof that Simenon had been right when he described, in his short stories, the colonialists' sexual domination of native Africans.

I asked him if he remembered when things were better in Kasongo and he nodded enthusiastically. He said after the shock of the Mulele Mai uprising in the early 1960s, Kasongo enjoyed a brief boom period in the early years of Mobutu's rule. High copper prices meant the country's working copper mines generated substantial earnings and *Les Grosses Légumes*, the fat cats of the Mobutu regime, had not yet plundered everything.

Towns like Kasongo were comfortably off, he said, and the tropical disease hospital – the one for which Vermond used to procure equipment – was a centre of excellence for the region.

'But things went wrong when Mobutu became interested only in clinging to power in the late 1970s and 1980s, to putting people in jobs just to win their support. These were people who took everything, but did nothing. The decline began when he created the cult of the personality and self-divination, describing himself as Man-God sent to help Congo, and when he nationalised everything – businesses, schools, shops, everything – and it all went down from there.'

I asked him how he kept in touch with his congregation. He pointed at his motorbike and explained it was how he completed his parish rounds, but only if he could buy fuel flown into Kasongo from time to time. Revving the engine, he raised his voice as the bike belched blue exhaust smoke that spoke of fuel filthy with impurity.

'This area around Kasongo has known all of the Congo's wars, one after the other, and the people use Christianity to survive. It's a struggle, but somehow they survive.'

Vermond led me down the slope at the back of the cathedral. It was badly overgrown, but gradually I made out symmetry in the trees on either side of us as we walked. We were following what had been laid out as an avenue of mango trees.

'This was the site of the big Arab villas during the slaving period, the main centre of the city,' Vermond said. I was sweating heavily, but he somehow retained his cool, even with the tweed hat on.

After a few hundred metres he stepped off the track into a particularly thick tangle of nettle, grass and reed, straining his neck. He was looking for something. I heard occasional words as he used his hands to clear a path. 'It's somewhere around here . . . I am sure of it . . . It's been such a long time. Cannot quite remember.' And then a cry of triumph. 'Come over here. I have found something to show you.'

I joined him, ripping through tendrils of ivy and thorn that snagged my clothes, before reaching an open section. Vermond was standing triumphantly looking at the ground, his right foot resting on a straining bunch of grass stems that he had pushed out of the way to reveal a sign that read 'Slave Market'.

'This was the place where the tourists used to come. These signs were made so they could see the old sites, like the slave market. Just over there is another sign marking the site of Sefu's villa, and beyond it the house where the two Belgians were staying when they were killed. Kasongo played a big part in the history of this place and people were interested enough to come all the way here to see. You must be the first visitor for decades.'

We wrestled our way back to the track, but I could make out nothing of the old villas, long since consumed by the jungle. I was finding the heat intense and we walked slowly back up the hill, talking about decay and decline. He told me about the grim days of the Mulele Mai rebellion. There was genuine terror in his voice as he described the feeling in town when rumours emerged from the bush that the rebels were coming.

'Some fled into the forest, others stayed to defend their homes. It was terrifying. There were still some white people here then, and I remember two of them decided to try to flee to the river and find a boat. They never made it. The rebels caught them on the road between here and the river.'

We were walking so slowly that I spotted something I had missed on the way down, a stone cross standing proud of the undergrowth, off to one side of the track.

'That's the old Belgian graveyard,' Vermond explained. 'I think the two men who tried to flee are in there.'

The graveyard had surrendered to the advancing undergrowth years ago, but several of the gravestones were so large they had not yet quite been swamped. The entrance was marked by two mango trees that had grown enormous in Kasongo's hot, humid climate. Their canopies were so thick that little grew underneath them and we scrunched through piles of dry, dead leaves as we made our way into the old cemetery.

Vermond performed the same trick as before, mumbling to himself as he searched. The first grave he came to had a metal plaque and I heard him scraping away dead leaves and reading out the details of a Belgian missionary who died here in 1953, before shaking his head and moving on to the next one, a Belgian woman who died in 1933. Finally he shouted out.

'Here they are.'

I climbed through the undergrowth and there were the graves of two men, Leon Fransen and Jean Matz. They were both in their thirties when they died and the inscription described them as agents of the Cotonco, the cotton company that used to be such a large employer here in Kasongo. Their gravestones confirmed that they died on the same day, 11 November 1964.

Tom took me to Kasongo's weekly market to show me what was available locally. It was pretty meagre. The market consisted of a group of women sitting in front of piles of leaves, or fruit or smoked river fish – tiny things the size of minnows – or white cassava flour, while gaggles of other women milled around, inspecting the wares. Some of the women had teased their hair into long, elegant tendrils. In his diary, Stanley had drawn just such hairstyles. I called the style 'antenna hair'. But the striking thing was just how painfully thin everyone was. There were no tubby faces. Everyone, seller and buyer alike, had the same haggard appearance, with faces so wan they appeared more grey than black.

'It's the cassava,' explained Tom. 'It is the only staple for millions and millions of people across the Congo because it is the easiest thing to grow, but in terms of nutrition it is not really any good because it lacks many basic nutrients. And without any large-scale farming or animal husbandry, the main source of protein is the meat of animals from the forest – monkeys, deer, that sort of thing. They call it bushmeat. But the animals have long since been shot out from densely populated areas like Kasongo, so really the only thing left is cassava with the occasional fish. We are seeing malnutrition levels here as if this place was suffering from a full famine.'

During my motorbike journey I had already seen just how pervasive cassava is, in spite of various attempts that have been made to encourage Congolese to adopt more nutritious crops, like maize. An American aid-worker friend spent two years in the province of Katanga during the 1980s working as a volunteer with village communities, on an ambitious national programme trying to wean people off cassava. It failed. The reality is that the ease with which cassava grows makes it the default crop in a country like the Congo where economic chaos makes it unviable to farm anything but the easiest plants.

After planting, cassava grows quickly into a small tree with edible leaves. You don't need to prepare a field for cassava. A burned patch of forest will do. The leaves are moderately tasty and palatable, but it is the tubers on its roots that are its most valuable asset. Without maize or corn or any other source of starch, the cassava root fills the empty belly of central Africa. The tubers are vast, bulbous things, with coarse, leathery skin stained the colour of the soil in which they grow. They have to be scraped and then soaked in water to leach away harmful toxins that occur naturally under the skin. As we biked over streams, I had often seen spots in the river beds that had been hollowed out and filled with soaking cassava tubers, pale without their skins. After it has been washed for a couple of days, the tuber is cut into fragments and dried. Again, most villages that I had passed through had piles of drying cassava fragments balanced on banana leaves drying on the thatched roofs of huts. By that time it is as white and brittle as chalk, so the next stage is simply to pound it with a pestle and mortar into cassava flour. This can then be made into a bread, known as fufu. I was not surprised to hear about its meagre nutritional value. It looked like wallpaper paste, smelled of cheese and tasted of a nasty blend of both. In the absence of any alternative, I ate a lot of cassava in the Congo and I was left feeling sorry for anyone whose daily diet never varies from the stuff.

Tom sounded downhearted as we continued walking around the market. 'I come from east Africa, Kenya, where people die of starvation because of drought. There is never enough rain for the crops or the animals. But here in the Congo, they have all the rain they need, rivers full of fish, and soil that is unbelievably rich. If you stand still here in the bush you can actually see plants growing around you, the growth is that powerful, that strong. And yet somehow people still manage to go hungry here because of the chaos, the bad management. It breaks my heart to see all this agricultural potential going to waste.'

We continued through the market. Under a tree a young boy was selling water pots made from red, earthy clay. And against the ruins of a building a woman had hung out some coloured cotton cloth for sale as wraps for women. I asked her where the cloth came from and she told me a story showing that even in a weak economy like the Congo's, the power of globalisation can still be felt.

'The best cloth used to come from Britain and Holland, a long time ago, maybe even a hundred years ago, but it became too expensive. Material from China is the cheapest now. It is not the same quality as the old material, but people buy what they can afford and that means the cheapest is best. So this material you see today has come to Africa by God only knows what route. It arrives in Kalemie somehow and from there people bring it all the way here by bicycle.'

I remembered the bike traders I had seen all along the 500-kilometre motorbike route I had just completed from Kalemie. It might beat feebly here in the Congo, but the free market is still strong enough to motivate people to drag bicycles laden with

Chinese cloth for vast distances through the tropical bush, to earn a living.

The colours of her display made for a strong photograph, but as I was fiddling with my camera I heard someone shouting.

'Stop there, stop there.' The voice came from a big man bustling towards us. 'This is a security zone, show me your permission to take photographs. Come on, show me.'

He was tall, well-built and clearly obnoxious. He jostled my arm and started to raise his voice again before Tom stepped in. In English, Tom told me firmly to put my camera away and in rudimentary French he charmed the stranger, before nudging me out of the crowd and back to his house.

'You see that is all that is left of the state. People who have no jobs or income, trying to make money by creating problems for outsiders.' Again, he sounded very forlorn about the Congo.

Back at Tom's house, I slowly got my strength back. Living conditions were bleak and I could not stop thinking about the contrast with the luxurious villas the Belgian soldiers found when they conquered Kasongo. Tom's house was the smartest in town, but even so its comforts were modest. A barrel of rainwater had been set up over a grimy old bath; in the sitting room a collection of old car batteries was connected to a generator that ran only when there was enough fuel; and the kitchen had basically been relocated outside to where Yvonne Apendeki, Tom's maid, cooked over a charcoal burner. She kept an African grey parrot for company, and most mornings I heard him whistling along with the kettle as she boiled water and fiddled around with the few pans and plates that Care International had shipped in for Tom.

She was only twenty-five but had lost count of the number of times rebels and mai-mai had come to Kasongo, forcing her to flee to the forest.

'I have one son and one daughter, and I carry them with me

when we have to run away. I don't know who is fighting who here any more. Everyone says they are against the government or for the government. It is not important. We all know it is not safe to stay here, so we just flee.'

As we spoke the parrot started to jump on his perch and become more animated as a man walked around the back of the house and sat down with the air of someone very familiar with the set-up. I introduced myself and asked him his story.

'My name is Pierre Matata. I was a garden boy when Belgians still lived in Kasongo and I have worked in this house since 1976. Back then the person who lived here was an Italian doctor working in the hospital.' Like the other denizens of Kasongo he was skeletally thin.

'When do you think the problems began here?'

'It was the first rebellion, the Mulele Mai revolt in 1964. It was anarchy, complete chaos. These guys came from the bush and they basically settled grievances that reached back years and years against the outsiders, the Belgians, the Arabs, everyone who was not what they regarded as a real Congolese. But it was not just the whites they targeted. Any Congolese like us who lived in the town were an object for their hatred. They saw us as collaborators with the whites and they were cruel with us. They killed absolutely anyone connected with the white world, the modern world. You see that flask there on the floor?'

He was pointing at an old vacuum flask Yvonne used to keep boiling water hot.

'If they saw you with that, they would kill you. That would be enough for them to think you belonged to the modern world.'

It was a gruesome story. I thought of the Khmer Rouge in Cambodia and their attempt to drag their people back to the Year Zero, to rid themselves of external, colonial, foreign influences.

'And since then we have rebels come through the town every so often. We flee into the forest, they steal everything and we come back and survive on what little is left. That is the cycle of our existence.'

After I had been in Kasongo for three days I noticed Tom becoming more nervous. His satellite message system kept bringing him news from Kinshasa about problems in the transitional government, in the aftermath of the recent killings in Burundi. Various rebel commanders, whose presence was essential to the long-term success of the government, had flown out of Kinshasa to return to their bush headquarters in the east of the country. Tom said he had been ordered to prepare to withdraw his ex-pat staff and close his operation in Kasongo.

'What happened back in June was bad. We are not going to go through that again. The safest place for you right now is to get to Kindu. At least they have a UN base there. So if you are feeling strong enough, I will send you there by motorbike. Is there anything else you would like to do here?'

The one thing I had to do was give my thanks to Benoit. I found him at the Care International office. It was a short walk from Tom's house, in an abandoned school building in the old 'white' suburb of Kasongo. Care International was the only aid group functioning in Kasongo, but working conditions were grim. They relied on air deliveries for all their supplies, so they could only attempt relatively modest projects such as track clearing or well digging. This was primary-level aid work. More complicated work, like running a clinic, was a far-off dream for Kasongo.

Benoit was wearing crisp, clean clothes and looked totally recovered from his 1,000-kilometre round trip to collect me from Kalemie. I owed him a great deal, but all I could offer was my thanks and a few hundred dollars. He had not asked for a penny, but I felt I owed him a huge debt for his skill, stamina and efficiency.

'What happens if they have to evacuate this office?' I asked before we parted.

'Well, I will have to make my way home. I am not ex-pat staff, so there will not be a place for me on any plane that comes. I will have to go home by myself. I am not from Kasongo originally. I come from the town of Bukavu itself, the one which had the problems in June. I guess I will have to make my way there. I don't know how. It will be difficult, but I will find a way.'

I leaned forward to shake Benoit by the hand, but could not stop myself feeling guilty as if I was abandoning him to an awful fate. I found it heartbreaking that a man as decent and talented as Benoit was trapped in a Congolese life lurching from crisis to crisis. I tried to sound positive.

'If anyone can find a way, you can, Benoit. Thank you for everything.'

Benoit could not be spared by Tom, but Odimba was available. I set off from Kasongo once again riding as his passenger, surrounded by numerous plastic bottles of specially cleaned water. Careering along the track, my head clattering every so often against Odimba's motorbike helmet, I thought more about Kasongo. During the slavery period it had peaked as a capital city, and during the colonial era its strong agriculture and tropical medicine hospital had kept it alive. But in the chaos since the first Mulele Mai uprising it had been slipping backwards.

As I approached the Congo River I found myself on the same track that the two Belgian cotton agents had used when they tried to flee that first rebellion in 1964. I thought of their graves back in the overgrown cemetery in Kasongo and shuddered. There is something about the violence of Congo's post-independence period that is seared into the minds of those whites who call themselves African – second- and third-generation colonials whose ancestors took part in the Scramble for Africa that Stanley's Congo trip precipitated. They remember dark fragments of what happened in the Congo after independence in 1960 – killing, rape, anarchy. The two cotton traders of Kasongo were just a small part of a much larger number of victims whose deaths still cast a sinister shadow through the older white tribes of Africa.

I tried to imagine the panic of their flight that day. How they felt as the worst nightmare of living deep in the African bush became a reality; the rumours in town of the rebel advance; the terrible understanding that nobody was coming to the rescue; the desperate hope that if they made it from Kasongo to the Congo River they might find a boat to safety; venturing out of the ordered precincts of the town only to be swallowed up by the vengeful rage of Congolese tribesmen settling decades-old scores.

7.

Up a River Without a Paddle

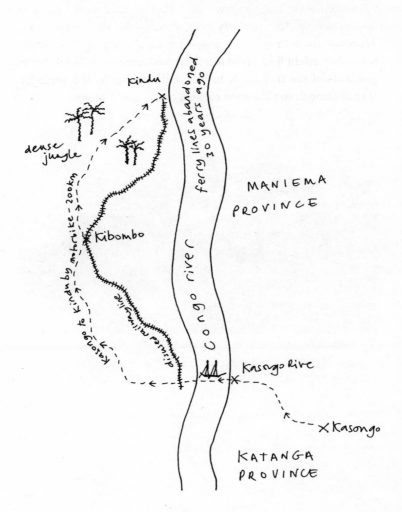

Abandoned paddle-steamer, upper Congo River, August 2004

I wish I could say my first glimpse of the upper reaches of the Congo River was a moment of dramatic revelation. For days spent clinging to the back of various motorbikes and plodding up hills through Katanga and Maniema, I had tried to picture the scene when I reached the river. In my imagination I hoped for an instant when the rainforest would fall away from a craggy hilltop to reveal, spread out before me, Africa's mightiest river churning through rapids, cloudy with spray, as it gathered itself for a 2,500-kilometre descent to the Atlantic.

I was disappointed. The moment came during another long day of motorbiking as we picked our way along a section of track not noticeably different from the 600 kilometres that went before. We simply turned a corner and there, unheralded, in front of me, lay one of the natural wonders of the world. The object of so much mystery for generations of outsiders, and the thing that had fired my imagination through years of research, oozed lazily down-stream between two thickly forested banks almost a kilometre apart. The midday sun was directly overhead, my least favourite time of day in the Congo when all the colours of the trees are washed out and the heat is at its most suffocating. In the flat light, the river appeared viscous and still. Conrad likened the river to a serpent uncoiling right across Africa. In these upper reaches, the snake was fat and lifeless.

I struggled to recognise Stanley's lyrical description of his first sight of the river:

A secret rapture filled my soul as I gazed upon the majestic stream. The great mystery that for all these centuries Nature had kept hidden away from the world of science was waiting to be solved. For two hundred and twenty miles I had followed one of the sources to the confluence and now before me lay the superb river itself! My task was to follow it to the Ocean.

I was vainly searching for the rapture in my soul when our track petered out on the river bank. My first encounter with the Congo River and it was already an obstacle. Our track continued over on the other bank and there were no boats in sight.

I watched as Odimba propped the bike on its stand and went off to negotiate with a group of men sitting in the shade of some nearby trees. Odimba was quiet, even shy, in comparison with Benoit, but over the days we spent biking together I found him utterly reliable. To be entrusted with one of Care International's precious motorbikes was a matter of prestige and Odimba responded with pride. He looked after the bike meticulously, insisted on not sharing the riding with me, and rode with great skill in spite of appalling conditions. Sometimes I would notice that his eyes were rheumy and sore. The concentration needed to avoid obstacles was intense and all day long his straining eyes were bombarded with dust and tiny insects. When I tried to offer him water to wash his eyes, he shrugged me away almost as if it was too much to take help from a white man. He played the role of the stoical sergeant to Benoit's commissioned officer. I detected that he was a little self-conscious that Benoit spoke much better French than he could, and throughout our time together Odimba appeared comfortable with a dignified silence. He was one of the many Congolese without whom I would not have been able even to attempt my trip so I owed him a great deal, but he did not attempt to exploit this position. For those white doomsters who grumble that corruption is in some way a natural African trait, I would hold up Odimba as evidence that they are talking rubbish.

As he went in search of a way to cross the river, I walked to the water's edge. The red soil of the jungle turned to a paler, sticky mud, which I could feel gumming up the soles of my boots. I walked slowly along the high-water line for a few hundred metres trying to picture the old port of Kasongo Rive that the Belgians built here. In its day it was a large enough town to support a church, shops, and warehouses for various steamboats and paddleboats that worked this section of the river. I had email exchanges with a Belgian who was born here in the 1940s and who remembers the neat quadrangle of brick buildings that formed the town centre, and the endless coming and going of river traffic.

All of that had long gone. There was not a single riverside building left and all the port facilities had vanished, spirited away over the years by a combination of looters and floodwaters. Areas of hard standing and numerous cranes and moles had all disappeared, leaving nothing but a rusting engine block from a car – too heavy to wash away and too valueless to steal.

Suddenly a man's voice disturbed the midday torpor. He was one of the men with whom Odimba had negotiated and he was summoning help from way over on the other side of the river. His shouted message was a single Swahili word, repeated and repeated. The river was much wider than I expected, broader than the Thames in central London. We were still 2,500 kilometres from the sea and the river was yet to be joined by any of its major tributaries, but it was already a huge body of water.

Way over in the distance I saw movement. A brown shape slowly flaked off the opposite river bank and began edging silently towards us. It was a pirogue, or dugout canoe. It was slender and elegant, and seeing it gave me a feeling of connection with Stanley. It was no different in design from those he would have seen on 17 October 1876 when he first reached the Congo River at a spot not far from where I was standing.

It took twenty minutes for the boat to make its way across. Pirogues come in a range of sizes, but this one was on the large side, a dreadnought made from the hollowed-out trunk of a large tree. It looked like the husk of a gargantuan seed, streamlined against the river current and without a single join or blemish along the hull. It was at least fifteen metres long and deep enough for its passengers to sit concealed by its sides, with only their faces peeking over the gunwales. It had no engine and was moved by three paddlers, two standing at the bow for power and one at the stern, in charge of steering.

Eventually its bow slid onto our bank with the lightest of kisses. The dreadnought was heavy and the river too inert to make it swing downstream, so it just sat there like a compass needle pointing in the direction I needed to go, straight across the Congo River. A dozen or so passengers disembarked, carrying bundles of fruit wrapped in banana leaves trussed up with cords made from vines. One man had with him a type of home-made bicycle where part of the frame, the front forks, were made of rough branches of wood still in their bark. There was a brief moment of negotiation between Odimba and the oldest paddler, before a tariff was agreed and our motorbike, still laden with luggage, was picked up bodily by four men and dropped into the canoe. The hull was deep enough for one of the paddlers to sit on the bike and freewheel it down to the lowest and most stable point.

We were not the only passengers. A woman carrying a very sickly child squashed in next to me. The baby was wide-eyed with fever and clammy to the touch.

'Malaria,' she said.

'Do you have any medicine?' I asked. She shook her head. Shortly after we pushed off one of the paddlers caught a crab, causing the canoe to lurch, but while everyone else onboard reacted in reflex, the mother and baby did not stir.

Most of the lives still claimed by the turmoil in the Congo are not the direct result of fighting. Only a tiny fraction of the 1,000-plus lives lost each day are ever caused by military action. It became clear to me that the vast majority of deaths are the result not of combat, but of the Congo's decay – children dying of avoidable diseases because field clinics have been abandoned; cholera epidemics among communities of refugees driven out of their homes into squalid camps by the threat of violence; malnutrition because of the failure of modern agriculture, and so on. I looked at the sickly child and tried to think of another country in the world where a baby born in 2004 was more at risk than one born in the same place half a century earlier.

That moment when I left the east bank of the river was special for me. I had achieved something that many people had thought impossible by crossing overland from Lake Tanganyika all the way to the Congo River, through some of the most dangerous terrain on the planet. With my own eyes I had peered into a hidden African world where human bones too numerous to bury were left lying on the ground and where the life of villagers pulsed between grim subsistence in mud huts, unchanged from those seen by nineteenth-century explorers, and panicked flight into the forest at the approach of marauding militia.

But I found the Congo a relentlessly punishing place to travel. It never let up, never allowed me to fully relax, feel comfortable or at ease. My thrill at having made the overland crossing was more than outweighed by thoughts about where I would next find clean water, food and safe shelter. It had basically taken me two weeks to cover 500 kilometres, but I still had five times that distance to go to the Atlantic, down a river that had not been safe enough to travel along for years. Sitting in that canoe on the Congo River for the first time was a moment for only modest celebration.

The pirogue deposited us on the west bank of the Congo River, but it took another two days of hard biking to reach the port of Kindu. The terrain was flat, but as the rainforest became thicker the humidity and climate grew more uncomfortable. Our track followed the line of a railway that the Belgians built at the start of the twentieth century to connect Kindu, their largest port on the upper Congo River, to Lubumbashi 1,600 kilometres to the south. We kept criss-crossing the old rails as the bike track picked its own erratic course past thickets of giant bamboo, elephant grass and jungle undergrowth. The rails sat on cast-iron sleepers and on some it was possible to make out their year of manufacture, 1913, and the location of their foundry, Antwerp. The railway ran almost parallel with the river, although it was so far away I never caught a glimpse of the water. In the town of Kibombo we passed an old station, where I stopped to find that the stationmaster diligently turned up for work even though only one train had been through in the last six years.

It was a sadly common feature of my journey through the Congo, the desperate willingness of people to cling to the old vestiges of order as an anchor against the anarchy of today. Here was a man who had not seen a train for years, yet he still kept his station house in a state of readiness, passing his time in an armchair on the platform next to the tracks that lay redundant and silent in the baking heat. On occasion he would even don the old stationmaster's cap, in the blue and red of the old national railway-company livery. We got talking about the old days and he showed me how he would inform the townspeople of Kibombo that a train was coming. He walked onto the platform, reached up and heaved an old bell that still hung over the platform. The clapper swung violently, but the bell let out the ugliest clang. I could see it was almost cleaved in two by a rust-rimmed crack.

Kibombo had once been a large town, large enough to support a substantial Catholic church and seminary that I had seen as we motorbiked in on the southern approach road. The sun was low in the sky, bronzing the seminary's unplastered brick façade, and after another long, dusty day it was a pleasure to pause a moment to enjoy the tranquillity. Shaggy-headed palm trees nodded deferentially towards the straight lines and angles of the abandoned building. It was long and thin, stretching for more than a hundred metres, and in some places it had two storeys. It looked like the front of a military academy rather than a religious training establishment, but spreading religion was a tough business in the Congo, so maybe the hundreds of novitiates who studied were drilled into shape, not just spiritually, but physically, here in Kibombo, before being unleashed to carry their pastoral message deeper into the African bush.

The church was impressive, but the thing I will not forget from Kibombo is the spectre of the town centre after dark, when it was lit entirely by slow-dancing flames from palm-oil lamps. I had been offered a floor to sleep on in an abandoned building where I had set up my stinking mosquito net before eating another grim meal of cassava. After dark I walked through the relic of a town centre where the lamps cast shadows on the few fragments of wall still standing. Palm oil burns with a low, fat flame and this seemed to make the shadows all the more slow, macabre and sinister. I knew that during one of the 1960s rebellions three Europeans were slaughtered here in Kibombo just hours before a rescue party reached the town. I wrapped myself tight in my mosquito net that night.

Again, we saw no other traffic on the track apart from pedestrians near villages of thatched huts and the occasional trader with a bicycle laden with goods. I stopped to look at one particularly gruesome bicycle payload – five black monkeys destined to be sold at market for eating, their hands and feet bound with vine, their black fingernails oily with some sort of bodily fluid excreted when they had been killed by hunters earlier that day.

We crossed one astonishing bridge near a village called Difuma Deux. The village had seen some recent fighting between government troops from Kindu and rebels attacking from the south. The original bridge had been blown a number of times and what was left was an amazing feat of ingenuity. Various branches, planks and pieces of timber had been lain across the few remaining piles of the bridge, but they were not anchored. As I put my weight on

the first plank, the whole disjointed structure sagged dangerously. I felt as if I was playing a life-and-death version of that
children's game where you have to pick up sticks from a pile
without moving others. It took me ages to summon the courage to
trust the bridge. I need not have worried. When I turned round I
saw this higgledy-piggledy construction was strong enough to
take the weight as Odimba skilfully wheeled our heavily laden
motorbike across.

After so long on the back of a bike watching the forest reel by, I
was thrown when suddenly I saw something metallic and man-
made next to our track out in the jungle. It was dark with rust and
almost submerged in the undergrowth, but there was something
about the straight lines and sharp edges that caught my eye. I dug
Odimba in the ribs and he stopped.

I had found the remains of an armoured car, a very primitive
1950s military vehicle, but an armoured car nonetheless. The
track I was travelling along had been unfit for regular road traffic
for decades and it took me some minutes to work out what this
once-modern and sophisticated war machine was doing out here,
quietly rotting in the forest. It was a relic of one of the Congo's
more chaotic periods – the age of the mercenaries.

In the early 1960s, during the chaos after the end of Belgian
colonial rule, the Congo was the world's epicentre for mercenary
activity. Soldiers of fortune came here to fight, at different times,
for the government, against the government, against the United
Nations, alongside the United Nations. Some of the mercenaries
liked fighting so much they fought among themselves. There were
those, like Che Guevara, who dressed up their involvement in
ideological terms, arguing that it was part of an effort to spread
socialist revolution, but many others (mostly, but not exclusively,
white) had more venal motives – a passion for violence and
loyalty that was transferable to whoever paid most.

As the Mulele Mai rebellion worsened in 1964, huge numbers

of mercenaries arrived in the Congo, many of them under the command of Mike Hoare, a former major in the British Army dubbed 'Mad Mike'. He sought to justify mercenary activity in Africa as a necessary bulwark against the spread of communism. For some time this earned him a good press in the West and nowhere better than in my paper, the *Telegraph*, due to his close relationship with my 1960s predecessor in Africa, John Bulloch. Today, Hoare prefers not to talk about what went on. I tried to contact him at his last-known address in Switzerland but failed, and John has not heard from him in years.

In those early days of the post-independence period, the Congo government had enough money from mining to promise the mercenaries extravagant pay packages, but they often ended up paying themselves. It became routine on operations when entering a Congolese town for the mercenary forces to hurry to the local bank, blow open the safe with dynamite and take whatever was inside. This was not small-scale stuff, or the work of just a few psychos and hotheads. Without a functioning army of its own, the government of the Congo came to rely on men like Hoare and a huge mercenary militia that grew to hundreds of men, spread across three battalions with their own cap badges, unit names and structure. For several years the Congo's combat troops were all foreign mercenaries.

Their activities peaked in 1964 when they were unleashed on the east of the country with carte blanche to deal with the rebels. The vehicle I had found was the relic of a skirmish during the combat assault on Kindu by Hoare's mercenary column. In a 1967 book, *Congo Mercenary*, he described what happened:

Our leading armoured car was face to face with three enemy armoured cars, evil-looking mock-up affairs, and the gunners were slugging it out toe to toe . . .

'Bazooka, sir?' enquired a soft voice behind me in the dark. It was Captain Gordon . . .

'OK,' I said reluctantly 'give it a bash. Watch yourself.'

Wham! A brilliant flash of yellow light lit up the tunnel of the track as an almighty bang reverberated down the length of the column and the front of the leading enemy armoured car flew into a thousand pieces . . .

The crews of the other two cars, panic-stricken, tried to bale out, but all were caught in merciless machine-gun fire . . .

The bodies of the dead were strewn on the track ahead of us, but nobody got out to remove them and the column continued after its fright, each vehicle bumping over the bodies in turn until they were reduced to a squashy pulp.

I was standing at the exact spot described by Hoare. In the 1960s this was a major thoroughfare down which a mercenary column comprising jeeps, trucks, armoured cars and command vehicles could easily pass and where their enemies could plan and execute an ambush. Today it is pristine forest crossed by a single-file track with only a war-damaged armoured car to hint at its bloody past. As I walked back to the motorbike to continue on to Kindu, I wondered if I was stepping where those bodies had been crushed to a pulp.

I knew Kindu had a large UN base and I was looking forward to feeling truly safe for the first time in two weeks. I had great hopes for the place. Maybe I could even have a wash and a decent meal. I should have known better. A good rule of thumb for my Congo journey was that the more I anticipated arriving somewhere, the more disappointed I was. By that formula, Kindu did not let me down.

'You came from where?' Marie-France Hélière, who ran the UN operation in Kindu, was astonished when I turned up in her office. She had never heard of any foreigner reaching her town overland and was amazed when I explained the route I had used.

In her experience, outsiders only ever flew to Kindu, using the UN-controlled airport, and she seemed initially a little sceptical about my claim to have arrived by motorbike.

Only my filthy state seemed to convince her I was telling the truth.

'Well, at least you look like a real traveller,' she said slowly, her gaze creeping from my dirty boots up to my dust-frosted hair. I suddenly felt very uncomfortable, as if I was spoiling the air-conditioned perfection of Marie-France's office. It was spotless, although she complained she was still retrieving shards of glass from her riot-damaged computer keyboard. Like all other UN bases around the Congo, the one in Kindu had been attacked by mobs angered by the failure of peacekeepers to protect civilians two months earlier. Near the door in her office I noticed a small overnight snatch-bag with her UN livery-blue body armour and helmet. She followed my gaze and explained, 'We have to be able to leave quickly if we need to.'

Her door opened and she welcomed two Italian aid workers. I felt slightly embarrassed when she introduced me as an 'adventurer'. I squirmed, but the two Italians were not that interested. One of them was thin and haggard, and the other fresh-faced and eager. The healthy-looking one was taking over from the ill-looking one, who had just finished a year of service in Kindu.

'What was it like?' I asked the older hand.

'The Congo is like nowhere else. After a year here, I cannot wait to leave.'

I thought of the thirteen Italian airmen who died here in Kindu in November 1961. They were flying routine shuttle flights for the original UN mission in the Congo, the predecessor by forty years of the mission that Marie-France worked for. They arrived in two planes at Kindu's small airport to deliver equipment to the local detachment of Malaysian troops, but for some reason they left the secure confines of the airstrip and headed into town, where they fell into the hands of an angry mob of government soldiers. They were dragged through the streets to the town centre just a short distance from where we were sitting and beaten to death. They were then butchered and eaten. Body parts were seen for sale days later at local markets. I don't even know if the exhausted, disease-ravaged aid worker I met was even aware of the story.

I was trapped there for days, struggling to find a way to travel downriver. In 2004 the river was viewed more as a hindrance than as a transport asset, a completely different reality from the town's heyday in the first half of the twentieth century when Kindu was a principal component of a carefully constructed Belgian transport network. Kindu was a major junction on the route between Kisangani (the colonial river town of Stanleyville) and Lubumbashi (colonial Elisabethville). River boats would arrive here from Kisangani in the north, to connect with trains that would head south to Lubumbashi.

I have a book by a Belgian hunter, André Pilette, about a safari he went on, just before the First World War, across this part of Africa. Most of the book is standard Great White Hunter stuff – descriptions of how he shot his way through hundreds and hundreds of game animals, dodging death from various wounded beasts – and it contains a fantastic photograph of him looking completely shameless in a suit, shoes and topi, being carried through the Congo on a hammock strung along a pole between two African bearers. But by the time M. Pilette reached Kindu in August 1913, he basically viewed his adventure as over, describing a modern town fully connected to the outside world. His journey home to Belgium began here with a routine ferry downstream:

All day long you could hear the whistles from railway locomotives or the sirens of riverboats; the sound of cargo being loaded and unloaded. On a Sunday or any weekday, you could see endless industry in the town and you could think yourself transported to one of Belgium's most important industrial centres.

By the time I reached Kindu ninety years later, it was a squalid imitation of a Belgian industrial centre. There were some buildings that once belonged to railway officials and built, just as M. Pilette described, on the crest of the hill behind the station, now decrepit and tatty. And I saw my first motor traffic since Kalemie, 700 kilometres to the south and east. The vehicles were almost all UN-owned or jeeps belonging to aid agencies, and at the junction outside the repainted rice warehouse where the UN had its headquarters, a Congolese traffic policeman diligently stood in the middle of the road all day long, whistling and signalling with gloved hands, peering out from beneath a bright-yellow helmet. I found the heat in Kindu grim, but every time I passed that junction I never saw the policeman without those delicate white gloves.

They were deeply incongruous in this otherwise filthy town. Roads that had once been smooth with tarmac are now potholed and uneven. There are a few shops in the town centre, but they sell nothing but the samizdat tat of low-end trading – cheap, Chinese goods that are brought here on the back of bicycles or on the occasional unregistered flight to Kindu's small airport. The town had grown up on the west bank of the Congo River, but over on the east bank and about 100 kilometres into the bush there were large deposits of cassiterite, the ore from which tin is made. If Lubumbashi is a cobalt town, Kindu is a tin town, although the relatively low profit margins on mining cassiterite make the whole operation more low-key than the more sexy diamond, gold and cobalt mines elsewhere in the Congo. Along the main drag in town, you can see a few buildings where cassiterite traders do business, buying sacks of ore from artisanal miners who drag it here by bicycle through the bush.

But without mains water or power, Kindu is a dismal place. Among the UN and aid community Kindu has one of the highest attrition rates for disease out of all towns in the Congo. The Italian aid worker who had looked so eager and healthy in Marie-France's office at the UN base fell sick almost immediately and, when I next saw him just a few days later, he was pale with a plaster on his arm where a drip had been attached. Without mains water, people use the Congo River as a giant sluice, to rid themselves of all types of waste. During recent fighting, war dead had been tipped into the river, continuing a tradition from the mercenary days of the 1960s when the mercenary commander, Mike Hoare, described the river waters turning red with blood when a boatload of rebels was hit by machine-gun fire.

Most frustrating for me was the utter collapse of the ferry system. There was not a single working Congolese motorboat left on the entire upper reach of the Congo River. I walked down to the old port to find the carcasses of various boats from the mid-twentieth century lying rusting on the river bank. I encountered the same suspicious, money-grabbing hostility that I had experienced many times over in the Congo, as my curiosity was met with demands from self-styled 'policemen' for money and threats that I must pay or get into trouble for violating a 'security zone'.

I was beginning to feel lonely and depressed, but I still could not avoid being impressed by the scale of the decay in Kindu. Some of the abandoned boats were enormous, with chimney stacks that reached up through four rotten decks. I struggled to imagine the planning, effort and expense involved in bringing the ships' components all the way here for assembly in the early twentieth century. But all of that effort lay in ruins, flotsam from a forgotten age.

'You must not give up hope. God will provide.' The optimism of Masimango Katanda perked me up a little bit. He was the local Anglican bishop and my host during my time in Kindu. I had

arrived unannounced at his house and yet he immediately offered
to put me up. I was curious about what a Church of England
representative was doing in the predominantly Catholic Congo.

'It was the British missionaries in Uganda who are to blame.
They crossed the border into the Congo and brought with them
their message into the east of the country. We do not have the
biggest congregation, but I am still responsible for 20,000 church
members in Maniema province alone.'

After a grace delivered in French, which the bishop tailored
specially for me by asking that travellers receive God's protection,
we ate a meal of cassava bread garnished with cassava leaves,
before moving outside to talk in the evening cool of his courtyard.
The town of Kindu had no power, although I could see a distant
glow from the UN base, lit up by its own generators.

'We have had so many rebellions and wars it is difficult to
remember them all, but I remember exactly where I was when the
latest one started in 1998. I was at the summer Lambeth
Conference in London when I heard of the fighting here, so I flew
to Uganda thinking I could come overland like those early
missionaries.'

I fidgeted on my plastic chair, trying not to break the bishop's
flow. After the fierce heat of the day the temperature had dipped
nicely outside, but I was anxious not to be bitten by mosquitoes
swarming in the gloom. I kept moving to make sure my ankles and
wrists were not exposed. The bishop's house was perhaps the
finest in town, but it was still basic, without running water or
power. As a treat I had bought a plastic bottle of petrol to run his
small generator and I could hear the delighted screams of his
children gathered around a television inside, watching a low-
budget Nigerian-made film about adult women falling in love
with a magical eight-year-old boy.

'We stayed in Uganda a month or so before it became clear the
fighting was too bad to make it back that way, so we had to come
up with another plan. We flew all the way to Zambia and headed

north until we crossed into the Congo and reached Lubumbashi. There we took the last train that ran from Lubumbashi to Kindu before the war. It was September 1998 and a journey that used to take thirty-six hours or so lasted nine days. It was grim. No food, no water, no bathroom. But at least we got home to Kindu.'

During the war the two banks of the river were held by rival militia.

'The town was completely cut off for years. No trains. No bicycle traders. Nothing. You could not even go down to the river because of the shooting sometimes. Our church had land for an educational centre over there on the east bank, but it was in no-man's-land. It was very dangerous, but now things are better.'

'Do you think it would be safe for me to travel downriver by canoe?'

'It will be very risky. If it was safe there would be regular river traffic, but, even today, there is nothing.'

One afternoon I crossed the river and went in search of the last English missionary still working in eastern Congo. Louise Wright was sixty-one when I met her, living in a mud hut, speaking Swahili fluently and claiming to miss nothing from home except for a daily cryptic crossword. A former English teacher at a girls' high school in Norfolk, she had turned her back on a comfortable Western life and spent the last fifteen years in the eastern Congo working as a teacher for the Church Mission Society.

Clearly loved by her congregation, she had committed herself to one of the least comfortable and most dangerous places on the planet. Even though she was much too modest to accept the comparison, to my eye she was living the life captured so power-fully in *The Poisonwood Bible*, an award-winning novel by an American author, Barbara Kingsolver, which tells the story of an evangelical Baptist and his family working as missionaries in the Congo around the time Belgium granted independence in 1960.

'I was working in my school as head of the English department in the late 1980s when I saw an advert from the Church Mission Society which read: "Is God calling you to stay where you are?" I don't know quite why it had such a powerful effect on me, but it made me think that perhaps I could be doing something more constructive to help the work of God.'

We were speaking inside the educational centre described by the bishop, set up by the Anglican Church on the east bank of the Congo River near Kindu. Outside I had seen a grim feature of local life as militiamen beat up bicyclists and stole their bicycles – there were no cars or trucks to speak of on this side of the river. But inside the compound, things were more peaceful. There were no modern buildings, just traditional mud huts and a large clearing in the bush where women were tending a crop of cassava. I could hear the murmur of voices from an open-sided thatched hall where trainee priests were being taught about the Bible. Louise gave me a tour.

'We have to be self-sufficient,' she explained as we passed a group of Congolese women clearing the forest so that more cassava could be planted, and another threesome who were milling cassava roots in a large wooden tub. Inside the tub there was a blur of motion as the three women skilfully wielded a thick timber pole each, pounding them like synchronised pistons so that the brittle cassava crumbled into flour. Another woman was sorting the ripe fruit of a palm tree so it could be crushed for oil. I had seen palm oil used in candles, but this woman had another use for it – washing her infant son, who beamed at me naked, but glowing with a fresh sheen of oil. Louise spotted my interest. 'Pretty impressive stuff, palm oil,' she said. 'You can cook with it, eat it, wash with it or light your house with it.'

Returning to a thatched boma in the centre of the compound, she said something that later I could not stop thinking about.

'The thing about the east of the Congo is that even during the Belgian colonial period, it really was not that developed. Today things are very basic, but the important thing to remember is that things have always been like this here – a very tough, rural self-sufficient lifestyle.'

This did not fit snugly with my image of the Congo as a once-functioning country that has slipped backwards. I responded, 'But surely the war and the chaos have made a difference. At least there was some sort of society before, an exploitative and cruel society, but one that was peaceful. Now people are dying in an anarchic free-for-all from things that would not have killed them before – starvation and avoidable disease.'

Louise thought for a second before answering.

'The war has had one major effect in that there are only two real ways left for Congolese people to get on. Before, there was at least a system of schools to go to paid for by the state, a transport system so that people could reach other parts of the country, a health system so that if you were ill you could stand a chance of recovery. But today all of that has gone, so that you only have two real options – you join a church, the only organisation that provides an education, a way for someone to develop, or you join one of the militias and profit from the war.'

I found her analysis depressing. The collapse of the state in this large swathe of Africa meant that its people either relied on the charity of outsiders or took to violence. I must have looked bit dejected because Louise tried to lighten my mood.

'From my point of view as church worker, it's great,' she said. 'When I go on leave back to the UK and I go into a church on Sunday, I am the youngest person there by a long way. But here in the Congo, I am always the oldest.'

As our discussion continued, she made one other important point about how the Belgian colonial way of doing things in the Congo lasted long after independence in 1960.

'The Belgians ran their colony almost on military lines. Black Congolese were only allowed to travel if they had passes from the Belgian authorities, and nothing could be done without the blessing of what was effectively the local Belgian commander. By the time I got here in the 1980s, the colonial era had long gone, but I found that under Mobutu everything was run along exactly the same lines. Nothing had really changed.

'I remember going to see the head of a big mine in the east of the country to ask if one of the congregation could be treated at the mine's clinic. Well, when I turned up at the director's office, it was as if the Belgians were still running things. The director, a white man, an old colonial type, was treated like royalty. I remember sitting outside his office for hours waiting for him to grant me an audience. It was as if the Mobutu regime had taken over and decided to use exactly the same methods of control and military discipline that the Belgians had used.'

Her story reminded me of something written by Conor Cruise O'Brien, the Irish author and politician, about his time serving with the UN in the Congo back in the early 1960s. He served as point man in Katanga for the UN Secretary General, when the province tried to secede, and in his subsequent book *To Katanga and Back* he writes scathingly about the attitude of Belgian colonialists to the Congolese:

If the attitude of the Belgian administration and the industrialists and missionaries had been genuinely paternal . . . there would have been much to be said for it. A good parent, after all, wants his children to grow up. He does not want to stunt their intellectual growth; he encourages them to take on responsibilities progressively; he steps aside, and stays aside, as soon as he reasonably can. There is little evidence that Belgians in the Congo generally were paternalist in this good sense. The priest who, in the presence of a Congolese colleague, emphasised not only the gravity but also the ineradicable nature of Congolese defects, was 'paternalist' in the manner of a father who enjoys sneering at a son's awkwardness, and keeps impressing on him that he is congenitally and incurably defective. I found this form to be, on the whole, the prevalent type of paternalism in Katanga.

As I prepared to say goodbye to Louise, outside the thatched hut where she lived in the Kindu training centre, I thought how her attitude of warmth and respect for Africans differed from that shown by so many outsiders over the decades in the Congo. Just as O'Brien had suggested, this dominant, negative attitude had left the Congo stunted.

I lay under my mosquito net that night in the bishop's house being kept awake by a terrible sound. Like all other Congolese towns I visited, Kindu fell silent at night as if people were too scared to move around after dark. But outside my room I could hear the deranged ramblings of the bishop's father-in-law, an elderly man suffering from acute dementia. At night he would stumble round the yard, crashing into things, wailing inco-herently. It added to my distress as I thrashed around on my sweat-sodden mattress, feeling trapped by history. When Stanley reached the Congo River in October 1876, he too had struggled to find a way to descend the river. Of the 355 expedition members who set out with him from Zanzibar in November 1874, only 147 were left by the time he got here. The rest had either deserted or died. Frederick Barker and Edward Pocock had both been killed by disease, leaving Francis Pocock as Stanley's last white companion.

In terms of nineteenth-century exploration, his party had already achieved great things, using his collapsible boat, the *Lady Alice*, for the first full circumnavigation of Lake Victoria and mapping other major features of the Great Lakes region. But the overall success or failure of Stanley's mission depended on him finding a way down the Congo River.

With good reason, the Arab slavers were unwilling to help. They were reluctant to let any outsider into territory they claimed for themselves, fearing – quite rightly as it turned out – that they might lose control of the land. They dressed up their explanations with warnings about hostile tribes and dangerous cataracts on the river, but it seems obvious they were reluctant to risk losing their exclusive control of the upper Congo River. Stanley was the third white man to reach the river after Livingstone and Cameron, but they had both failed to persuade the local Arabs to let them proceed downstream. Livingstone had turned back towards Lake Tanganyika, while Cameron had abandoned the river and struck out overland towards the west coast of Africa.

By the light of my head torch that night, I reread Stanley's account of the colourful warnings issued by the Arabs to dissuade him from heading downstream:

There are monstrous large boa-constrictors, suspended by their tails to the branches waiting for the passer-by or a stray antelope. The ants in the forest are not to be despised. You cannot travel without your body being covered with them, when they sting you like wasps. The leopards are so numerous that you cannot go very far without seeing one. Almost every native wears a leopard-skin cap. The gorillas are in the woods, and woe befall the man or woman met alone by them; for they run up to you and seize your hands, and bite the fingers off one by one, and as fast as they bite one off, they spit it out.

I felt a strange empathy when I read how Stanley had seen this as a crisis point for his journey. Amid warnings from the Arabs and demands from his Zanzibari porters that they turn round and go home, Stanley describes in his book how he and Francis Pocock turned to the toss of a coin to decide whether or not they should head downriver. Heads would be for the river, and tails for retreat. Six times a rupee coin was tossed and six times it came down tails. In Stanley's book this moment of great drama is captured in a black-and-white etching that shows a pipe-smoking Pocock preparing to flick the coin with his thumb while Stanley, in full tunic and knickerbockers, stands poised for the result.

Somewhat strangely, the pair decided to completely ignore this six-toss omen, badgering, cajoling, threatening and bribing the Arabs until they eventually agreed – for a price – to provide protection for Stanley's party for sixty days' march downstream.

The expedition initially set off on foot, slogging through the forest on the east bank of the river. There is no explanation as to why Stanley wasted effort going overland when he was right next to a perfectly navigable stretch of river. It is most likely that he could not find enough local canoes for his expedition – with his Arab protectors, the expedition had swollen to around 700 souls. Having experienced the climate myself and seen the thickness of the rainforest, I realised that Stanley's description of the rigours of the overland trek rang horribly true:

> We have had a fearful time of it today in these woods and those who visited this region before declare with superior pride that what we have experienced as yet is only a poor beginning to the weeks upon weeks which we shall have to endure. Such crawling, scrambling, tearing through the woods! . . . It was so dark sometimes in the woods that I could not see the words, recording notes of the track, which I pencilled in my note-book . . . We arrived in camp, quite worn out with the struggle through the intermeshed bush, and almost suffocated with the heavy atmosphere . . . Our Expedition is no longer the compact column which was my pride. It is utterly demoralised. Every man scrambles as he best may through the woods; the path, being over a clayey soil, is so slippery that every muscle is employed to assist our progress. The toes grasp the path, the head bears the load, the hand clears the obstructing bush, the elbow puts aside the sapling.

It was in this section of forest that Stanley came across village after village decorated with skulls, often arranged in two rows sunk into the soil running the entire length of the village. The inhabitants told him, through translators, that they belonged to apes trapped in the forest and eaten, although Stanley smuggled two samples home to Britain, where a medical expert studied them and concluded they were definitely human. The same image was used by Conrad twenty years later in *Heart of Darkness* when his narrator arrives after a long and terrible river journey in central Africa in search of a white colonial agent, Mr Kurtz, to find his bush house decorated with human skulls.

Eventually Stanley abandoned the land route, sent his Arab guides back towards Kasongo and committed his expedition to the river. Behind the *Lady Alice* came a flotilla of twenty-two pirogues – one he named the *Telegraph* after our employer – that he had stolen at gunpoint from riverside villages. He saw them as spoils of war after a series of skirmishes with the Wagenia, the tribe living along the river. The only contact the Wagenia had ever had with outsiders had been raids by Arab slaving parties, and it is no surprise that they treated Stanley's arrival with hostility, attacking with bows and arrows and suffering heavy casualties from the modern weaponry fired by Stanley's Zanzibaris. By late December 1876 Stanley's entire expedition was floating down the Congo River, anxiously peering out over the barrels of their Snider rifles, percussion-lock muskets and double-barrelled shot-guns at a forest that concealed dangers both real and imagined.

When I eventually left Kindu, I did so in circumstances very similar to Stanley. I was on a boat crewed by non-Congolese outsiders, heading nervously downriver and looking out from behind a phalanx of rifles and machine-guns.

I had hitched a ride on a UN river patrol boat, a swanky, sleek-looking thing with powerful engines and comfy padded white seats more suited to the French Riviera than combat riverine operations. It was the property of a tiny detachment from the navy of Uruguay. They were MONUC's sole military presence on the 800 navigable kilometres of the upper Congo River. I was lucky to have been given a place on their downriver patrol and I owed my good fortune to Lieutenant Commander Jorge Wilson, an impressively bulky Uruguayan naval officer who commanded the Kindu unit.

I don't know whether it was because, as a descendant of nineteenth-century British immigrants to the Americas – Scottish miners who mined salt in Uruguay – he felt an affinity with Stanley, another British nineteenth-century immigrant to the Americas, but Cdr Wilson was very knowledgeable about Stanley's journey and happy to play a small part in helping me re-create it. My target was Ubundu, a town 350 kilometres downstream from Kindu at the head of a series of rapids that make the river impassable. The cataracts make river travel downstream from Ubundu impossible, so I would have to travel overland to the next major town, Kisangani. That would be dangerous enough, but for now my main concern was getting to Ubundu.

'There's no way we can get you all the way to Ubundu. We don't have the fuel to make it even halfway. But on our next downstream patrol we can at least give you a head start.' He was shouting above the sound of the Village People's 'In the Navy' being played at full volume during a Saturday night booze-up at his unit's base next to Kindu's old railway station.

Sailors from his unit were wearing the Uruguayan national soccer strip and comedy sombreros, jiving drunkenly, pausing every so often to gulp down more beer and steak – all imported on UN flights. While the rest of Kindu was in darkness, the Uruguayan naval-unit compound fizzed with bright lights and loud music. As I left to walk through the silent streets to the bishop's blacked-out house, I saw a large halo effect around the compound perimeter lights. Walking closer, I saw thousands of tiny flying insects attracted from the nearby river by the light, shimmying backwards and forwards in a thick cloud. And on the ground beneath the light, millions more lay dead in drifts.

Cdr Wilson's offer was the best I could hope for. My plan was simply to go as far downriver with the Uruguayans as possible and then try to find some villagers to paddle me the rest of the way to Ubundu by pirogue. I would face another raft of problems when I reached Ubundu, as the war had cut links with Kisangani, the next major port 100 kilometres downstream. Marie-France and the bishop both thought my pirogue plan risky, but I was desperate to get moving again.

The next time I saw Cdr Wilson was the morning we were due to leave. As he climbed down from the river bank to the boats, the gangway sagged and so did my spirits. There was something in his expression that was not quite right and, after dumping his webbing on the pontoon, he led me out of earshot of his crew.

'We have big problems today. I have just heard the rebel commander here in Kindu is angry about the way some of his men have not been given well-paid promotions, and he is threatening to pull out of the peace process and to take all his fighters with him. Unfortunately for you, he comes from the area you want to travel through and that is where his men are assembling. Are you sure you want to carry on?'

It was one of those moments in the Congo when fear threatened to overwhelm me. Throughout my journey fear had been a constant, nagging away like a ringing in the ears. After hearing from Cdr Wilson, it welled up and threatened to deafen me.

I looked out over the Congo River. The sun had risen, but was yet to lift the layers of sweaty mist blanketing the water. In the half-light the river looked like a motionless slick frozen by torpor – the same torpor threatening my entire journey. The Uruguayan crew was busy preparing the two patrol boats for departure as I mulled over what to do. A broom scratched noisily on the foredeck, while three machine-guns were mounted in their firing positions on each boat, making a deep metallic clunk as they were bolted home. I noticed that by some wonderful quirk of historical circularity, their guns were Belgian-made. Brussels might have been forced to cede its Congo colony in 1960, but its guns were still master here in 2004.

A Congolese woman paddled calmly by in a small dugout. She looked up disinterestedly at the activity before disappearing out of view behind an old tugboat, abandoned, rotten and motionless, next to our pontoon on the river bank. Motorboats come and go on the Congo River, I thought, but the pirogue remains.

'Come on,' I said to myself. 'You can always make a decision when the moment comes to be dropped off. If it doesn't look safe, you just come back to Kindu with the Uruguayans.'

I shouted for help from one of the sailors already on board the patrol boat and passed him my luggage, including a grubby yellow plastic jerrycan. I was not going to make the same mistake from my dehydrated motorbiking days. The can contained enough drinking water for four days, carefully boiled and filtered by the bishop's wife.

Our flotilla of two pushed off as the sun finally folded back the morning mist. I felt the traveller's surge of satisfaction as the propellers whipped up a wake. I was on my way again after five frustrating, uncomfortable days in Kindu.

The river might be more than 1,000 metres wide on this upper stretch, but it is not deep. We were at the end of the region's dry season and I noticed fishermen wading thigh-deep hundreds of metres out from either bank. The Uruguayan navy helmsmen had also noticed, and the engines barely ticked over as they nosed their way through sand banks in search of a navigable channel.

It gave me time to look at the rusting wrecks of the old boats that used to ply this reach, but which now lined the left bank for well over a kilometre. Some were huge, others more modest, but all were in ruins. One ship had been completely overrun by a reed bank and its old smokestack could just be seen poking from the vegetation with ivy, not smoke, spewing out of the top. Another hulk was lying on its side clear out of the water, the panels eaten away by rust to reveal bulkheads like ribs in a whale carcass. But my favourite was an old stern-paddler, a rust-red X-ray image of the Mississippi steamboats of my imagination. The panels were all gone, but the superstructure remained in skeletal form. At the stern was the octagonal tubular frame on which the wooden blades of the paddle once stood.

'It was the biggest boat on this section of the river.' I looked over my shoulder to see the Congolese pilot employed by the Uruguayans following my gaze. 'The Belgians brought it here in the 1940s and called it the *Chevalier*, or something like that, but after independence it was renamed the *Ulindi*. I started work here on the river in 1977, but that boat has not moved since long before I arrived.'

The voice of Kungwa Mwamba was flat and free of emotion. There was no sadness, no sense of anger at the waste, no hint of shame. He was fifty-two years old and came from Kabambarre, the town that I passed through en route from Lake Tanganyika to the river. Stanley had spent time there, so I asked him about the explorer Stanley, but he shook his head. He knew nothing about that period. He did, however, know a lot about boats.

'They bought it all the way here from Belgium, piece by piece, by ship and train, and assembled it here on the upper Congo. And they did not stop there. It was one of a pair, with a sister ship, the *Prince Charles*, I think, but that was sunk downriver from here in the 1964 rebellion. If the river is low, you might even be able to see the remains.'

A single, enormous transport company was created by the Belgians during the colonial period, covering its vast interests in the Congo River basin. The Great Lakes Railway Company laid thousands of kilometres of track, but it was much more than just a railway. Its emblem was a swirling white-and-red ship's pennant, which somehow conveyed the importance of boats to the company along the Congo's long river system and on the lakes that form the territory's eastern frontier.

'After I left school I joined the company. By then it had changed its name to the Congolese Railway Company, but it did the same job and after I was trained they moved me onto the boats on the upper river. But the money to maintain the engines was all stolen, there was no fuel and the system just fell apart.'

There was something terribly matter-of-fact about Kungwa's delivery. He said he had not been paid a penny in wages since 1998, but was still supposedly on the books of the company. No wonder he was moonlighting as a pilot for the UN.

'I have seen the river die here. Without the boats, life closes in for everyone, they just go back to their villages and have no contact with the outside world.'

He was right. Just a few river bends downstream from Kindu and life did indeed close in abruptly. Every so often a chink would open in the jungle to reveal a few thatched huts and some shadowy figures, but they were as cut off and remote as they had been when Stanley passed this spot in late 1876.

The sun was now cruelly strong and I retired under the shade behind the cockpit leaving Kungwa uncovered up on the foredeck of the patrol boat. As a trained river pilot, he was meant to know the lie of the deep water and spent the whole day concentrating intently on the river in front of him, pointing left and right to the Uruguayan at the helm just behind him.

Looking over the shoulder of the helmsman, I watched as he slowly turned the pages of an old river chart. Printed in 1975, its marked channel had long since been shifted by underwater currents and for the purposes of river navigation it was pretty useless. But I was impressed to see the number of towns, plantations and settlements it identified. According to the map we were passing through a busy river thoroughfare full of navigation buoys and buildings once maintained by the the Great Lakes Railway Company.

I did see one navigation bollard. It was made of rocks set in concrete, but half of it had been washed away by flood water. It was bestrewn with rotting flotsam and capped with a bright-white dollop of dry guano. Kungwa told me the bollards used to carry working navigation lights. Not for decades, I thought, as a black, long-necked diving bird prepared to leave its latest mark.

As the heat grew, I began to dwell on Cdr Wilson's warning. He advised me it would be suicidal to venture alone into such a remote part of the Congo at a time of increased tension. But I kept thinking of how awful it would be to abandon Stanley's route so early in my journey.

As the day's heat built up, I began to doze. Images in my mind began to blur. I thought of Stanley coming down this same stretch of the river, his boat bristling with guns pointing at the river bank. And here I was, almost 130 years later, with a Uruguayan sailor peering down the sights of a General Purpose Machine Gun trained on the same river bank. And the gun he was using came from Belgium, the country that had colonised the Congo on the back of Stanley's discovery. It all seemed a rather strange amalgam of history folding in on itself. I fell asleep to the throbbing of the diesel engines.

'Cocodrilo' was the word that roused me. I did not have to understand Spanish to understand what they were talking about. The engines had stopped on both patrol boats and the crews had gathered on the port side pointing at a distant sand bank.

'We have not seen a crocodile before on the river, so we will go to investigate,' Cdr Wilson was grinning broadly as he spoke. He then looked over my shoulder and ordered a rubber dinghy to be made ready for a river safari.

It was the highlight of the day for the five or so sailors chosen to come along. They joshed and giggled like Girl Guides on a field trip as we headed towards the basking crocodile, a large specimen at least three metres in length. Commander Wilson let out a sigh as he peered at it through his binoculars. 'It is so big, so big,' he whispered and ordered the engines to be cut.

Crocodiles, hippos and other river wildlife were once a common sight along the Congo River. My mother told me of large pods of hippos she saw from her river boat in 1958, sending up jets of water as they shifted their bulk out of the way of the boat. But the Congo's collapse has led to nearly all river life being shot out by starving riverside villagers desperate for protein. Our crocodile sighting was a rare treat.

As the day wore on, I grew increasingly anxious. I would soon have to make a decision: stay with the Uruguayans and head back to Kindu, or leave the sanctuary of their boat and risk everything on a river descent by pirogue.

By the time Cdr Wilson summoned me shortly before sunset, a wonderful sense of confidence had settled on me.

'This is as far as I can take you, I am afraid. We are still a long way from Ubundu. Are you sure you want to go?' he asked.

I nodded.

Barking orders to his men, he gestured to the side of the patrol boat, where a small, black rubber dinghy with an outboard was being readied by a crew member. As I clambered down into the dinghy with the commander, all the other Uruguayan crew members gathered on the side of the larger boat. They had obviously been told I was planning to go it alone. Several of them silently shook their heads as we peeled away and headed towards the shore.

The commander said nothing as the river bank approached. We were heading to where some pirogues had been drawn up on a beach beneath a high river bank. The sound of the little outboard engine had stirred some villagers into life and I could see them hurrying down to the water's edge.

Cdr Wilson raised his eyebrows, said nothing and nodded. The dinghy slid up onto the west bank of the Congo River and I jumped out with my gear. He shook me by the hand and told me that, according to his map, we were near the village of Lowa. He wished me luck and pushed off. The sound of the dinghy's engine slowly fading into silence as the boat disappeared in the twilight is a memory that will stay with me for the rest of my life.

8.

Pirogue Progress

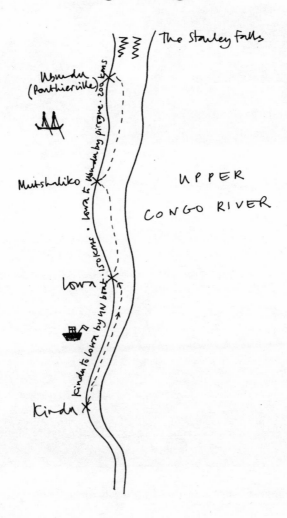

The Stanley Falls

Ubundu
(Ponthierville)

Mutshaliko

Lowa

Kinda

Lowa to Ubundu by pirogue. 200 kms.

Kinda to Lowa by un boat. 150 kms.

UPPER

CONGO RIVER

THE DESPERATE SITUATION OF ZAIDI, AND HIS RESCUE BY ULEDI, THE COXSWAIN OF THE BOAT.

Stanley Falls as recorded by H.M. Stanley in 1878

Author approaches Stanley Falls by pirogue, August 2004

The Congo had already taught me one clear lesson: towns bad, open spaces good. It is a country where gatherings of people promise not sanctuary and support, but threats and coercion. As I stood lonely and terrified on the river's edge that evening, I knew the safest place for me was out on the river, away from Lowa and its potential for trouble.

My legs ached with fear, but I tried to stride up the river bank with confidence, approaching a group of men sitting silently on the ground next to a quiver of beached pirogues.

'I need to reach Ubundu by the river. Who can take me?' I asked in French.

My question stirred an immediate flurry of discussion and after a few minutes a tall, wide-faced man in his twenties signalled for me to join him a few paces away from the group. For negotiations, he wanted privacy.

'It is more than one hundred and fifty kilometres to Ubundu. That will take four days if I come with you alone. It will be quicker if we take more than one paddler.'

'How many dollars will it cost?'

He paused and tried to look away, but my fixed gaze held his attention.

'The maximum number of paddlers on our pirogue is four. That will cost one hundred dollars for everything.'

Now it was time for me to pause. I did not want to seem gullible by accepting his first offer, so I countered.

'I will pay fifty dollars if you get me there in four days, and double if you get me there in two. But I want to leave now – right now.'

My offer met with immediate approval. He span on his heel,

shouted back that his name was Malike Bade, ordered me not to speak to any other paddler and ran over towards the others, snapping instructions. Three of them immediately jumped up. All four of them jogged up a steep muddy ramp cut into the river bank and disappeared out of sight. Darkness was gathering quickly and I wanted to be on my way. I did not like the look of an armed man who had just arrived on the beach wearing the tatty remnants of a uniform and clutching a firearm. He started to approach me. Remembering the trick used by my pygmy friend, Georges, back in Katanga, I rummaged in my bag and offered him a UN pamphlet. It had the desired effect. He grabbed it and walked away triumphantly as a gaggle of children mobbed him to demand a peek.

My crew of four reappeared, each carrying nothing but a paddle and something small bundled up in banana leaves. In the failing light I could not quite make out what it was until they formed a circle, dropped onto their haunches and unwrapped what was effectively a fast-food meal. Inside the leaves was a wedge of cassava bread and some small, bony fish. The men were fuelling up for the journey. Apart from their paddles they brought nothing – no change of clothes, no cooking pots, nothing to eat or drink. The journey back upstream from Ubundu, against the current, would take at least twice as long as the descent, so they could be leaving their home for more than a week, but they were empty-handed.

They wolfed down their meal, still managing to sift and spit the fish bones from each pulpy mouthful. Within a few minutes they stood up and walked together to the river's edge. They had a cocky swagger, like a gang of urban punks in a city. Strange, given that on the muddy bank of the upper Congo River we were about as far away from an urban environment as it is possible to be. They approached the pirogues drawn up on the water's edge. There seemed nothing special about the one they chose. Like the others it was just a bare, hollowed-out tree trunk containing a puddle of water from a rainstorm earlier that day. One of the paddlers used his hand to bail it dry, before I lugged my gear on board and prepared to settle myself in the middle of the boat.

'Wait,' Malike shouted and hopped back onto the river bank before looking for something among the grass. It was almost pitch-black, but he grunted with satisfaction and came back to the pirogue offering me a low, home-made wicker tripod seat. I thanked him and sat on it. It made me feel a little self-conscious. Did this special treatment make me no different from the Belgian hunter from 1913 with his hammock borne by porters?

With two paddlers taking up their station at the helm and two at the stern, we pushed off. There was no current to speak of, but within a few strokes the pirogue was far enough away from the beach for the militiaman to be lost from sight in the failing light.

After a day of looming anxiety over whether to leave the safety of the Uruguayan patrol boat, that moment of slipping out onto the river provided a blissful release. I arranged myself on my little stool. The low wicker seat was smaller than my backside, but it was surprisingly comfortable and as the paddlers began to find their rhythm, I let my fingertips trail in the river water. It was as warm and soothing as a bath.

I ran my wet fingers across the coarse hull of the pirogue, tracing gouges left by the boatmaker's adze. They felt like a rough-hewn braille, charting the history of a river nation both blessed and cursed by this great natural phenomenon. It is a waterway that offers much, but which has run with blood from the moment Stanley paddled past here aboard the *Lady Alice* at the head of a flotilla of stolen pirogues. At every stage of the Congo's history, the river had sluiced away its dead – natives shot on their war canoes by Stanley's people in the 1870s; agents of Leopold drowned during clashes with Arab slavers in the 1890s; Belgian officers killed by disease as they toiled to build a modern colony high up an African river in the 1930s; Congolese rebels mown down by white mercenaries in the 1960s; civilians slaughtered in 2000 by African armies sent to the Congo by its greedy neighbours.

The modern world had used this river for its toehold in central Africa. Towns had been built along its banks. Motorboats had been assembled here. But while the towns were now abandoned and the boats left to rust, the one constant was the pirogue. It gave the river its pulse, moving people and goods across a swathe of central Africa that was all but abandoned by the outside world.

I sat in the darkness, thinking of my journey so far and how remote this area had become. A yachtsman on the southern seas or a climber in the Himalayas had more chance of rescue than I did. The Uruguayans were long gone and would not be back to this stretch of water until their fuel supplies were replenished in another month or so; anyway, I had no way of communicating with them. High on the Congo there were no helicopters to summon, no rescue teams to call on. I felt very alone.

But instead of being overwhelmed by helplessness, I found it liberating. My journey through the Congo had its own unique category. It did not quite do it justice to call it adventure travel, and it certainly was not pleasure travel. My Congo journey deserved its own category: ordeal travel. At every turn I faced challenges, difficulties and threats when in the Congo. The challenge was to assess and choose the option best suited to making progress. But there were moments when there were no alternatives, or shortcuts or clever ideas. At these times, ordeal travel became really no ordeal at all.

That evening on my pirogue was one such moment. I felt I had no alternative other than to commit myself utterly to the river. There was nothing left other than, quite literally, to go with the flow. I felt horribly alone, but more than at any moment on my trip I also felt relaxed and content.

My sense of well-being grew as a full moon rose brightly in the east, its beam perfectly reflected in the broad, still waters of the river. I pushed the stool out of my way and stretched out on the gritty bottom of the boat and, to the gentle sound of scraping as the paddles rattled down the side of the pirogue, I fell into a deep sleep.

A clap of thunder woke me. I opened my eyes and at first I could see nothing. The moon was long gone, but a flicker of lightning gave a nasty snapshot of busy, angry-looking clouds overhead. Pulling myself upright, I could no longer hear the scraping sound of the paddles on the hull. They were drowned out by the pounding of freshly whipped waves that made the hull of the pirogue shudder and vibrate.

There was an urgency in the strokes of the four paddlers that I had not noticed when we set off from Lowa.

'We must find shelter, or the rain will fill the pirogue and we will capsize,' shouted Malike, struggling to make himself heard above the noise of the wind and waves. I thought of the crocodile I had seen the day before. Capsizing would not be good.

As the paddlers made for the shore, we raced a curtain of rain that I could hear, but not see, approaching from behind. We lost the race by only a short distance, but it was still enough to see me soaked through, struggling to keep my camera bag clear of the water welling in the bottom of the boat. I had felt sorry for the paddlers when I saw how little they brought with them, but now I was the one with the problem of having to deal with wet equipment.

The paddlers had spotted a break in the riverside forest and some tied-up pirogues being clattered by the waves, so I knew we were near a village. Slithering up a muddy bank, we found ourselves at a thatched hut shuddering in the wind. There was nobody to ask permission from, so we just bundled in through the small door and collapsed on the floor. By the time I had retrieved my soggy head torch and cast a light around the room, my four companions were asleep, their limbs all folded together for warmth like the blades on a Swiss Army knife. I turned off the torch and settled myself on the ground, watching as every so often the mud-hut walls glowed to the flicker of lightning outside.

A very watery dawn broke over the village of Mutshaliko. We were on the west bank of the upper Congo River and by the time I emerged from the thatched hut, where we had gained sanctuary, the sun was clear of the horizon, but struggling to break through the remnants of the storm clouds. I sat down outside on a large log and tried to spread out some of my wet gear that so it would dry.

Three of the paddlers slept on, but Malike was already awake.

'I must go speak with the village chief, to pay our respects,' he said before disappearing down a track leading away from the river bank.

There was nobody around. From the top of the river bank I had a perfect view out over the full breadth of the river. With the sun so low in the sky, the greens of the forest on my side were picked out perfectly. There was the bright emerald green from banana leaves, all ribbed and symmetrical with a bright waxy sheen; a lighter peridot green from reeds swaying in the muddy water's edge; and a green so dark it was almost black on menacing-looking palm fronds, the same shape and sharpness as a broadsword. Eating biscuits given to me for the journey by the bishop's family back in Kindu, I watched a pied kingfisher, its black body flecked with white, as it darted along the river's edge before it picked a suitable overhanging branch from which to spy. For minutes it sat motionless, before plunging into the storm-churned water and emerging with a silver morsel in its beak.

The bird flew away when Malike returned. He was not alone. Behind him trouped a group of children and an elderly, grey-haired man wearing a baseball cap. I turned round and stood up to shake the man's hand.

'My name is Liye Oloba,' he said. 'I am the administrative secretary for the village.'

He joined me at my jumble sale of drying clothes and I asked him about the village and how it had fared during the war.

'When I was young, the ferryboats used to come by here almost every day, up and down, but they never stopped in our village. Our place is too small. So even though I have not seen a boat for years, I don't think there is any great difference. The only difference is that gunmen come from time to time and take everything. They came through here a few times in the last few years, but we don't know where they come from or who they are fighting for. They just take our chickens and our goats and our cassava and then leave.'

His baseball cap bore a message in English: 'Not Perfect But Damn Close'. It came from the busy trade in donated clothes that has grown up between the developed world and Africa. Clothes given in the West to charity shops are sold for peppercorn sums to traders more interested in quantity than quality. The traders bale them up and ship them here in bulk for sale in street markets. No matter that they are so tatty or unfashionable in Western eyes as to have no value, here in Africa people are willing to pay good money for them, and the bizarre clothing I saw all over the Congo suggested it was big business. My favourite was a T-shirt that had obviously been given to contestants in a 1994 pistol-shooting competition in Dallas, Texas, only to end up, more than a decade later, as the main component of a Congolese villager's wardrobe. I wondered by what meandering path Liye's baseball cap ended up on the banks of the Congo River.

I asked him about the houses.

'The river floods every year, so we must be able to rebuild our houses,' explained Liye. 'The waters sometimes carry everything away, so we must start again using what we find in the forest. Those modern houses built during the colonial period do not last. They are not suitable for our conditions.'

He explained that flooding was regarded as an occupational hazard for the subsistence farmers of his village. The village had to be built close to the river because it was here that the best soils were found, washed down by seasonal floods. But those same floods meant the houses were threatened with destruction. It was a classic development trap – to survive, these villagers lived somewhere that any attempt to build bigger, better homes was wasted because of the flood threat.

Liye had been friendly enough, but suddenly he changed. Leaning forward he started to whisper, 'I have a lot of work to do as the administrative secretary here and I need money to pay for our work.' His face was almost touching mine, and this first request was made sotto voce. He almost seemed embarrassed to be asking. But when I hesitated he started to threaten me, demanding to see written permission from the local militia commander for my presence in the village. In the face of these threats I caved in, slipping a ten-dollar note into his hand, but I was not happy until Malike and the crew returned to the pirogue and whisked me back out into the safe anonymity of the river.

The daylight hours passed very slowly on my pirogue. The paddlers chatted and sung in Swahili. The sun was as strong as I have ever known. We were just a short distance from the Equator and the storm had washed the sky clean of any screening clouds. While the crew were impervious to the sun's force, it had me cringing in a puddle of shade under my wide-brimmed hat, pathetically splashing my face and arms with river water the same colour and warmth as tea, praying for the evening shadows to reach us.

The paddlers would josh and cajole each other, sure-footed as they danced up and down the delicate pirogue working their long-handled wooden paddles. About three metres long, they were shape of spades from a deck of cards, only stretched out to mansize, with shafts that were thin and shiny, polished by years of being slid through calloused hands. The leaf-shaped blade spread broad and fat before tapering gracefully to a point. It was no surprise when later on the journey I saw them being used both as trays for food and as weapons for fighting.

The foursome worked in harmony, with just the faintest of deliberate lags between the actions of the two up front and the two behind. Standing upright they would lean forward to plunge the blade into the water, before heaving it backwards with a dip of the shoulders and a shimmy of the hips. The deft, feathering flick at the end of the stroke to clear the blade from the water would have impressed the most skilful Oxbridge oarsman and each time they did it I felt a faint surge in the pirogue as it inched forward.

My pirogue was about ten metres long and was nothing but a tree trunk, halved and hollowed out, completely bare, without shelving, seats or compartments. Someone had scratched the name 'Sandoka' at the stern, but when I asked the four paddlers what it meant, they shrugged their shoulders and said it was not normal for pirogues to have a name. Many different types of tree are used to make pirogues, but some have wood that is so heavy the pirogues sink if they are overturned. I did not want to put the *Sandoka* to the test, so every time I clambered aboard I squatted as low as possible and mentally rehearsed how I would grab my small camera bag if the boat tipped.

I did not have many other possessions to worry about. Apart from the camera bag, all I had was my rucksack and the yellow, plastic jerrycan of boiled water. Someone had stolen the can's stopper, so I had made a botched repair with a piece of plastic and an elastic band. I could not afford to fall ill out here. The paddlers watched me in polite silence as I drank from the jerrycan only after wiping the spout with one of my sterile baby-wipes.

At twenty-seven, Malike was the oldest of the four paddlers and clearly the leader of the group. He had enough French to communicate with me as the three others looked on unknow-ingly, and it was through him that requests for cigarettes and food were channelled.

I had so much time to myself that I actually measured their stroke rate. Every thirty seconds they averaged twelve to fourteen strokes. They kept this up for hours at a time, but when the rate began to fall Malike would suddenly declaim, 'We must stop, we must eat.'

And with that they would head to the next village for a fuel stop.

To drink they would squat down while we were out in midstream, lower their faces over the edge of the pirogue until their lips were suspended maybe ten centimetres above the river and literally throw the water into their mouths with their hands. They peed over the edge of the boat and were as sure-footed as if they were standing on terra firma. I was more ungainly, so when I tried, the effort of standing up and keeping my balance made me way too tense. Only after hours of discomfort could I build up the pressure required to overcome my nerves, and then only if I kneeled on my rucksack. Standing on the wobbly pirogue was much too nerve-racking ever to enable me to pee.

As the stern paddler, Malike could control the pirogue's steering and at one point he veered us towards the river bank where I could see nothing but dense jungle. He must have spotted something because, as we approached the shore, the trees opened up and there was the village of Babundu.

Tying up alongside one of the village pirogues, Malike disappeared with his three mates up a four-metre-high sandy bank, leaving me to get my breath back in the shade of a tree. I was finding the heat and humidity difficult to bear, and the suddenness of standing up after so long made me giddy. I panted heavily as my breathing settled back down again and plucked the sweat-sodden clothes from my skin.

Venturing out of the shade, I faced the same dilemma that I encountered in every place I visited in the Congo. I wanted to nose around, ask questions and take photographs, but I did not want to catch the attention of the local authorities with all the attendant hassle of having to explain who I was, pay bribes and beg not to be arrested as a spy. Also, I was feeling so enervated that I was happy to skulk into the same hut where the crew were restoking and simply avoid the midday heat.

They ate in silence. Without cutlery, they skilfully set about a lump of cassava bread the size of a rugby ball delivered on a broad, glossy banana leaf. In turn they would pinch enough for a mouthful and roll it into a ball, which they would then dimple with their thumbs. Into the cavity they popped the garnish – fried river fish, no bigger than a stickleback, coloured red by hot palm oil – before eating it eagerly.

'Are you hungry?' Malike offered me the remains of the lump. I toyed with a marble-sized piece, struggling to overcome a gag reflex brought on by the rotting cheese smell and wallpaper-paste texture.

There is something primordial about Congolese villages. The villagers themselves wear modern clothes, often in tatters, but modern nevertheless in that they are factory-made and delivered by the occasional trader who ventures along the river. But the houses are at the base level of simplicity. There is not a single pane of glass, metal hinge, cement plinth or fitting that connects this place with the modern era. There is no litter, no plastic bags, empty cans or cigarette butts. Without any painted signs, it is a place of browns, greens and duns, a settlement built in the jungle and out of the jungle, utterly separate from the modern world.

The doors are made of split cane, held together by a rope of woven vines and kept in place by wooden sticks. The walls are mud thrown against a cane trellis, baked hard by the sun and fissured with a crazy paving of cracks so intricate it looks almost man-made. And the roofs consist of layers of wide, dry banana leaves held down by lengths of split bamboo.

This region is one of the rare places in the world that fails what I called the Coca-Cola test. The test is simple: can you buy a Coke? I have been to many remote places where Coke is an expensive and rare luxury, but it is still almost always possible to find a trader who, for a price, can procure me a Coke. Out here on the upper Congo River, where a hundred years ago a Belgian hunter could buy ferry tickets, I could no more buy a Coke in 2004 than fly to the moon.

Back on the river I tried in vain to spot the remnants of the paddle steamer that the river pilot had told me about back in Kindu, the one that had been sunk during early post-independence fighting. His story echoed a terrifying account of the 1964 rebellion written by an American teenager, Murray Taylor, whose father had lived his own *Poisonwood Bible* existence, working for twenty years as a missionary near this section of the upper Congo. In his account of the incident, Murray described how the local tribe that his father had sought to convert to Christianity, the Mitukus, tried to defend his family when the Mulele Mai rebels approached and how scared his family had been when the rebels chugged into view on the river on a boat stolen just before Mike Hoare's mercenary force reached Kindu:

Soon a rebel steamer came up the river from Kindu and began shelling the main river settlements. I was really scared. This was the first time in my life I'd heard big guns. Besides, we weren't sure who the rebels were firing at. We prayed that God would protect us. Later we learned that the guns were aimed at the Mitukus on the other bank of the river.

Murray went on to describe how he saw two warplanes as they flew over the mission station searching for the rebels' boat:

I heard what I thought was thunder. Suddenly it dawned on me that it wasn't thunder; it was the explosion of bombs hitting their target! Little did I realise then what effect those bombs would have on our family. But that air attack proved to be the beginning of our trouble with the rebels, for they suspected that my parents had called the planes!

That afternoon, some rebels arrived at our mission station. They told us that the planes had sunk one of their riverboats. Soon more rebels came and confiscated our two ordinary radios. Later, more rebels returned to the mission. Their faces were ghastly and frightening and they were very hostile. Again they searched our house for the transmitter they were sure we had. They threatened to kill us if we didn't reveal it.

The Taylor family were eventually moved by the rebels to Kisangani, the large port downstream, where the Mulele Mai rebellion reached a bloody conclusion in late November 1964. Murray was lined up against a wall with his father and various other male prisoners. A guard opened fire with a machine-gun, killing Murray's father. The boy described how he survived by ducking behind an arch. When the rebels came to remove the bodies, one took pity on the fourteen-year-old boy and he was ordered downstairs to join his mother and sisters.

I must have passed the spot where the boat was sunk, but I had missed seeing any remains.

After their fuel stops, my crew would return to the water at full power and full voice. Their Swahili harmonies reached from bank to bank as Malike led his colleagues in song. He would begin and then the refrain would be picked up in turn by the others, with choruses and verses lasting hours.

As my pirogue journey went on, my sense of unease began to build as I neared my next ordeal. The river was navigable only as far as Ubundu, at which point I would have to continue overland for 100 kilometres around a series of rapids and cataracts, still commonly referred to as the Stanley Falls, until I reached Kisangani, the large port city built at the bottom of the seventh and final set of rapids and the model for Conrad's Inner Station in the *Heart of Darkness*. In the early twentieth century the Belgians had built a railway around this unnavigable reach, although when I researched my trip I discovered it had not run in years. Worse still, the road between Ubundu and Kisangani had disappeared into the equatorial forest, and peacekeepers from the large UN base in Kisangani never ventured this way.

I knew Ubundu had witnessed some of the worst fighting in the region during the war. In the forest between Ubundu and Kisangani, there had been clashes between Hutu refugees, who had made their way here for sanctuary in the aftermath of the 1994 genocide in Rwanda, and Congolese militiamen backed by the now Tutsi-dominated regime in Rwanda, seeking revenge against the Hutus. And its local mai-mai home guard had then clashed with Ugandan troops sent to secure Kisangani and its lucrative diamond trade. All in all, I knew Ubundu was always going to be one of the major troublespots on my journey, far removed from its more genteel days during Belgian rule when it was known as Ponthierville.

In 1951 Katharine Hepburn, Humphrey Bogart and a forty-strong Hollywood film crew arrived in Ponthierville by train. They were on their way to the jungle, riverine set for the filming of *The African Queen*, the story of two colonial misfits taking an old boat down a river to attack a German warship. In the actress's diary she describes a charming railway town where the local missionaries enthusiastically helped in the filming, showing the crew the best spots along the nearby cataracts from where to capture shots of models of the *African Queen* being pounded and battered by the white water. The book, written by the pre-First World War Belgian hunter, described the town as a pretty colonial outpost.

My main hope for getting through Ubundu lay with a team of motorcylists from an American aid group based in Kisangani, whom I had contacted by satellite phone from Kindu. They told me they would be making a rare visit to deliver vaccines to a field clinic in the town. Towards my second evening on the pirogue I began to fret, because I knew that if we did not make Ubundu that night I would miss the bikers, when they headed back to Kisangani early the following morning.

Malike could tell I was becoming more worried and kept reassuring me: 'Don't worry, we will get to Ubundu by nightfall.'

He was utterly unfazed when one of the other paddlers quietly lay down at my feet and went to sleep. Kago Arubu was the thinnest of the team, but had given no sign of being unwell before he stopped paddling, let his paddle clatter to the floor of the pirogue and collapsed.

I looked round anxiously at Malike. 'He has fever. He will be all right.' There was no shade for Kago to lie under. He did not drink any water. He just lay down out in the baking sun and within seconds was fast asleep. Malike would not even let me try to paddle as I would mess up the balance and the rhythm. So effectively we had now lost an engine and with it, I believed, all hope of making Ubundu that night.

As the sun began to sink, the river bank came alive with other river travellers. I started to make out dozens of pirogues making their way back upstream, clinging to the bank where the current was weakest and the shadows longest. Our progress downstream was slow – I reckoned we were making only ten kilometres an hour – but at least we had the current with us. The pirogues heading upstream could not have been going faster then five kilometres an hour, and in many places the paddlers were using their paddles in the shallow water to punt the pirogues.

One pirogue passed us going upstream and I saw a small dog asleep on the bow. 'Hunters,' whispered Malike. I looked further down the river bank and the other members of the hunting pack were running along the foreshore yapping and frolicking. Their muzzles were covered with blood and then I could see why. In the pirogue behind the sleeping dog was a butchered antelope with soft Bambi-style white spots on its russet coat.

The hunter saw me reach for my camera and then put on his own *danse macabre*, enacting the hunt that had taken place earlier that afternoon. In his tattered clothes he jigged about on the water's edge, barking like a dog to show how his pack had chased the animal down before he had dispatched it with a spear. As a grand finale he posed dramatically with his spear and the antelope's head.

I don't know if it was the smell of the recently killed meat that stirred him, but the feverish Kago suddenly arose. A discussion between the paddlers then ensued, followed by negotiations with the hunter. Within minutes one of the blood-soaked quarters was onboard the *Sandoka* wrapped in leaves and ready for cooking once we reached Ubundu.

The presence of the meat seemed to energise all four paddlers. They worked their blades with added vigour, churning up the river water into small mocha whirls, inching us closer and closer to Ubundu. For the first time in days, I started to look at my watch, anxiously calculating and recalculating how long it might take, but Malike kept on reassuring me we would make it.

Almost astride the Equator, night fell like a portcullis. The sun dropped below the horizon and suddenly all was dark. My arms and face had been cruelly sunburned out on the river and I convinced myself I could actually see my skin glowing, as I peered into the gloom, anxious to spot the first sign of the town.

Ubundu is a large town and a strategic port, so I was expecting to see at least a few lights from the shoreline. I was wrong. The first evidence I had that we had reached Ubundu was the sound of the rapids. For hundreds of kilometres the Congo River had been mute and yet suddenly, as we rounded a headland, I could make out the sound of rushing water. It was terrifying.

'There is Ubundu,' Malike pointed over to the left bank.

'I see nothing. Are you sure?' My voice quavered.

'You cannot see anything at night, but it is there.' With that he spun the head of the pirogue towards the right bank and prepared to tie up for the night.

'It is too dangerous to cross above the rapids during the dark and there are soldiers over there too. We will stay the night here.'

'Wait a minute,' I said. 'I must get there tonight. The motorbikes leave early in the morning, we have to cross now.'

I heard Malike negotiating with his three colleagues in Swahili. In the darkness I could not read their faces, but I could tell the other three were not happy with the idea of the night-time crossing. The debate continued for minutes and then I thought of the dollars hidden in my boots.

'If you get me there tonight, I will double the pay.' My offer was desperate, but effective. Malike translated and suddenly the pirogue was spinning round through 180 degrees and darting out into the open river.

The noise of the cataracts grew. Somewhere out there to our right was the start of the Stanley Falls. When Stanley encountered these rapids for the first time he tried to shoot them. Various members of his expedition drowned and he ended up dragging his canoes around each dangerous section of water. The sound had a dramatic effect on the paddlers. They dug their blades in the water with studied effort and I sensed that on each stroke they looked out right, peering for the first signs of white water.

We surged across the river. In the darkness I could not tell how quickly we were being washed downstream, but my legs were tense, my heart racing, anticipating what I would do if the pirogue toppled. Peering forward, I was desperate to make out the first signs of the opposite bank and suddenly, as an almost full moon emerged from behind the clouds, I started to make out some dark shapes up ahead.

'This is the harbour of Ubundu,' Malike whispered. All I could make out was a jumble of broken concrete from an old slipway. 'And that . . . is a soldier,' he added in a voice trailing into silence.

I looked up. A dark figure was moving towards us and the gun-metal grey of his rifle had a pale moonlit sheen.

He was small, only a boy to be honest, and I did something completely unplanned. I jumped onto the broken jetty and began to bark orders.

'Who are you? Where is your commanding officer?' My voice was firm. It was meant to camouflage my terror and could have backfired horribly. No white man had arrived here for years, let alone by pirogue in the middle of the night, and the soldier had every reason to treat me with suspicion.

I could not believe what happened then. The gunman shuffled respectfully to attention and saluted me.

9.

The Equator Express

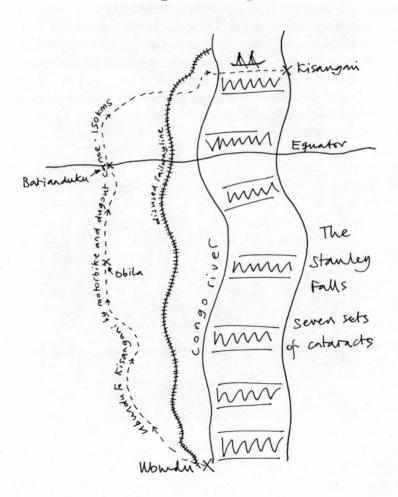

I knew my bravado to be a fragile thing with an unreliably short half-life. I also knew it would not be long before the Congolese gunman worked this out. Stomping off purposefully through the undergrowth, I was desperate to maintain the illusion of control. Thankfully the darkness hid the fear in my eyes. Days earlier I had tried to relay a message through the closest major town, Kisangani, 140 kilometres to the north, to the last remaining Catholic priest in Ubundu, that I might pass this way. My best hope for sanctuary was to make it to the priest's house and pray my message had got through.

It was already the middle of the night. Beneath clouds weakly backlit by the waning moon, our small column set off for what passes as Ubundu town centre. Uninvited, Malike, the leader of the paddlers, grabbed my rucksack, balanced it on his head and led the way up a thickly overgrown track between two banks of dense vegetation. I could make out large trees lurking overhead. At times the shadows merged so thickly I thought we had entered a tunnel. Malike said he knew the way to the priest's house and I was banking on him being right. I followed next, trying to convey an air of control. Falling flat on my face would not have helped, so I took extra care as I picked my way through the web of roots and tendrils underfoot. And behind me came the gunman. I could not see him, but the sound of his footfall was clear and threatening.

As we left the other three paddlers at the riverside, so we left the roar of the cataracts. I was still being deafened, but this time it was my adrenalin-spiked heartbeat that was pounding in my ears. Sweat poured down my back in the clammy night heat as fireflies began to flicker in the gloomier puddles of shadow.

Under one particularly thick knot of foliage I could just make out a carved stone madonna. It fitted with the only detailed description I had been able to find of the town, one written by Katharine Hepburn in a diary entry describing an afternoon idled away here while waiting for the train north during the filming of *The African Queen*.

> I wandered out the main avenue toward the monks' church . . . On the way there was a nunnery. Quite high walls lined the avenue. Plaster – mud-coloured – sometimes painted white. Great vines growing over them. Just opposite the nunnery was the nuns' cemetery . . . I went in through the gate and stood thinking by the sweet gravestones. Lives of total service . . . I am not in any sense a Catholic, but one couldn't help being moved by the dedication of these men and women.

In the gloom I could not make out any nunnery or cemetery, but the madonna suggested I must be near.

Malike ploughed on uphill and after a few more minutes we came to an area where the undergrowth had been cut back and in the darkness I could make out the loom of buildings. All was silent.

'Hello, hello, is there anyone there?' I tried to conceal the tremble in my voice as I broke the silence with a shout.

Nothing.

And then a shambling human shape emerged.

'I am the housekeeper. The priest is asleep, but he told me someone might come one of these nights. I will show you where you can sleep.'

My sigh of relief was so deep that, for a second, I felt dizzy. Malike put down the rucksack and I spent a few minutes in the dark rummaging through its innards to recover my head torch. Under its glare, I carefully unrolled four $50 notes and handed them to him. This was four times more than the price we had agreed, but all my usual nervousness about not appearing too foolishly generous was lost in the thrill of having made it to Ubundu. Malike was silent. He turned the notes in his hands. I flashed the head torch a second time so that he could check each note and confirm I was not fleecing him. My largesse clearly troubled him. Maybe he was disappointed that he had not driven a harder bargain. If I could afford to quadruple our original price, then surely I could have been persuaded to pay even more. Maybe he suspected the notes were counterfeit. A single fifty-dollar note represented a fortune in his riverine village, now several days' paddle back upstream on the upper Congo. Four was wealth untold. He turned on his heel without shaking my hand and, with my plaintive thanks in his ears, disappeared back down the track to the river. I was closely watching the gunman from the corner of my eye. To my great relief, he decided to go back to his sentry position on the river's edge, fell in behind Malike and was soon lost to my sight.

The housekeeper told me to follow him to an outbuilding. As the door opened with a creak I could hear the scuttle of cockroach legs scrabbling on the cement floor. It was a curiously lovely sound. It meant I had made it to the safety of a place connected to the modern world: a place of cement floors, dirty, cracked, vermin-infested cement floors, but cement nonetheless. I fell asleep with a grin on my face, wrestling with my mosquito net, planning how I would cope with the next ordeal.

The room where I slept was in the precincts of a church, but it was the sound of a drum, not bells, that woke me. In *The Poisonwood Bible*, one of the child narrators describes the 'loggedy' drums of the Congo that she heard while growing up at her Baptist father's mission station. It was a perfect description for the large, wooden instrument I heard that morning. It was located just inside the door of the church of Saint Joseph's looking like an oversized piggy-bank. It was made from a two-metre length of tree trunk, stripped of bark with just a single slit in the top. Through that aperture, carvers had scraped out the innards of the trunk to leave a hollow wooden tube. When drummed on the outside, a sound as thick as treacle oozed from the slit.

A cloudy dawn had broken and I could now see where I had arrived in the middle of the night. The church itself was a large building, dating from the 1950s. Older brick buildings comprising a school and prayer centre stood in front of it, but the whole place was overgrown and badly looked after. When known as Ponthierville, this town had been another important hub in the Belgian colonial project, connecting the upper Congo River with a railway skirting the 100 unnavigable kilometres of the Stanley Falls.

'Nothing is working right now.' The priest, Adalbert Mwehu Nzuzi, sounded deeply troubled. He had welcomed me in front of his church, but from the moment I saw his cold expression, I knew I was dealing with a worried man. 'This place is not safe for you. I really think you should leave as soon as possible.'

After surviving three weeks' travel through the Congo, I was beginning to feel a bit cocky, so I assured him I was all right. He looked me in the eye, slowly raised his eyebrows and repeated his warning.

'This is a terrible place where terrible things happen. You really must leave before they find you.'

'Who are "they"?' I asked.

Before he answered he looked around over his shoulder to check no-one was in sight and whispered a reply. 'The rebels, the mai-mai, the ones who are under the command of . . .' At this point he dropped his voice so that it was barely audible. 'Kufi.'

I had not heard the name Kufi before. It was a name that left Father Adalbert petrified.

'I lock myself in at night. We hear the most terrible things. Sometimes it is the sound of gunfire, but sometimes we hear nothing but the screams. That is when they are using "white weapons".'

I had never heard the expression 'white weapons', so I asked him to explain.

'The old weapons, the ones that do not make a sound: knives, machetes, spears. Once they kill, they throw the bodies in the river and they are washed away.

'There is just no law here. That is what we need more than anything. A sense of the law and the sense that there is someone to enforce it. Without that there is chaos. These mai-mai kill for no reason at all. One day you are okay, the next day you are dead. There is no sense to it. If they are angry with you or don't like your clothes, they kill and they know they will never face justice.'

It was a brief but eloquent lament for the Congo. What the country needs above aid shipments or charitable donations is a sense of law and order.

Entering the priest's house, I saw on a table a portrait of one of the main culprits for Congo's legal anarchy. It showed the dictator Mobutu Sese Seko. When the Congo won independence from Belgium on 30 June 1960, the African continent viewed it as a moment of great optimism and hope, a time when eighty years of colonial control and exploitation would end and a new era of black emancipation would begin. More than any other single person, Mobutu made sure this dream was never fulfilled.

Mobutu's dictatorial reign between 1965 and 1997 created the violent free-for-all of today's Congo. It was Mobutu who robbed the country of its wealth, plundering national reserves on a scale economists have still not been able to gauge accurately. When he came to power, the Congo had a thriving mineral industry, reliant on copper from the south-eastern province of Katanga and diamonds from the central province of Kasai. When he was driven from office in May 1997 to die in exile a few months later, the country was broke and the output of the mines a fraction of what it had been fifty years earlier. Estimates of what he stole vary from millions of dollars to billions, but the truth is nobody will ever be able to arrive at an accurate figure. Dictionaries cite Mobutu's rule as the perfect example of a kleptocracy, a state where rampant greed and corruption erode normal economic activity.

Like many other African dictators, Mobutu won power by presenting himself as the only leader strong enough to unite the country. For five years after independence, the Congo had been in a state of near-permanent rebellion, with the attempted secession by Katanga, the Mulele Mai uprising in the east and various coup attempts in Kinshasa. In one of the clumsier features of Belgian rule, Brussels had groomed no Congolese politicians to take control of the vast country at independence – Belgian colonial law barred Congolese from reaching senior positions in the army, civil service, judiciary or other organs of state, and by the time the colonialists left, the country had barely a handful of graduates. Control of the Congo fell into the hands not of a cadre of trained, experienced, educated leaders, but of young turks who suddenly found themselves vying for positions of enormous influence.

Mobutu had not yet turned thirty when independence came to the Congo but, as violence gripped the country for five years, he used his senior position in the army to artfully convince America and the West that he was the only Congolese leader capable of controlling the fractious giant at the heart of Africa. It worked. The coup that brought him to power in 1965 was tacitly approved by Washington, if only because it promised an end to the turmoil. Mobutu obliged by establishing stability in the most brutal way possible, publicly executing rivals and detaining possible plotters. Pierre Mulele, the rebel leader responsible for the Mulele Mai uprising, was lured back from exile with a promise of an amnesty, only to be disposed of by Mobutu's troops. He died under torture, after his genitals and limbs had been cut off. What remained of his body was then tossed into the Congo River.

Democracy was shunned by Mobutu, who defied calls for free and fair elections and centralised power into the hands of a close-knit cabal of friends, family and cronies.

There was a certain brilliance to Mobutu's evil. He was the consummate showman, luring George Foreman and Muhammad Ali to his capital, Kinshasa, for the most famous bout in boxing history, the 1974 'Rumble in the Jungle'. Concorde, the world's only supersonic airliner, would be chartered specially to fly supplies of pink champagne from Paris to his jungle palace complex at Gbadolite in the north of the country. The runway was specially extended so that the jet could land. Symbolically, Mobutu was the first leader of the Congo to tame the mighty river, building the only bridge to span the Congo River, the Marshal Mobutu suspension bridge. And with his leopardskin hat and a sense of the dramatic, he established himself as one of the most iconic African figures of the Cold War. I have a journalist friend who remembers Mobutu flying to the scene of a bush atrocity deep in the Congolese jungle back in the 1980s, quoting Conrad. With the press within earshot as he looked at the mutilated bodies of his countrymen, the Congolese leader effortlessly quoted Mr Kurtz's last words from *Heart of Darkness*: 'The Horror! The Horror!'

But his showmanship should not disguise the corrosive effect his rule had on Congolese society, destroying completely any national sense of order or justice.

Long before Stanley passed through here, the Congolese had their own system of tribal justice. Onto these roots eighty years of Belgian colonial rule had grafted its own skewed, white-dominated legal system. Mobutu's most damaging achievement was to undo this, to create the sense of anarchic self-help that characterises today's Congo. Under the pre-colonial tribal system, no single chief was powerful enough to hold dominion over the entire Congo River basin. There were scores of tribes – 200, according to early twentieth-century anthropologists – each responsible for a chunk of territory, but the power of any chief was held in check by his people. If a chief grew unpopular, his people could oust him. Oustings were often bloody and brutal affairs, but the point was that a chief could not ignore his people completely.

These checks and balances were done away with in the post-colonial period as African dictators like Mobutu adroitly used Cold War rivalries between the superpowers to skew the system. Aligning himself with the West, Mobutu enjoyed such generous financial and military support from Washington that he became untouchable. He used these resources to do something no Congolese leader had ever been able to do − to run the vast country as one single fiefdom, centralising so much power that it became effectively impossible for any dissenting rivals to oust him for decades. By distorting the old rules, the post-colonial period became one of anarchy and decay.

Modern weapons made it almost impossible for Mobutu to be removed, so if you could not beat Mobutu's methods, there was only one realistic option − copy them. By raiding the national treasury he made sure government employees went without pay. How could one expect an unpaid soldier in the army of the Congo to behave correctly when every other member of the military system followed the country's leader and simply helped themselves to whatever they could get away with? The corruption that travellers to the Congo have experienced since the early Mobutu reign is an exercise more of self-preservation than of exploitation. If government officials at the airport were not being paid, then it made sense for them to graft cash from anyone unfortunate enough to cross their paths.

The picture on the priest's table was the first official portrait of Mobutu I had seen during my trip. Mobutu spent his thirty-two years in power inflating the cult of his own personality, claiming this country as his own personal plaything. His picture hung in every official building; newspapers covered every detail of his life, no matter how mundane; his name was attached to any large bridge, sports stadium or other construction project embarked on during his rule; and national television broadcast his image day in, day out. Just seven years after Mobutu's departure I found that almost all traces of his cult had disappeared.

It was rather unsettling to see him there in the priest's house. Here was an icon of modern African evil, an individual who did more than almost anyone else to set the Congo and the wider region of central Africa on its downward spiral.

It was an early official portrait, taken in the first few years of his rule when he still called himself Joseph-Désiré Mobutu and described himself as President of the Congo. Some years later, in the 1970s, Mobutu embarked on an Africanisation programme to strip away the remnants of colonial nomenclature. He reinstalled the river's ancient name, Zaire, and named his country after it. Western Christian names were ordered to be replaced by authentic, tribal names, so Joseph-Désiré Mobutu became Mobutu Sese Seko Kuku Ngbendu Wa Za Banga, which translates as 'the all-powerful warrior who, because of his endurance and inflexible will to win, will go from conquest to conquest, leaving fire in his wake'. And he dropped Western clothes, preferring what he presented as a more genuine African look of short-sleeved, safari-style tunic, capped with his trademark leopardskin hat.

'I keep it to remind me of the old order. Back in the 1960s this country still had hope. But then, around the time of this picture, it began to go wrong,' Father Adalbert said.

I looked closely at the portrait. Mobutu had adopted a very presidential pose, turning his bespectacled and very young face – he could only have been in his thirties when the picture was taken – away from the camera with studied nonchalance. He was wearing the uniform of a lieutenant general, a rank he thought more appropriate for a head of state than the rank he reached as a colonial paramilitary under the Belgians. Under their rule, he made it to sergeant major, still an impressive feat in a colonial force where black recruits were banned from holding the rank of officer. There was a gold chain of office hanging across his smart military tunic, red flashes on the tips of his collar and rank after rank of medals. This man had almost single-handedly destroyed any chance Congo once had of developing as a normal nation. I found myself shivering in spite of Ubundu's tropical heat.

The priest could offer me no food or supplies. He apologised but explained that every two months he would send someone on the roughly 300-kilometre round trip by bicycle from Ubundu to Kisangani to buy essentials like flour, sugar and oil. When I arrived, he was at the end of his two-month cycle and his supplies were out. All there was to eat was some banana fried in palm oil. I noticed that he kept every door locked in all the church buildings, including his house.

'You have to remain prudent every day. Really, you must leave as soon as you can.' He did not sound inhospitable. He sounded genuinely worried that it would be safer for me if I left Ubundu.

When I explained my plan to meet up with the aid workers from Kisangani delivering vaccines, he said he knew where they would have spent the night and sent a messenger on foot. While waiting for the messenger to return, I flicked through a pile of old magazines that I had found in the front room of the priest's house. One was called *Zaire Afrique* and clearly came after Mobutu's temporary name change from Congo to Zaire. Inside were earnest articles about some of the crazier aspects of Mubutu's misrule, such as the period in the early 1990s when he thought it a good idea to allow one of the country's provinces, Kasai, to issue its own currency in parallel to the main national currency, the Congolese franc. It was cloud-cuckoo-land economics but it met with the approval of the Congolese economist writing in the magazine, who praised Mobutu's sagacity and grasp of macro-economics.

Ubundu had no working cars, so when I heard the sound of engines approaching later that morning, I guessed they belonged to three motorbikes from the International Rescue Committee. This was the same aid group that had put me up in Kalemie, on the shore of Lake Tanganyika, so I felt as if I was meeting members of the same family when they circled in front of the house. The riders, all local Congolese from Kisangani, had exactly the same Yamaha bikes that Benoit and Odimba had used to bring me from Lake Tanganyika to the Congo River, complete with the same livery of mud splatters and crazy luggage arrangement of jerrycans and plastic bags strapped down with old inner tubes.

'We were told to look out for someone staying with the priest, but to be honest I did not think you would make it. Where have you come from?' Michel Kombozi grinned as he shook my hand. When I told him I had come from upriver, his eyes opened wide in amazement. 'We come here every two months or so to deliver medicines to the local clinic, but we have never heard of anyone coming here along the river. I thought it was much too dangerous.'

Michel was a big man, a father of nine children back in Kisangani. He was as purposeful and efficient as Benoit, ordering one of his colleagues, a cool-looking man who wore a reversed baseball cap, and wrap-round sunglasses, to strap my gear to his bike as quickly as possible. Father Adalbert continued to look anxious. He was genuinely worried that my presence in Ubundu would cause trouble, so after thanking him I urged Michel to leave as soon as possible. He did not argue. Above the revving engine I heard him shout, 'The distance is only a hundred and forty-three kilometres to Kisangani, but the track is bad so it takes all day. Let's go.'

The three IRC riders showed the same skill and strategy as Benoit and Odimba. Once we got going, they were reluctant to stop for anyone or anything. So after leaving Saint Joseph behind, they started threading their way quickly through the narrow footpaths criss-crossing Ubundu, splashing through puddles, sending chickens squawking out of our way in feathery explosions, and using the momentum from the bikes to surf along the lips of huge muddy furrows carved in the track by rainstorms. I saw a man with a gun take a second look at us after he spotted my white face riding pillion, but before he could raise his weapon we had already moved out of sight. After the torpor of Kindu and the crawling pace of the pirogue, I relished the sense of being on the move again, even though our progress was hardly swift.

Within moments of leaving Ubundu we entered full rainforest. There were trees so high I could not make out any detail of the leaf canopy tens of metres over my head. Some of the trunks were pleated into great sinews that plunged into the earth, as massive and solid as flying buttresses on a Gothic cathedral. And high above my head, but beneath the gloomy leaf canopy, I could make out boughs as square and broad as steel girders.

The going was much slower than in Maniema and Katanga because the forest here was that much more fecund. Stanley had had a grim time of it here too, dragging his canoes around the seven stretches of cataracts that make up the Stanley Falls. Whenever he left the river, his expedition had to expend huge effort hacking a path through the fringe of the rainforest, along which they could portage their canoes to the next stretch of navigable water.

The track I was travelling along was the remnants of the main road between Ubundu and Kisangani, which used to have regular four-wheeled traffic back in the 1950s. During my research for the journey, I had had a bizarre exchange with officials from the British government's foreign-aid arm, the Department for International Development (DFID), in which they assured me the road still existed and was already being upgraded, following the 2002 peace treaty, using British government funds.

This sounded like good news for my plan to travel through

here, but when I pushed them a little harder, the DFID people admitted that they had no further information and that I should speak to a UN official appointed as their agent. In spite of various messages and telephone calls, no-one at DFID was able to track down this mysterious agent and the whole experience left me feeling despondent at the efficacy of the aid effort in the Congo. Here was an important piece of infrastructure – a road around one of the biggest sets of cataracts on the river – and here was one of the world's most experienced aid providers, DFID, and yet there was a terrible disconnect somewhere. I was saddened by the thought that the DFID people back in London were attending meetings, summits and seminars at which they assured the colleagues in the aid community that the Kisangani–Ubundu road upgrade was in hand when, as I was finding out, this was not the case.

There was absolutely no work taking place on the road. The advancing jungle had choked it to a single-track footpath, snaking around mature trees growing up from the centre of the old carriageway and past vast mudslides and dramatic rockfalls. Bridges had been washed away, making us pick our way down to the bottom of water courses and then charge up the other side. Recent rains made the whole exercise a dirty and dangerous one as the bikes slithered in the glutinous mud time and again, often pitching me onto the deck. One fallen tree caused a twenty-minute delay as the only route for our convoy of three bikes was up and over the top. This meant unloading everything, carting it over to the other side and then heaving the bikes over the fallen trunk, all the time sliding in mud that stood no chance of drying out because the dense leaf cover kept out any direct sunlight. The sticky heat felt as if we were toiling inside a hothouse.

At one point an obstacle made us stop in a thicket of giant bamboo. Canes as thick as my leg sprouted close together before splaying out as they grew longer and thinner. I spotted a long, thin black line that looked like a gunpowder trail from a western movie. Walking closer, I saw the line begin to move. At first it shifted as one, but as I got nearer it separated into millions of component parts – a column of ants.

'Get away, get away,' Michel shouted at me. I had heard stories of Congolese ant columns descending on villages and eating everything in their path. Infants, the elderly and the infirm will perish if left to be consumed by the column. A hunter told me that he would prepare the trophy from an antelope hunt by deliberately finding one of these ant columns and then throwing the dead animal's skull into its path. When he came back the next day, the bone would be spotless, stripped of every last piece of flesh and gristle, tendon and tissue.

Stupidly ignoring Michel, I approached to what I took to be a safe distance and started taking photographs. Within seconds I had a bite on my knee, and then one on my thigh, then another on my back. As I ran back to the bikes, the ants were so thick on my trousers I brushed them off like soot. It took ten minutes to undress and rid every last ant from the creases in my clothes. The worst of the bites stung for days.

From time to time we would spot other road users, pedestrians carrying heavy loads or pushing bicycle frames laden with food. Just as earlier on my trip, these people carried possessions that belonged not to today's world, but to an earlier time. Loads were wrapped in old leaves and then bundled up with woven grass into primitive rucksacks carried on a headstrap reaching round the forehead. Several of the walkers had large African snails stuck to the side of their leaf bundles. The snails did not have to be tied on, as their gooey, muscular foot kept them firmly attached until the moment when they were taken off and cooked. The only other food we saw was cassava paste tied in small rectangular leaf packets. Cassava smells pretty rich even when it has just been cooked, but this stuff was even more rank having been carried for days, unrefrigerated, along the sweaty jungle floor.

I saw a husband and wife plodding along at the pace of one of these mealtime snails. Both were carrying heavy loads borne on headstraps of fibrous bark reaching under the baskets and then around their foreheads. They were sweating heavily and after I persuaded Michel to stop, I took a hold of the man's basket. I could barely lift it and he was carrying it for 143 kilometres, the distance clocked by my bike's odometer between Ubundu and Kisangani, with the entire weight borne by his neck.

I asked the man about an atrocity that happened on this very track in early 1997. Thousands died when a column of Hutu refugees from Rwanda was attacked by rebel forces loyal to the new Tutsi regime in Rwanda. For a few weeks around the end of March and beginning of April, aid workers described what happened here as one of Africa's worst war crimes. I wanted to know what impact it had had on the local community.

The man listened to my question and thought for a moment before shaking his head.

'I come from Ubundu, but I don't know what you are talking about. There have been many attacks and many massacres. When it happens we flee into the bush, but nobody ever knows the details.'

I was stunned. An hour later we stopped in a trackside village called Obila. The IRC maintained a solar-powered fridge there inside a thatched hut to preserve vaccines and medicines, which are given out at a clinic of other thatched huts. Again, I asked about the 1997 massacre. Again, my question was met with shrugs.

It taught me a lesson about one of the Congo's chronic problems, its lack of institutional memory. The loss of life during the slaughter on the Ubundu–Kisangani road was of the same order of magnitude as the 11 September 2001 attacks in the United States, and yet in the Congo there were no repercussions. There was no memorial, or historical account of what happened, or court case to hold the perpetrators to account, or international response. The killings simply got lost in the Congo's miasma of misery. I wondered what hope there can be for a place if such lessons from the past are never heeded.

It was during this part of the journey that I had one of my most profound Congolese experiences. Since we left Ubundu several hours earlier we had seen nothing but forest, track and the occasional pedestrian or thatched hut. The scene I saw in the twenty-first century was no different from that seen by Stanley in the nineteenth century or by pygmy hunter-gatherers over earlier centuries. It was equatorial Africa at its most authentic, seemingly untouched by the outside world.

Suddenly, our convoy stopped. One of the bikes needed refuelling, or one of the riders had taken a tumble, I don't remember. What I do recall was the sense of Africa at its most brooding. The engines had been switched off and the silence was absolute. There was no birdsong, no screech of monkeys. Everything edible had long since been shot or trapped for the pot by local villagers, and the thick canopy way above our heads insulated us from any sounds of wind swishing branches or rustling leaves.

The ground was brown with mud and rotting vegetation. No direct sunlight reached this far down and there was a musty smell of damp and decomposition. Above me towered canyons of green, as layer after layer of plant life filled the void between forest floor and treetop. I felt suffocated, but not so much from the heat as from the choking, smothering forest.

I took a few steps and felt my right boot clunk into something unnaturally hard and angular on the floor. I dug my heel into the leaf mulch and felt it again. Scraping down through the detritus, I slowly cleared away enough soil to get a good look. It was a cast-iron railway sleeper, perfectly preserved and still connected to a piece of track.

It was a moment of horrible revelation. I felt like a Hollywood caveman approaching a spaceship, slowly working out that it proved life existed elsewhere in time and space. But what made it so horrible was the sense that I had discovered evidence of a modern world that had tried – but failed – to establish itself in the Congo. It was a complete reversal of the normal pattern of human development. A place where a railway track had once carried trainloads of goods and people had been reclaimed by virgin forest, where the noisy huffing of steam engines had long since lost out to the jungle's looming silence.

It was one of the defining moments of my journey through the Congo. I was travelling through a country with more past than future, a place where the hands of the clock spin not forwards, but backwards.

The railway track belonged to the Equator Express, a line built by the Belgians to circumvent the Stanley Falls, cutting straight through the Equator. Katharine Hepburn described taking the train to *The African Queen* set, and the grim conditions during the eight hours it took the train to cover just 140 kilometres. Some of the film crew members tried to deal with the heat by pouring buckets of water over themselves, but she judged it a waste of time because the effort of raising the bucket made you sweat even more, so she sat in a puddle of inertia willing the journey to end.

I heard a rumour that an enterprising Belgian official had placed a plaque alongside the rails to mark the exact spot where they cut the Equator. I would have liked to have tried to find the sign, but our bike track had deviated far from the overgrown railway line at the relevant place. I had to make do with holding my GPS device in my hand as I bumped along behind Michel on his motorbike and praying that it would work. I had used it to follow my journey from Kalemie, six degrees south of the Equator, and wanted to know the exact spot where I would cross from South to North. But to function it needed to pick up signals direct from a satellite and the thick tree cover meant the machine had trouble registering a signal. I cursed.

Then all of a sudden we reached an opening in the tree canopy and a clearing on the ground for a village. The machine pinged into life and the screen registered a long line of noughts. I was smack on the Equator on the noughth degree of latitude. I tapped Michel on the shoulder and asked him to stop so that I could find out the name of the village, Batianduku, which enjoys the status of straddling the Equator and being in both the northern and southern hemispheres.

The journey continued with the same rhythm of all my Congolese motorbike experiences. I would peer over the shoulder of the rider, trying to read the track so that I could brace myself for the next pitch forward or lurch to one side, through a blurred tunnel of forest green whipping past the periphery of my vision. Green, green, green, broken only occasionally by the brown of mud huts in a village clearing before more green, green, green. The odometer on the bike's handlebars counted down the kilometres to Kisangani, but the more I stared at it, the slower it seemed to move. In the end I stopped looking, my mind too numb to care.

And then, with a rush of light, the forest curtain was lifted and we reached one of the great jungle cities of Africa. Initially I felt excited, but disorientated. The buildings, the wide roads, the crowds of people and moving cars made me feel a little giddy. Kisangani was built mainly on the right (eastern) bank of the river and our track had brought us to the less-developed left bank. Pirogues ferried people backwards and forwards and these were special pirogues, very different from the ones I had used upstream, because they had outboard motors.

The sun was setting behind us by the time we had found one to ferry our bikes across the Congo River and, with the sun on my back, I had time to prepare myself for the big city. It felt like a moment of discovery. After weeks of mud huts, jungle tracks and hollowed-out canoes, I had found a pocket of modernity. The city docks glowed in the soft light to reveal a line of crane gantries on the wharf, an impressive cathedral with twin towers, a miniature version of Notre-Dame, and even some high-rise buildings. And in my pocket my mobile phone chirruped back into life.

10.

Bend in the River

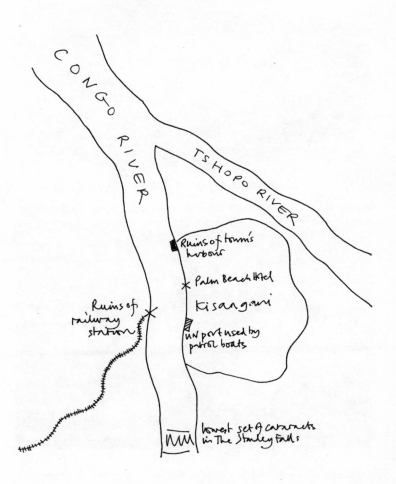

THE SEVENTH CATARACT, STANLEY FALLS.

Final cataract in the Stanley Falls as recorded, also by H.M. Stanley in 1878 and, below, by the author in 2004

My euphoria at reaching Kisangani did not last long. The gentle sunset on that first evening might have given it the appearance of a regular city, but as I explored I found it to be a shell, prone to spasms of brutal anarchy and chaotically administered by inept, corrupt local politicians. And it owed what little stability it had to the artificial props of a large UN force and foreign aid workers.

For the first days I was in recovery mode. I checked into the most lavish hotel the town could offer, the Palm Beach, which at $75 a night gave me comforts I had not enjoyed for weeks: a bed with laundered sheets, a shower, a door with a lock. It was built at the end of the Mobutu era and was already more than ten years old, but the two-storey structure was the most modern in the city. Skirmishes during the wars following Mobutu's death had imbued the hotel with quite a reputation – the bodies of eleven Ugandan soldiers killed in the grounds were stored for days in a bathroom because the kitchen refrigerator had been destroyed, and I kept hearing sketchy and unverifiable accounts of a foreign journalist whose dead body had recently been discovered in one of the rooms.

None of this mattered much to me during those first euphoric days. The hotel was my sanctuary. I felt I had earned a break from the hardship of Congo travel, so I locked the room down, with the shutters blocking out the light and the noise of air-conditioning drowning out all sounds of the Congo's second city. The bathroom plumbing worked and I took my first proper shower in three weeks. A few minutes later I took my second. It was only after my third that the water stopped running off me milky with grime. I looked at myself in a full-length mirror for the first time in weeks. I had lost more than a stone in weight. My face and forearms were brown as teak, but the rest of my body had the pasty pallor of unpolished marble. My spindly arms did not look as if they belonged to my body. And at the end of these unfamiliar limbs were something even stranger – claws. Ever since childhood I have not been able to stop biting my nails, but in the Congo some subliminal fear of its bugs and diseases made me stop biting. I scrubbed them time and time again, but for weeks they would not lose a grubby tinge of brown. None of these bathroom shocks could keep me from sleep. To the hum of the air-conditioner, I collapsed onto the bed and did not stir for fourteen hours.

The hotel even had a functioning restaurant. On my first morning I thought I had slept through breakfast, but a waiter in a black bow tie assured me all was in order and ushered me to a table with a clean, white tablecloth. The breakfast menu was short – fruit and eggs – but that was not the point. I was ordering food from a functioning kitchen, a very different experience from what I had encountered so far. The waiter brought me a place setting and on the saucer was a paper sachet of instant coffee. Some of the best coffee in the world used to be grown near Kisangani, but now the finest hotel in the city served only imported Nescafé. I had been longing for a cup of coffee and I felt a bit crestfallen. But all was forgotten when a plate of pineapple arrived. It was the sweetest, smoothest pineapple I have ever tasted. I could feel my internal battery indicator flickering from the red to green as the sugars ran into me.

I spent the first day or so in Kisangani locked in my room. I slept a lot, washed repeatedly, and laundered my filthy clothes in the bathroom. But most of all, I gathered my thoughts about what I had been through and primed myself for the next challenge. I wrote up my daily notes and used the luxury of the hotel's electricity supply to fire up my computer to edit the digital photographs I had taken. I unfolded my maps and tried to estimate how much more time I would need. It had already taken me three harrowing weeks to cover 1,200 kilometres and I was still not even halfway towards my endpoint, the port of Boma near the mouth of the Congo River. But I consoled myself that nobody had expected me to make it this far and, anyway, the really dangerous bit was now behind me. Surely, my ordeal could not get any harder.

When I planned my trip, I pictured Kisangani as a major milestone on my attempts to follow Stanley, not least because for sixty years the city had borne his name. As a cartographical tribute paid to the explorer for his role in staking the Congo for the Belgian king, the city was called Stanleyville, until it was changed to Kisangani in the 1960s.

Sitting in the dark and cool of my hotel room, I reread Stanley's account of his trip and how he dared not dawdle when he first passed here.

It had taken him weeks to descend the seven sets of rapids in the Stanley Falls. There were chaotic moments when some of the expedition canoes were caught by the current and dragged into the white water, drowning crew members. Stanley expressed regret whenever he lost one of the crew, but he sounded just as annoyed when one of the expedition's rifles was lost overboard. One lucky man survived only because he clung to a rock in midstream, just above a cauldron of white water. It took Stanley and the other team members several hours to rig up a rope long enough to reach the man and persuade him to let go of the rock and trust they would pull him to safety. Time after time Stanley's team had to portage the *Lady Alice* and its flotilla of canoes around white water, and time after time the expedition fought with local tribes.

The river was inhabited by the same Wagenia fishing tribe that Stanley had clashed with hundreds of kilometres back upstream near today's Kindu. Jungle drums used by the Wagenia had brought news of an expedition of outsiders coming downriver. Earlier raiding parties by Arab slavers had taught the Wagenia that strangers brought trouble, so when Stanley's expedition came into sight the first reaction from the locals was hostile. As war canoes were launched from riverside villages, Stanley lined up his flotilla in attack formation, with the *Lady Alice* in the lead and his pillaged canoes, including the *Telegraph*, spread out behind. During his river descent Stanley described thirty-two pitched battles and, while he enjoyed a military advantage in the modern rifles his expedition was equipped with, when he ventured ashore to portage his boats he often lost members of his expedition to tribesmen, expert at using the jungle as cover and deadly with bows and arrows carrying poisoned tips.

The town begins right at the bottom of the last set of falls, and when Stanley reached this place he described how he took immediately to the open water, safe at last from attack on the river bank. The expedition paddled as fast as it could out into the middle of the river and did not set foot on the right bank where the city of Stanleyville was to grow. Instead the expedition began the longest river stretch of their journey. It would be 1,734 kilometres before the river was blocked again by rapids near the country's capital, Kinshasa.

I sat in my hotel room, a hundred metres or so from the river, and plotted how I would follow him downriver. First, I would go and look for a Wagenia fisherman called Oggi Saidi.

A South African television reporter had recommended Oggi to me. In 2003, after the peace treaty was signed, he had flown to Kisangani to travel downriver in a kind of homage to Conrad. The river passage from Kisangani to Kinshasa has been one of the great African journeys since Conrad immortalised it in *Heart of Darkness*. Conrad began life as a merchant sailor and, more specifically, a professional skipper of steamboats. Steamboat crew in the late nineteenth century played a pioneering role in the Scramble for Africa as the continent fell under white rule, and in the early days of the Congo Free State, when Leopold's agents developed the colony for the Belgian monarch, skippers were at a premium. Conrad was one of many hired for duty on the Congo River.

In the first part of the twentieth century, regular ferry services covered the 1,734 kilometres between Leopoldville (Kinshasa) and Stanleyville (Kisangani) in less than a week, for those who wished to emulate Conrad. But the journey became more hazardous and intermittent after independence in 1960, and during the war that began in 1998 river passage was utterly impossible.

The South African television reporter had spent months of pleading with corrupt government officials before he found a boat descending the river, but he only got as far as Bumba, a few hundred kilometres downstream from Kisangani.

'It was the worst experience of my entire career reporting on Africa,' he said. 'But if you are going to stand any chance, then go and find Oggi. He knows the river as well as anyone.'

After several days of recovery in the Kisangani hotel, I felt strong enough to search for Oggi. My advice had been to go to the main fishing village closest to the falls and ask there. The village was located just above the cataracts that could be seen from the town centre, so one clear, sunny morning I set off on foot. I walked past the Falls Hotel, once the most glamorous establishment in Kisangani, but now a ruin swarming with prostitutes. Several of them were out on their tatty balconies and when they saw me, the only white man on the street, they started wolf-whistling and cooing terms of endearment in fluent Russian. Clearly, the charms of the Falls Hotel were enjoyed by the aircrew from the former Soviet Union, who fly contraband in and out of Kisangani. Opposite the hotel was a large plinth where a statue of Stanley had once stood. It was taken down shortly after the Congo became independent, and the plinth now bears a plaque commemorating not the nineteenth-century explorer, but the aid group that recently refurbished a water spring below the spot where

Stanley's likeness once stood. When I passed by, some of the women from the hotel were scrubbing their underwear in the spring water.

Behind me I heard a tramping of feet and a chorus of chanting male voices. The street cleared of pedestrians and the washer-women scuttled back across the road to the hotel. Round the corner came a terrifying sight. About fifty men, wearing ragtag clothes and scraps of military uniform, jogged slowly past in formation, responding as one to the calls of their leader running alongside. Their synchronised footfall and voices had me cowering behind the plinth where the statue of Stanley once stood. It felt for a moment as if the spirit of the old man, my *Telegraph* predecessor, was looking out for me. Kisangani was supposedly run by a mai-mai general promoted to city commander under the terms of the 2002 peace treaty, but in reality various military formations still lurked in the shadows. From time to time different units would go on the rampage, killing and looting with impunity. No wonder the people I saw on the street fled when they heard the approaching soldiers and it took several minutes for the street to return to normal once they had passed.

It had been a mistake to search for Oggi on foot. The air was still and the heat difficult to bear. Within minutes I was covered in a slick of sweat. My skin was as slimy as a cake of soap left too long in water. For a short distance I followed a tarmac road, the first I had been on since Lubumbashi. I could see it was being eaten away at the edges. Locals were using the hard surface of the road to sharpen their machetes, knives and other blades, rubbing away the tarmac surface little by little, slowly sending this modern road the way of the railway track I had seen lost under the forest floor. After a kilometre or so I picked up a footpath snaking through a patch of tall grass in the direction of the falls. The sun was fierce and the humidity cruel. The pace of my walking slowed as the rate of my breathing surged.

Stanley left this spot in a hurry when he passed here in January

1877, but he found time to describe the fishing methods of the Wagenia around the main cataracts and even illustrated his book with an ink drawing of the scene. I held up the sketch and found nothing had changed. There were the same wooden frames erected near the water's edge, made from entire tree trunks driven into cracks in the rock. Attached to the frames, suspended four or five metres above the ground, were specially made tapered rattan baskets, with a wide opening at the upstream end, but narrowing to a tight knot in the downstream direction. When the water level rose, fish would be washed past the gaping mouth of the basket and would become trapped in the narrow section, unable to swim back up against the weight of water.

I was there in early September, when the water level was at its lowest. The dry season south of the Equator was nearing its end, so this was off-season for most Wagenia fishermen, but I had a good view of the wooden frames hung with their basket traps. Fishermen were already clambering over them, reattaching baskets and refastening joints in preparation for rising river levels later in the year.

I walked across exposed flanks of the black rock, which, in a few weeks, would be underwater. Eventually I came to the edge of the lowest rapids, where the entire upper Congo River came crashing through a 200-metre-wide cleft in a rock shelf, throwing up a pleasantly cooling spray and churning the brown water into a creamy white lather of eddies and wavelets stretching hundreds of metres downriver. Stanley took great pride in the discovery of the falls that even today bear his name, describing them as more impressive and powerful than any others he had seen during his African wanderings:

> The river at the last cataract of the Stanley Falls does not merely *fall*; it is precipitated downwards. The Ripon Falls at the Victoria Lake outlet, compared to this swift descent and furious on-rush, were languid. The Victoria Nile, as it swept

down the steep declivity of its bed towards Unyoro, is very pretty, picturesque, even a sufficiently exciting scene: but the Livingstone [Stanley's name for the Congo River] with over ten times the volume of the Victoria Nile, though only occupying the same breadth of bed, conveys to the sense the character of irresistible force, and unites great depth with tumultuous rush.

The 'tumultuous rush' was a stark contrast to the placid body of water down which my pirogue had travelled. Enjoying the cool of the spray, I watched a few bold fishermen working their pirogues from below the falls into the white water, paddling furiously to make progress against the current and then launching small hand-nets over the side.

'The fish that live in the biggest current are the strongest,' said a voice. It belonged to a barefoot fisherman wearing torn red shorts who had joined me on the ledge.

'Do you know Oggi Saidi?' I asked.

'Of course. Everybody here knows Oggi. Come with me.' He put down his hand-net and led me back across the black rock. We had only walked about a hundred metres when we approached a small man with a tiny head, wearing a smart blue shirt.

'I am Oggi. How can I help?' His words startled me. He was speaking fluent English.

Oggi could see I was struggling in the heat, so he invited me to his home, a thatched mud hut in the main fishing village, Binakulu, within a few hundred metres of the cataract. We were just two kilometres from the city centre, but the village was as primitive as the settlements I had passed deep in the jungle. Oggi explained there was no mains water in the village and so the entire community used the river for drinking, washing and sewage. He shrugged and explained that dysentery was common and malaria endemic. In fact his first son, just four years old, was suffering from a bout of malaria.

He gave me a small wooden stool to sit on in the shade of a tree as I explained my journey, following Stanley's route all the way downriver from Kisangani to the Atlantic Ocean, still more than 2,000 kilometres downstream. When I told him how his name had been given to me by the South African journalist, he dropped his gaze for a second and rocked his upper body forward.

'Yes. I remember that journey to Bumba. It was a bad journey, a really bad journey.'

Undeterred, I said that I had spent three weeks slogging all the way here from Lake Tanganyika and I was anxious to find a way downriver. When I finished speaking, he hesitated before replying.

'I know this river as well as anyone. The reason I speak English is that back in the 1980s and early 1990s there were tourists who used to come here, English-speaking tourists. I would take them down the river on boats or sometimes I would take them fishing on pirogues, but the war brought chaos to the river. I have never known it as bad as today. There are no regular boats from Kisangani, and at this time of year, with the water level so low, boat owners do not like to risk their boats. There are sand banks and if you make a mistake you can lose your boat for ever. We can go down to the main port in the city and ask if any boats are moving, but you must understand, it is going to be difficult.'

My euphoria at reaching Kisangani was now fully spent. I might have made it further than any foreign overland traveller in the Congo for decades, but Oggi suggested that my ordeal was far from over.

The next day we went in search of a river boat heading downstream. I had expected we would need to go to the large concrete quayside that I had seen when I first reached Kisangani, the one with the line of cranes. But it turned out this was the property of the Congolese armed forces, who were hostile to anyone trying to tie up alongside, so civilian boats were tied up a kilometre or so downstream along a muddy stretch of river bank. To get there we walked past the remnants of the two-storey hotel where the stars and film crew of *The African Queen* had stayed in the early 1950s. At the time it had the rather sweet name of 'L'Hôtel Pourquoi Pas?'. On arrival, Katharine Hepburn had been incensed to find she had been fobbed off with a ground-level room and had immediately pulled rank over the film's accountant, who had been given a first-floor room with a balcony overlooking the river. She had the bean-counter summarily evicted before installing herself in what she described as a charming room with a pleasant view.

Today 'L'Hôtel Pourquoi Pas?' is a broken ruin, home to scores of squatters who sleep on the bare floor next to walls stained with damp, and who light fires where the Oscar-winning actress once unpacked prodigious amounts of luggage, full of the latest tropical outfits designed by the smartest London couturiers.

A little further along the river bank, I saw what I initially took to be a graveyard of wrecked river boats. There were rusting hulks haphazardly tied together by a web of knotted hawsers and cables, bedecked with large pieces of plastic, which had been stretched out to provide shade for gaggles of wretched-looking people living on the decks. It was a floating shanty town.

'Welcome to the port of Kisangani,' Oggi said formally.

The stench was incredible. The people under the shades had been living here for months. The river bank was sloppy with raw sewage and I could see a malodorous slick that leached into the river downstream from the boats, too viscous for the current to disperse. Stepping delicately through a minefield of human waste, I made it to a wobbly-looking gangplank connecting the river bank with the first hulk. It creaked under my weight, but with a lunge I reached the rust-brown deck and looked around.

Faces, faces, everywhere. A few turned to look at the white stranger, but most just stared forlornly out over the river. Mothers breastfed babies. Other women stirred pots of cassava on wood fires lit straight on the deck. Men sat in dirty singlets, eyes dull with boredom. It was crowded, chaotic and grim. Only one area of the deck was free of people and I saw why. Some sort of gummy oil had weeped from a split rattan basket onto the deck and the sticky, sweet mess had attracted a thick cloud of angry bees.

I heard Oggi questioning various people and saw them all pointing in the same direction, to the outermost hulk, furthest from the bank. Jumping over hawsers and stepping between the different deck heights of the parallel boats, I followed Oggi. By the time I arrived, he was already in earnest conversation with a man who introduced himself as Simon Zenga and described himself as the Person Responsible for the motorboat *Tekele*. I queried him. Does that mean you are the captain? No, he replied. I am the Person Responsible.

It was a term that carried the stamp of Belgian colonial rule. The Belgians ran the Congo on a strict hierarchy, from white bosses down to black underclass. The level of Person Responsible was a middle-ranking tier that was neither as powerful as the boss nor as weak as the underling. The Mobutu regime had made a lot of noise about ridding the Congo of the old trappings of empire. But in reality the old colonial hierarchies had proved to be just as useful for the African dictatorship.

As Oggi and Simon continued their discussion, I slowly made sense of the chaos around the port. The boats were, strictly speaking, not boats at all but barges – vast, flat-bottomed hulls with roofs, but no engine. These were the things that I had taken to be abandoned hulks. They had no cabins, no fittings, no furniture, no lighting, no portholes, no paintwork. They were just floating boxes made of sheet metal, rusting away in the tropical heat. For power they relied completely on tiny tugboats, or 'pushers' in the vernacular of Congo boatmen. Dwarfed by the barges, the pushers were much more important as they actually had engines and could both drive and steer the barges.

At the end of the barge I was now standing on, attached by some taut hawsers, was the motorboat *Tekele*. It was old, rusty and very, very small. Against the river vastness it looked like a toy, and yet the Person Responsible promised me that with enough fuel and a skilful navigator it could push its barge for 'the 1,734 km'. He was referring to the journey from Kisangani to Kinshasa, where every last kilometre had once been marked on river charts.

'We are the outermost boat because we are the next one planning to leave,' Simon said, stirring my interest.

'When?' I asked eagerly.

'In the next few weeks.'

'How long will it take you to go the whole 1,734 km?' Excitement was welling inside me.

'At least four months, but we will have many stops and we might not even go all the way down to Kinshasa . . .' He was still speaking, but disappointment had temporarily deafened me.

Back at the hotel, Oggi and I found solace in a bottle of Primus, the local beer. It has been brewed in Kisangani since the colonial era, and across the Congo it enjoys the status of a national institution. During my research most people with any direct experience of the Congo mentioned Primus. During the various wars and periods of turmoil here, just about the only thing that remained open in the city was the brewery, churning out Primus lager in large, brown litre bottles that bore the name not on a paper label, but on a stencil of white letters glazed direct onto the glass. There were legendary stories about bottles of Primus being opened to reveal human nails inside, or insects, or other detritus too gruesome to go into. But the point was: while every other factory in Kisangani collapsed, the Primus brewery plodded on, filling, recycling and refilling the bottles, time after time, year after year, crisis after crisis.

Each bottle I drank seemed to have its own story. The tiny chinks on the lip or missing letters on the stencil told of boozing sessions and bar fights through the city's turbulent past. Drinking a bottle of Primus in the sweaty heat of Kisangani made me feel more in touch with the country's recent history than almost anything else I did in the Congo. And another thing – it tasted great.

Smacking his lips lavishly after a gulp direct from a bottle, Oggi reiterated that the low water level meant the larger boats rarely moved up as far as Kisangani for fear of being beached on a sand bank at this time of year. He said he was not surprised that the smaller boats like the *Tekele* were the only ones that attempted the journey and that four months was a normal journey time.

'A small boat like the *Tekele* does not make money from a single cargo. It is too small to carry a large amount from Kinshasa to Kisangani. So it makes its money on a thousand small cargoes, cramming in people and their possessions for just a few kilometres here and a few kilometres there. If you ever see a river boat like the *Tekele* moving, there will be a hundred pirogues hanging off it at any one time, their paddlers using it to save the effort of paddling a few kilometres. But it means a boat like the *Tekele* would stop at every town, every village. There will be problems with fuel and navigation. A journey on a boat like the *Tekele* takes a long, long time.'

I ordered another Primus, discarding the old bottle and with it the hope of travelling with the *Tekele*.

'Okay, so what are my options for going downriver?'

Oggi thought for several minutes.

'We can try to find a way to get you to Bumba. It is the first large town downstream, three hundred and fifty kilometres away from Kisangani. If you went by pirogue it would take at least a week, but maybe we could try to hire a motorised pirogue from the local priests. I know they have one, but they would charge eight hundred to one thousand dollars for the fuel alone. But the problem would remain that when we get to Bumba, we would have to wait there for another boat like the *Tekele*.'

I could feel my Congo despondency beginning to resurface. And then Oggi made a final suggestion.

'Or you could ask the UN. Every few months I see one of their barges and pushers arriving here. Maybe you would be lucky with them.'

Like all other UN buildings I had visited in the Congo, there was something unearthly about the headquarters in Kisangani. The tidiness, the cleanliness, the flicker of computer screens all belonged to a world very far removed from planet Congo. I was welcomed by Ann Barnes, a tall, elegant British woman who worked as senior administrator. She was too charming to say anything about my malodorous, grubby appearance and seemed genuinely interested as I explained that I was trying to follow Stanley's original route and that passage downriver was the key. Like every other foreigner I met in Kisangani, she expressed astonishment that I had arrived here overland rather than via the city's airport. She could not have been more helpful, promising to make a formal request through the UN channels, but also pointing out something I was familiar with already: that the organisation's bureaucracy worked very, very slowly.

So began weeks of waiting in Kisangani. Like a supplicant on a daily ritual, I would begin each morning plodding between Kisangani's port and the UN office, begging for news of a boat heading downstream. My overland ordeal reaching Kisangani had given me a strange feeling of superiority. It was a much stronger version of that felt by the rucksack-carrying overlander, recently arrived at a remote location, over another traveller who arrives at the same spot by air. I felt something similar, only much, much more powerful – a sort of cockiness, almost an aloofness. Without regular river traffic or road connections, Kisangani had been effectively cut off for years. This had made it shrink in on itself, most of its people never venturing far beyond the city confines. Except for a web of dangerous footpaths used by a few tough, foolhardy bicycle-porters, it had no overland connections with the outside world. And the foreigners who come here did so by aircraft.

Just a few months before my arrival, people had died on Kisangani's streets during rioting sparked by the Bukavu incident. Congolese people were venting their anger at the killings committed there by Rwandan-backed rebels. The Congolese government might be inept at running the country, but it is adept at dodging blame, so it used the government-controlled media to direct the people's rage against the United Nations, blaming foreign outsiders for failing to protect Bukavu. Popular anger against the UN spread across the country, but nowhere was the anger more intense than in Kisangani, where UN buildings were torched and property looted. The peacekeepers fled and an unknown number of local Congolese died in rioting as the mob's anger was turned against all things foreign. Aid groups had their offices and warehouses ransacked and what passes for the Congolese authorities did nothing to stop it. Indeed, there was plenty of evidence of the local soldiers and police taking part.

The violence was simply the latest in a long series of spasms that had wrecked Kisangani over the last fifty years. Squabbles between occupying soldiers from Uganda and Rwanda had developed into all-out battles on the streets of Kisangani on several occasions between 1999 and 2002. The troops had come here as part of their respective homeland's pillaging of the Congo's resources. Witnesses described the river nearby running red with blood when bodies scraped off the roads were tipped into the water. On another occasion, Rwandan-backed rebels slaughtered dozens of Congolese in the city after a series of protests at Rwandan occupation.

Those killings were just a continuation of what had gone before. In the early 1990s when Mobutu's rule began to crumble, Kisangani suffered as much as any Congolese city from what locals refer to as the Mass Lootings or *Grands Pillages*. These were the episodes of anarchy sparked by the growing sense that Mobutu's corrupt rule was spiralling towards collapse, when the army and police followed the example of the country's leader and simply helped themselves to whatever could be pillaged. Local people in Kisangani cannot agree on how many Mass Lootings took place there. Some say three, others four. And no-one agrees how many bodies, yet again, were collected from the streets of Kisangani and cast into the river.

And in the decades before – the 1960s, 1970s and 1980s – the city suffered bouts of anarchy, captured by V.S. Naipaul in his book *A Bend in the River.* He described the bloodletting when ancient tribal anger clashed with the modern regime of 'The Big Man', the soubriquet given by Naipaul to the African dictator, who plundered the riverside city deep in the jungle, allowing mercenary forces to run amok, killing with impunity.

But the most notorious violence to grip the city came when it was still known as Stanleyville, in the turbulent years just after the Belgians reluctantly gave independence to the Congo. Here was established one of the most brutal, even clichéd, snapshots of African violence: the slaughter of missionaries and the rape of nuns. And the person who gave me an account of exactly what happened was a venerable, timeworn Belgian missionary with a throaty chuckle, who had lived through the whole horrible episode.

Father Leon has called the Congo his home since arriving here in 1947 at the age of twenty-six. Born in Brussels, he followed a well-trodden path exporting Christian enlightenment to his country's African colony. Historians have found plenty of evidence of collusion between Belgium's established Church and the colonial authorities in the Congo, of the Church being used to justify cruel acts of subjugation, but I was prepared to believe the man I met in the Kisangani headquarters of the Missionaries of the Sacred Heart of Jesus was just a well-meaning foot soldier in Christianity's long battle for the soul of Africa.

I met him in strange circumstances. After five nights at the Palm Beach Hotel in Kisangani my cash had begun to run low and I had grown fed up with the din from hookers, aid workers and assorted hangers-on who gathered nightly in the hotel restaurant. I needed to find a place to stay that was cheaper and more peaceful.

The Missionaries of the Sacred Heart of Jesus were one of the first Christian communities to reach Stanleyville. They arrived here shortly after the turn of the twentieth century and have witnessed every subsequent episode in the history of the city. Other missions had come and gone, but the Missionaries of the Sacred Heart of Jesus were still hanging in there in 2004, running a skeleton operation, but obstinately refusing to surrender a century's work. They ran the last, large mission in the city and they had a few guest rooms at the back of their property where I was offered accommodation. On the first afternoon in my new digs, I heard a chuckle in the courtyard and went out to investigate.

Father Leon was having his snow-white hair cut by Father Wilson, a tall, strapping Brazilian missionary in his late forties. The old man looked tiny as he bent his head forward meekly so that his colleague could get at his neck, and the pair were clearly in high spirits. I could see the shoulders of Father Leon shuddering as he laughed.

'Yes, of course I remember what happened in those dark days in 1964,' Father Leon said later as we shared a bottle of Primus on the steps of the mission station. His sharp, spiky haircut made him look younger than his years.

'By that time I had been in the Congo for almost twenty years. When I first arrived as a missionary, I was met by my brother, who was already working in the Congo as a colonial officer. For my first year or so I lived at the mission station in Ponthierville. It was very peaceful, very pleasant.'

His description made me think of what I had found when I had passed through what was once Ponthierville, the ruined town I knew as Ubundu and from where I had been told to flee for my own safety. I struggled to recognise Father Leon's description.

'And then I was moved here to Stanleyville to teach. The Church decided where we would go and when I received my orders, I would go.'

He was describing an almost military hierarchy for the missionaries, who were deployed hither and thither from his headquarters in the city. The missionaries were expected to obey instructions like soldiers, sent off into the forest at a moment's notice, often for years at a time. It fitted with what I had already seen in the centre of Kisangani of the Church's main building, a vast, fortress-like brick structure right next to the river's edge. More of a bunker than a spiritual centre, it had survived all the riots, pillages and street battles that the city had seen.

'After five years' service, we are given six months' leave and I remember it must have been after my third leave that I got back to Stanleyville in 1963. My colleague, a Belgian missionary called Heinrich Verberne, was meant to go to the mission at Opiange, a very remote place many days' travel from the city. But he was ill and I was sent instead.'

For the first time, the twinkle dimmed in Father Leon's eye as he got to the point of his story.

'It cost Father Heinrich his life. I was sent to Opiange and he stayed behind here in the city and was caught up in the rebellion.'

He was beginning to lose his flow, so I tried to prompt him gently back on course.

'Which of the rebellions are you talking about?' I asked.

'The big one, the Mulele Mai rebellion after independence, when the Congo began its big decline.'

Weeks earlier, back in Kasongo, I had seen the graves of Belgians who died in the Mulele Mai rebellion. Here in

Kisangani, the bloodletting had been much worse. Father Leon explained.

'We heard on the radio there were problems, but we did not know how bad. I was with an Irish missionary out at Opiange and we thought we were safe because we were so remote, but then one day in October or November of 1964 some Congolese men with guns came and said they had orders to bring all missionaries to Stanleyville. This must have been at the end of the rebellion because, by the time we got here, the other missionaries like Father Heinrich who had been caught here in the city had been taken by the rebels from the city centre to the left bank of the river, just across the water there.

'We were held in a room, along with other white people for a few days, but the situation was not that bad. We had water and a bit of food. But then came the day of the twenty-fourth of November 1964. I can remember it like it was yesterday.

'It was a Tuesday. The Belgian paratroopers arrived, dropped by American planes, and the rebels just disappeared from the city centre here on the right bank of the river. There was some shooting in the city, but within a few hours we were free. But over on the other side of the river, the left bank, the rebels were still in control for another day or so. That was where the massacre occurred. That night they killed all the missionaries they had and, after they raped the nuns, they killed them too.'

I sat in silence, but Father Leon had found a second wind.

'Come, I will show you something.'

He led me inside the mission house, past the refectory table where the missionaries ate their meals and through a large salon lined with dusty books.

'It's in here,' he said, walking to a side-room that was full of furniture. 'This used to be a chapel, a long time ago, but we use it now for storage. Help me move this, will you.' I joined him heaving at a cupboard and, as it moved, I could see the wall had been decorated with hand-painted portraits of men's faces, each in a tile-like square, which were arranged in the shape of a cross. Some of the faces were young, others old; some with glasses, others with beards; and one was wearing a topi, in the style of Tintin.

'These were painted to honour all those who died that day, that evening on the twenty-fourth of November 1964.'

Right at the centre of the cross was the portrait of a man with round spectacles and a goatee-beard and moustache. Straining his eighty-three-year-old eyes, Father Leon settled on this image and pointed with his finger.

'That is Father Heinrich. If he had not been unlucky enough to be too ill that time, perhaps it would be my picture up there.'

My days in Kisangani entered a grim routine made all the grimmer by my not knowing how long I would have to stay there. My priest's cell at the mission house was small, with a cement floor and a single light bulb hanging from the roof. As the days passed, I tried to make it feel more homely. On the chair I propped the photograph Jane had presented me with before my trip. It was of her and our dogs sitting outside our Johannesburg home in bright sunshine. It was creased across the middle from where I had tucked it into my notebook. No photograph has ever given me more pleasure.

I would be woken at dawn by the sound of Joseph, the house-keeper, noisily scraping the charcoal burner clean before he prepared to light it for another long day of boiling water and preparing food. No matter how early I rose, I never managed to get up before the Brazilian priest, Father Wilson, who seemed to get even taller and more healthy-looking the longer I spent there. His energy levels were stunning. Each morning I would see him clean-shaven and in a fresh T-shirt wolfing down bananas and bread, freshly baked by Joseph, before he headed off into the tropical heat, walking several kilometres to a piece of land where he was preparing the ground for a primary school. And as the people of Kisangani deserted the city's dangerous streets each evening, I would head back to the mission house for my supper of bananas and cassava bread and find Father Wilson already installed in the mission chapel, wearing his vestments and readying himself for a long vigil of prayer.

Each morning I took breakfast with Father Dino, originally from Italy and now a robust-looking fifty-year-old. You clearly had to be physically strong to represent the Missionaries of the Sacred Heart of Jesus in the Congo. As the days passed, I began to joke with the priests about the special military-style selection they appeared to need for service in the Congo.

'Well, it helps if you are fit. We had two young Polish missionaries here back in 2000, but the first malaria bout really got one of them and the first round of fighting got the other. Neither came back,' Father Dino said. I thought of Father Leon arriving in the Congo in 1947 and of the disease, hunger and deprivation he had endured over the last six decades. 'Perhaps the young priests aren't as tough as they used to be' were Father Dino's last words on the subject.

The priests managed to acquire fresh beans from the last dregs of the once-thriving coffee industry in the area and they had one of those elegantly simple Italian coffee pots, with two tapered, hexagonal chambers screwed together. It was old and battered, but it worked. I have one at home and when I saw the one in the mission, steaming on Joseph's burner, it made me ache with homesickness for my morning ritual of fresh coffee as I surfed the Internet. Like a child in a sweet shop, I guzzled way too much on my first morning at the mission and paid for it with a sleepless night neurotically guessing the time between howls from a dog chained up in a nearby yard.

Whenever I left the sanctuary of the mission I felt a degree of fear. My Congo mantra – towns bad, open spaces good – was reinforced daily as I got caught up in the white noise of corrupt bureaucracy that mars life in any large Congolese town. In order to walk down a city street in the Congo you have to get your paperwork in order. And by paperwork, I don't mean a passport to prove who you are. You need permission from state-security apparatus to be in a certain place at a certain time. I found it all very tedious and coercive, but I was by now too used to it to get angry. I plodded between the various buildings claimed by the Congolese government machine – the provincial governor's secretariat, the director of the immigration office, the local military commander's headquarters – and had various pieces of paper stamped, counter-signed and authenticated. The offices were in run-down, water-damaged buildings with no computers or phones, but they were invariably occupied by an apparatchik quick to frown, shake his head and demand payment.

I was warned not to take any pictures in town. UN officials had been bundled out of cars and had their cameras stamped on by aggressive Congolese gunmen for having the temerity to take a souvenir photograph. So I plodded the tatty streets of Kisangani, honing my Congo Survival Skills, looking not staring, pausing not dwelling, chatting without questioning.

It was clear why the government apparatus extends to Kisangani – it is a place where easy money can be skimmed from local miners who dig diamonds out of alluvial deposits along local river beds. During the recent wars Ugandan and Rwandan troops had occupied the city to get their hands on its diamond wealth. And under the terms of the peace treaty that ended the recent war, Rwanda sought to keep hold of its diamond income through the well-armed militiamen it kept in the city.

The diamond industry in Kisangani was as chaotic as the cobalt mining in Lubumbashi. It relied on artisanal miners scouring through the shingle of river beds for rough stones and then bringing them into town to sell the diamonds to dealers. But even if it was an industry that worked in a piecemeal, hapless, chaotic way, it was clearly profitable.

The diamond dealerships were easy to spot. They were the only freshly painted buildings in town. The façades were decorated with brightly painted garish images designed to tempt anyone with a diamond to sell. My favourite had a two-metre-high cartoon image depicting a man, dirty and sad, carrying an angular diamond in his hand, followed by the same man, clean and with a sparkling smile, running along with a sack in his hand marked with a dollar sign. I stole glances inside these establishments, but was too scared to enter. They invariably had a phalanx of dangerous-looking Congolese men slouching on chairs in the shade out front, their eyes hidden behind sunglasses. A handful of Lebanese traders braved the gangster's life of Kisangani diamond trading, buying up roughs before smuggling them out of the airport north to Sudan or east to Uganda, and onward to be resold, cut and sold again, an industry dependent on a web of bribes, tips and pay-offs here in Kisangani.

There was only one city-centre restaurant, a drab, modest-looking place, which people came to more for its Primus than its food. It was run by Sridar, a deferential Indian in his late twenties who swayed his head like a bobbin when he spoke. He was a relic from a once-huge Indian-subcontinent community that first arrived by boat at port cities such as Mombasa and Dar es Salaam before percolating right across the continent. During the colonial era they filled a lower-middle-class stratum deemed too menial for the whites and too sophisticated for the blacks. They were the shopkeepers, the foremen, the general traders of colonial Africa and, when independence came, they were often persecuted by Africa's new native leaders, resentful of their once-superior status. The hero of Naipaul's *A Bend in the River* is one such trader, who drives from the coastal home where his family have lived long enough to regard themselves as African, all the way to the city on a great river, deep in the rainforest. Sridar made me think of this character and his struggle for identity as darker forces rip the city apart, destroying his sense of connection with Africa.

'Welcome, welcome, you are most welcome,' Sridar said when

I first met him. 'I have just opened this restaurant and we have big plans. I work for my uncle, who owns a general trading shop. But I told him we could make money from a restaurant as well.'

'Are you not worried about what happened here to your predecessors, shopkeepers and traders over the past few decades?' I asked.

'I know nothing of them. I have just got here. I am sure if we work hard we will make good business.'

Sridar did not have to look far for his first lesson in the perverse character of commerce in the Congo. Near his place I visited a few general stores, crammed with Chinese-made mattresses, flip-flops and imported tinned food. Everything was hugely expensive because, without any meaningful flow of river traffic or passable roads, it all had to be flown in. And the transport costs were then inflated by the need to pay off customs officials, immigration officers and the like. The crazy thing was that the shops that actually contained anything, the general stores, were deliberately tatty and unpainted, an inversion of the Western commercial model that uses bright lights and adverts to draw customers in.

In Kisangani, the last thing a shop owner wants to do is advertise that he has stock. This would only attract the looters and robbers. A general store has a lot to lose if it is raided, whereas a diamond trader, who would never be so foolish as to leave gems in his shop, brightly advertises his business. If his shop is looted, all the robbers would find are a few tatty chairs or pieces of furniture.

There was one other thriving business, a shop belonging to a mobile-phone company. Like many other cities in Africa, Kisangani had benefited from the communications revolution. No longer do African regimes have to spend vast sums maintaining land lines and telephone exchanges, exposed to the perils of looting or climate damage. A few mobile-phone beacons, powered by solar batteries, cost a fraction of the old, fixed system. And the cash earned by mobile-phone systems is much easier to control. Gone are the days of relying on a failing mail system to send bills to users of landline systems to chase up payment for calls already made. Top-up cards have to be paid for in advance. Mobile-phone networks are among the most cash-rich and fast-growing businesses in today's Africa. It is no wonder that the sons, nieces and confidants of Africa's dictators vie for ownership of mobile-phone companies.

In Kisangani, I learned the double-edged character of instant communication, the way mobile phones can make you feel both in touch and isolated at the same time. I would go into the phone shop in the city centre, closing the door behind me, and pause under the downwash of air-conditioning, before paying for my next top-up card. I could then speak to Jane back home and hear about a world I had been detached from for weeks. During my journey up to that point there had been occasions when I had felt alone, but I had never had time to dwell on them because of much more dominant feelings of anxiety, fear or exhaustion. In Kisangani I had plenty of time to myself, and being able to speak to Jane so easily served to magnify my loneliness. The presence of a phone in my pocket, on which I could speak to her at any time, left me feeling more powerless and alone than if I had no means of communication. To hear about her normal day, her frustrations with the Johannesburg traffic, how our dogs had played up on their walk in the park or any other mundane detail of home was pure agony.

Jane could tell something was up. She tried desperately to keep my spirits up, enthusing about my achievement in reaching Kisangani along Stanley's route and encouraging me to wait just a little longer to see if some sort of river boat might appear. But the Congo was such an abnormal place that I found it distressing to hear from her. I was in a world where Jane and our lovely shared life simply did not belong. I missed normality so much that it was painful and, as I spent long periods in my priest's cell staring at her photograph, for the first time on my journey I started to seriously consider giving up. Unlike the remote places I had been passing through, Kisangani was connected to the rest of Africa through its airport. As the days of waiting passed, it became more and more difficult to bear the knowledge that in just a few hours I could escape this Congolese chaos and rejoin the world of that photograph.

The nadir to my despondency came on one of my morning walks along the bank of the Congo River. I had been to check on the boats at the port, but the *Tekele* had not moved and there was still no certain news of when she might sail. Making my way up to the UN headquarters to see if there was any word about one of their barges heading downriver, I noticed the view over the river looked very different. It took a few seconds to work out what was different but slowly it became clear. An enormous boat had moored, a tanker so large it changed the entire shape and topography of the bank as if a new section of developed land had miraculously appeared next to the river bank overnight. Where there had been mud and water, there was now angular metal and broad, open decks, all painted blue in the livery of Cohydro, a Congolese petrol company, and the name *Mbenga* was printed clearly on the wheelhouse.

The sight alone made my heart race. This boat was larger and more riverworthy than anything I had seen in ten days. It had arrived unannounced and I had no idea when it might leave, but for the first time in days I felt a surge of optimism.

Then began the most wretched twenty-four hours. I boarded via a gangplank and a crew member pointed me in the direction of the engine room to find the skipper. I found him a touch officious – he refused to give me his name – but I was willing to overlook this when he said he would be leaving for Kinshasa the following morning. First I asked to be allowed to sail with him, then I pleaded and finally I begged. It was humiliating but, worse still, it did not work.

'I do not have the authority to let you travel on this boat. You must speak to the Person Responsible for Cohydro here in Kisangani,' the captain said, in a most irritatingly officious voice.

I ran back up the river bank and went in search of the offices of Cohydro. Cars are a rarity in Kisangani, affordable only by foreign aid groups and the occasional diamond trader, so I jumped on the back of a toleka, one of the bicycle taxis that swarm the streets. They are chunky, Chinese-made bikes, with a padded seat carried on a frame welded above the back wheel. In Swahili, *toleka* means 'let's go', so shouting 'toleka, toleka', I urged my pedaller to find the Cohydro offices.

News of the arrival of the *Mbenga* had already reached the Kisangani headquarters of Cohydro. It consisted of an old petrol-station forecourt and a nearby room. By the time I got there, a crowd of several hundred people had gathered at the petrol station carrying old plastic bottles and there were even a few sinister-looking cars in line, their windows too tinted to see who was inside. The boat's arrival indicated a rare delivery of petrol in Kisangani and people with motorbikes, generators and vehicles were anxious for fuel.

As I paid my toleka man, there was a fracas in the crowd. It happened in a flash, but I had a clear view of a woman standing in the queue squawking as she looked in amazement at her handbag on her hip, inside which was the hand of a street-boy, no older than ten. Immediately he tried to run. The woman squawked louder still. The crowd surged. A leg appeared and tripped the pickpocket. And then the crowd surged again, swallowing him up, and I could hear blows landing on the boy and a scream that started loud and clear, but then became faint and gurgling. Then the mob parted and there was the boy, with his arms twisted behind his back and the foot of a man, a petrol attendant in Cohydro cap and uniform, stamped firmly on his neck. The boy's mouth was bleeding and the side of his face was squashed flat on the uneven concrete of the forecourt. It was a scene I had witnessed numerous times during my stint covering Africa. Quick and brutal, African mob justice is a terrifying thing.

I was too preoccupied by my own emergency to worry about the boy's plight. The opportunity I had been waiting for was within reach, so I turned my back on the boy and went in search of the Person Responsible for the company. Eventually I found him, Mr Mosinde, and pleaded to be allowed to travel downriver on his company's boat. He was not interested. He referred me to his boss in Kinshasa, and though I was able to get through on my mobile phone, he referred me, in turn, to his superior, and then he to his, and so on.

It was heartbreaking. To know there was a decent boat about to leave for Kinshasa was just too tantalising. All afternoon I fretted over phone call after phone call, desperate to find the person with the right authority. But a slow, growing ache in my guts told me I was wasting my time. Still, I persisted, trying to ignore the gut-ache and wasting top-up cards, trying in turn to sound polite, obsequious, deferential. By evening the people I had been calling in Kinshasa had turned off their phones. I had failed.

It was masochistic, but I made sure I was there on the river bank the following morning when the *Mbenga* unmoored, swung into the current and set sail downstream. I was left staring sadly at a bare, muddy river bank, feeling lower than ever.

And so my wait continued. I passed my time in Kisangani trying to track down people who could tell me about its past, people like Clement Mangubu, a local historian and academic. I was trying to find out if Kisangani had any sort of institutional memory. The history of the city is rich and turbulent, but I wanted to see how well it was remembered by local Congolese. Clement worked at Kisangani's university, but I did not find him there. The buildings had been abandoned so long ago that three dormitory blocks, dating from the early Mobutu era, had mature trees growing from their roof gutters. When I eventually found Clement, he told me he had published a book on the history of Kisangani. Perfect, I thought. Here is the person to make sense of all the chaos.

'There can be few cities in the world with a history more bloody than Kisangani,' he said portentously, when we first met at the mission house. 'From the time of the Arab slavers, through the wars between the Belgians and the Arabs, the colonial era and to everything that has happened since independence, the one common theme is blood.'

He explained the city's early history well, how the land became known as Kisangani once the Arab slavers arrived here in the years after Stanley's expedition. The name means 'on the island' in Swahili. Clement explained how the city is surrounded on three sides by water: the Congo River to the west, and the Tshopo, a tributary of the main river, to the north and east. In effect, he said, Kisangani was really a synonym for Mesopotamia, the land between two rivers.

When Stanley came back here in the 1880s, commissioned by Leopold to set up the Congo Free State, he brought with him a Scotsman, Adrian Binnie, to build the first settlement on the land next to the bottom of the Stanley Falls. Binnie must have been extraordinarily tough to accept such a task, the real-life precursor for Conrad's fictional spectre, Mr Kurtz. Various wars followed: fights between the Wagenia and rival tribes connected with the advancing Europeans, and then skirmishes between the Arab slavers and Belgian colonial officers, two of whom drowned in the Congo River. The fighting got so bad that ten years after first crossing the Congo, Stanley sailed all the way to Zanzibar for a peace conference in 1887 with Tippu-Tip. The pair had met during Stanley's foot march from Lake Tanganyika to the upper Congo River and Tippu-Tip had since established himself as leader of all Arab slavers in eastern Congo. More than a century later in the summer of 2000, the UN Security Council met in not dissimilar circumstances, issuing a resolution specifically designed to end the bloodshed in Kisangani. It is a rare and dark honour for a single city to be the focus of its own UN Security Council Resolution.

Clement explained the racist character of colonial Stanleyville, where black Congolese had to apply for written permission even to walk the streets of the city centre, and how the rumblings of a national independence movement first stirred here. Patrice Lumumba, the Congo's post-independence Prime Minister who was later assassinated on the orders of America and Belgium, was based in Stanleyville in the 1950s, working as a post-office official, when he first began organising a national, Congolese political party calling for an end to Belgian rule. Again, there were killings here, this time by Belgian security forces cracking down on Lumumba's nascent Congolese National Movement (MNC), an event commemorated by the large Martyrs' Square in the city centre just next to the ruin of the main post office where Lumumba worked.

The square has seen plenty of martyring since independence. After his assassination in 1961, Lumumba's supporters set up their own parallel government here, and there were bloody skirmishes in the square between them and troops loyal to the capital, Kinshasa. Rebel groups came and went, white mercenaries stormed the city centre, and foreign armies invaded. Clement's account of it was hazy, but I could not criticise him for this. In a nation with little institutional memory, it would be wrong to blame him for not keeping track of this city's history. The numerous rebellions, uprisings, mercenary raids and invasions blurred into one grim, bloody continuum.

A few days later I dragged Clement to the city's main post office in search of any evidence of Lumumba. The country's postal system had not worked for decades and the same 1950s building where Lumumba had worked was a terrible mess. Windows were smashed, the sorting hall sorted nothing today but dust and cobwebs. Entire corridors and rooms had been surrendered to the ravages of tropical damp. But when I asked an old man hanging around the main entrance about Lumumba, there was a flicker of recognition. I was shown a dirty old office and told this was where he had worked. It was empty apart from a desk with an old Bakelite phone connected to a line that had not functioned in living memory. And when I asked if there were any other artefacts from Lumumba's time, I was shown the cover of a quarterly postal-union magazine entitled *The Postal Echo*. The innards had long gone, but on the cover was printed 'Managing Editor: Patrice Lumumba'.

From this now-ruined building Lumumba had dreamed of independence for the Congo and the end of eighty years of colonial tutelage that began after Stanley's expedition passed down the nearby Congo River. And it was outside this building that Lumumba's dream died, in round after round of bloodletting in Martyrs' Square.

Only a handful of foreigners remain in Kisangani today, from a population that once numbered more than 5,000. During my stay I saw plenty of outsiders, but they were almost all aid workers or UN people, working on short-term contracts, whose experience went back just a few months or years. Many were hard-working, deeply committed to helping the local people, but pretty much all of those I spoke to found the scale of the humanitarian problems simply overwhelming. I heard heartbreaking stories about corrupt Congolese officials pocketing aid money intended for local public-health workers, and local soldiers not just looting aid equipment, but brazenly asking for cash to hand it back to its rightful owners. Many in the aid community spent their time counting the days until their contracts were up and they could go back to the real world.

Yani Giatros's attitude to Kisangani was very different. He was born in the Congo in 1947, part of a once-huge Greek expat community who had set themselves up as traders, mechanics and farmers during the Belgian colonial period. So large was the Greek community in Kisangani that the city boasted a Hellenic Social Club with restaurant, bar and sports facilities. By the time I got there, the club was barely functioning, but its lunchtime moussaka buffet was one of the few palatable meals available in the entire city.

'Where logic ends, the Congo begins,' Yani said as he bent his face down to spoon up some moussaka. He peered at me over his spectacles as I made my notes.

'I was born here in the Congo. When my parents took me as a child back to Greece, it was more primitive than here. I used to look forward to coming back to the Congo because it was more advanced than Greece. Can you imagine that?

'This city alone used to have a regular flight by a plane spraying for mosquitoes. Every day trucks would drive around the city sprinkling water on the roads to stop the dust rising. You could pick from six cinemas. Eros was my favourite. The whole city centre was electrified. Right at the end of the colonial period, in the 1950s, they put in a hydroelectric power station on the Tshopo with four generators, which was enough for the whole city.

'But even if you accept the fighting, the wars and the struggle for control, what do you have today? Nobody with any interest in making this place work, apart from a few aid workers.'

Yani raised his eyes and a club waiter came running with a bottle of Primus. He lit a cigarette and drew heavily on it before leaning forward conspiratorially.

'You see him?' he asked quietly, flicking his eyes in the direction of a photograph of the country's president, Joseph Kabila, catapulted into the job in his twenties after his father, Laurent Kabila, was assassinated.

'What skills does he have to run a country like this, or even a place like Kisangani? In all his life he has never been here, and this is the second city of the country he is president of. It is ridiculous. Christ, before his father took over this country, the young Kabila was driving taxis for tourists in Tanzania, and now he is meant to be a national leader!' His harrumph of scorn was so loud it made the waiter jump.

'Who is there who actually wants this place to work? I don't see anybody. Let me give you an example. An aid group went to the Tshopo power station in the last couple of years. They found three of the four generators were broken, so they raised the money and shipped replacements to Matadi, the country's main port down near where the Congo River reaches the Atlantic. And they flew in engineers to Kisangani ready to fit everything.

'So what happened? The customs, the officials, the people down at Matadi blocked the generators from coming in. The foreign engineers got more and more frustrated until they eventually left, God knows where the new generators ended up, and the lights still go out here in Kisangani.'

He leaned forward again, fixed my gaze and whispered.

'The Congo was built with the chicotte, and the only way to rebuild it will be with the chicotte.' He was referring to a whip made from dried hippopotamus hide, which the early Belgian colonialists used savagely when dealing with their subjects in the Congo. Even today, almost fifty years after the Belgians left, the chicotte endures as a sinister symbol of their brutality.

After two weeks of delay in Kisangani, I finally got the news I had been praying for. A Congolese boat, under charter to the United Nations, was heading downriver to Mbandaka, more than 1,000 kilometres downstream. The journey could take a week, maybe longer. I did not care. I was on the move again.

To secure a place on the boat I needed the assistance of Robert Powell, the UN's transport boss for Kisangani and a former soldier in the British Army. He helped me through the final stretch of the bureaucratic paperchase needed to travel on the UN boat, before giving me the most unexpected experience of my fortnight in

Kisangani. Robert is a plain-speaking Yorkshireman and an advocate of the British Army adage 'any fool can be uncomfortable'. In the remote city where I had lived in an austere priest's cell on a diet of fruit and cassava bread, Robert made sure he was true to his word.

The house he occupied had been turned into a palace by local standards. He had a generator, a fridge full of freshly imported meat, South African satellite television, air-conditioning and no end of other luxuries. I spent my last night in Kisangani enjoying his ribald company and ploughing through a mountain of sausage and 'bubble and squeak', prepared, as my host boasted, 'like my mum taught me back home'.

After dinner we found a shared interest to talk about: fishing. In South Africa fishermen get excited if they catch a two-kilo Tigerfish. Robert explained how everything was so much bigger on the Congo River where a separate species, the Goliath Tigerfish, reaches upwards of fifty kilos. I was sceptical until he showed me pictures of specimens that had been caught in the nets of local fishermen. They were as big as children, with ugly-looking teeth and sinister eyes. We spent the rest of the evening plotting how to take one of these leviathans on rod and line, idly dreaming about running fishing safaris out of Kisangani for multi-millionaire anglers.

After my night of Yorkshire hospitality there was just one more thing I needed to do in Kisangani. I wanted to say goodbye to Oggi. We met in the bar of the Palm Beach Hotel. When I explained that I had got a place on a boat heading downstream, he smiled half-heartedly. He seemed a bit distracted as if he had something important to say to me, but could not quite come out with it.

As the Primus flowed, Oggi became more and more nostalgic. He told me stories of how hardy tourists arrived here in the 1980s, coming through the jungle on overland Africa tourist trucks all the way from Europe, and how he took them out for day trips on the river. It reminded me of an elegant film poster I had once seen advertising a French movie about a pan-African journey in the 1950s. The poster showed the continent in outline with a thick red line snaking down from Tangier, Africa's closest point to Spain, across the desert sands and then through the equatorial jungle before eventually reaching Cape Town at the southern heel of the continent. A few place names were marked on the poster, and I clearly remember that Stanleyville was one of them, just another waypoint on a road that once traversed the entire continent.

'Those trucks stopped coming in the late eighties,' Oggi said. 'The forest ate those roads, and the problems with corrupt officials meant our city was slowly written off the map.'

Oggi's fluent English was entirely self-taught. He was tough – he had lost count of the malaria episodes he had survived. And he was resourceful – somehow he fed his family and kept them clothed without any meaningful income. But just like Georges, Benoit and many other Congolese I had met, all his energies, skills and talents were spent on the daily struggle to survive. The failure of the Congo is so complete that its silent majority – tens of millions of people with no connections to the gangster government or the corrupt state machinery – are trapped in a fight to stay where they are and not become worse off. Thoughts of development, advancement or improvement are irrelevant when the fabric of your country is slipping backwards around you.

After enough Primus to make his eyes rheumy, Oggi found the inner strength he had been looking for. He put his hand on my forearm, leaned forward and made the most wretched of pleas.

'Please, Mr Tim, I have a huge favour to ask. My son, my four-year-old, has no future here. There is nothing for him in Kisangani. I know which way this city is going. Please will you take him with you to South Africa and give him a new life.'

There was no way I could smuggle a child onto the UN boat with me. I felt wretched having to turn Oggi down. But I felt more wretched that he had to resort to asking me, someone he had known for only a few days, to save his child from the Congo.

11.

River Passage

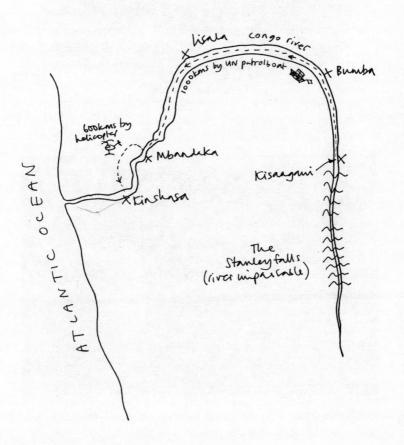

FIKE, STANLEY FALLS.

Goliath Tigerfish from the Congo River as recorded, above, by H.M.
Stanley in 1878 and, below, by the author in 2004

I stood on the deck of the river boat watching the gap widen between me and the crumbling Kisangani quayside. There was a gaggle of Congolese stevedores sitting in the shade of an idle crane, but next to them I could make out a solitary figure lift up his sunhat with studied extravagance, bow and wave me bon voyage. It was Robert. While he helped with my final, rushed preparations, buying bags of rice and boiling up a jerrycan of clean water, I noticed he seemed a little sad, jealous even.

'We've never had a civilian person travel downriver before,' he confided forlornly. 'I had always thought I would be the first to leave here by boat. But somehow I never found the time.'

Time is something you need a lot of to travel the Congo River. I was embarking on a 1,000-kilometre journey from Kisangani to Mbandaka and I had been warned it would take at least a week and potentially much longer if we ran out of fuel, hit a sand bank or became snarled on any of the river's other hazards. And even if I made it to Mbandaka, I would still have another 700 kilometres or so of river descent before reaching Kinshasa.

I stood watching Robert's figure get smaller and smaller as the boat made its way over to the deep-water channel on the far side of the river from the UN dock. We had started the journey pointing upriver towards the lowest cataracts of the Stanley Falls. I was straining to spot their broken white water in the distance when our skipper spun the wheel, pointed the bow downstream and ramped up the throttle. For a second I felt a bit unsteady as the boat's entire superstructure began to vibrate, but gaining my river legs I shifted position so that I could watch the Kisangani waterfront for the last time.

There were the cranes that had so impressed me when I first

reached the city, but which I had later discovered to be useless, broken beyond repair. And there was the cathedral, where Father Leon had led the memorial service in 1964 for his murdered missionary colleagues, whose bodies were brought by barge across this same reach of water to the stone steps that I could see leading down the river bank to the water's edge in front of the cathedral. And there were the squalid ruins of the 'L'Hôtel Pourquoi Pas?' with the balcony where Katharine Hepburn once took the evening air and, just to the left, the even more squalid collection of leaking, disease-ridden, overcrowded hulks of the port.

The city where I had been trapped for two frustrating weeks slipped steadily by until, without fanfare, it vanished. All that was left was a thin line of trees below an arch of empty sky. No buildings, no people, no smoke, nothing to suggest I was close to one of the great cities of Africa, home to one million-plus souls. Its disappearance was so immediate, so complete that I stood disbelieving for a few minutes, rocking gently with the motion of the deck. Perhaps I had dreamed it all. Perhaps the hollowed-out city had been nothing but a ghostly mirage all along.

Like the vessels that I had seen in Kisangani's port, the boat I was travelling on was, strictly speaking, two boats. The front was a massive barge, red with rust and slightly scraped and battered at each end. It was thirty-eight metres long, but had a draught of only thirty centimetres, crucial for the shallow water of the upper Congo River during the dry season, when sand banks loom dangerously close to the surface. The only permanent structure on its entire length was a grey cubicle that looked and smelled like a public lavatory. It protected a gangway down into the barge's storage compartments.

To the barge's stern was attached the second boat, the pusher, named *Nganing*. It was dwarfed by the hulking barge and had only three modest decks: an oily, smelly engine deck with two large, rattling diesel motors, a cabin deck with just one cabin, and on top a one-room wheelhouse where the helmsman sat. It had no radar equipment, no radio and only the most rudimentary control panel. There was a tiller wheel, an on/off switch and a throttle. The helmsman even had to bring his own high wooden chair to sit on. Next to the hulking barge, the *Nganing* looked tiny.

Both the barge and the pusher were genuine Congolese river craft, normally based in Kinshasa and leased by the United Nations as part of a strategy by MONUC to restore confidence in river travel. The Congo River and its many huge tributaries are as potentially useful today as they were when Stanley first charted them. He reported to Leopold the existence of a massive network of navigable waterways, waiting to pump modern commerce and economic development across a swathe of equatorial Africa larger than the entire subcontinent of India. The Congo River system is potentially one of the most valuable natural assets in all of Africa, but in recent years it has been choked to a standstill by war and mismanagement.

Since the 1990s, boats that once plied thousands and thousands of kilometres of navigable river have idled in the docks of Kinshasa as the Congolese authorities effectively ceded control of the river. During the Belgian colonial era various national institutions were established to open up the river network, but they had all been allowed to collapse. Ferries run by the national transport company, ONATRA, stopped running as the staff went unpaid and the poorly maintained boats broke down. The national navigation company, RVF, stopped marking and dredging a safe, navigable channel on the waterway, making passage hazardous. But the demand for river travel did not diminish. The collapse of the Congo's road system meant that the river was the only way to travel for millions of Congolese. So when the occasional boat did venture upstream, it would be mobbed by people. Overloaded boats would capsize or become trapped for months on sand banks. If passengers did not drown, they faced other hazards. Insanitary conditions on overcrowded hulks, like the barges I boarded at Kisangani's port, often proved fatal. Food poisoning and dysentery would break out on the slow, sweaty river passage and it was not uncommon for scores to die from disease on a single journey, their bodies tipped into the river as the boats crawled between towns where public hospitals had long since closed.

The wars of the late 1990s only made things worse. Various factions hostile to the Kinshasa regime began to attack any boat that ventured upstream, so by 2000 the river was effectively closed, plunging the Congo River basin back to the same state described by Conrad in the nineteenth century, 'the blankest of blank spaces on the earth's figured surface'.

After the 2002 peace treaty, the Congolese authorities declared the river open again, but there were few boat owners brave enough to risk sending their vessels hundreds and hundreds of kilometres upstream on journeys where it was impossible to guarantee fuel or security. The UN stepped in to try to reinvigorate the river. MONUC had flown in enough people and equipment to ensure fuel supplies in places even as remote as Kisangani, so it leased ten sets of pushers and barges and sent them chugging up the waterways of the Congo River basin, flying the UN flag and trying to give the impression that all was normal and safe. Each boat had a local Congolese crew, a small deployment of UN troops for protection and a MONUC naval officer in overall command.

To restore confidence was the mission. As my journey unfolded I saw the humbling scale of the Congo River and how a fleet of ten boats was much too modest to restore confidence across a river system largely in the same primitive state Stanley found when he paddled downstream for the first time in 1877.

As with so many projects on UN missions, money was no object. The tiny boat I was on had been leased for $35,000 a month, an obscene sum for such a basic vessel. The local crew –

a skipper and six deckhands, who all had experience of Congo river boats from the days before the war – were meant to be under the command of the senior MONUC officer onboard, a lieutenant commander from the Malaysian navy, Mohammed Yusoff Sazali, who liked to be known as Ali. But it soon became apparent who was really in charge. Ali struggled to communicate with the Congolese crew. He spoke only a few words of French and I watched as the Congolese skipper, Captain Jean Paul Mbuta Monshengo, an untrustworthy-looking man with a lazy right eye, carefully chose which of the words he would understand.

Our departure from Kisangani had been delayed by one day in mysterious circumstances. Captain Monshengo had declared there was a problem with one of the diesel generators on board, but he would task his best engineer to sort it out as soon as possible. After a delay of exactly twenty-four hours, without the need for any spare parts or, indeed, any apparent effort by the engineer, the problem was rectified and we left, a day behind the MONUC schedule.

As I got to know Ali, he took me into his confidence and explained what had really happened.

'We were due to sail on a Tuesday from Kisangani. We have been here for several months now, the only UN boat so far upriver, so the crew had plenty of time to get everything in order. But the problem was that Monday was the monthly payday and the Congolese crew had gone into the city to spend. They all have second wives and girlfriends here, parallel homes from their other homes downriver, so they had personal business to attend to. They were too busy to leave as scheduled, but once they had sorted out their mamas here in Kisangani, everything was okay and we could leave.

'I have been here long enough to know what the skipper was up to. And he knows I know what he is up to. But there is nothing I can really do about it. I carry no weapon and all I have is the authority of the UN mission, which does not count for very much when you are hundreds of kilometres away from a friendly face, far up the Congo River.'

He explained some of the other scams pulled by the Congolese crews on the UN boats. He said some skippers deliberately pretend there is an engine problem and reduce the speed of the boat. But this is done simply to lower the rate of fuel consumption, leaving a surplus at the end of the trip that the skipper then siphons off to sell. And the Congolese crew routinely use the UN boats to smuggle things up and down the river, goods from Kinshasa to be sold in Kisangani. Many suspect diamonds from Kisangani are smuggled back downriver to avoid having to pay bribes at the airport.

Ali was too philosophical to be angered by all this. His mission was to fly the UN flag up and down the Congo River. For months at a time his boat, which he preferred to call 'UN Pusher Number Ten' rather than the *Nganing*, would be deployed upriver, steaming to ports like Kisangani and then waiting there for weeks in between patrols. A day's delay here or there was not worth fighting over.

I have seen numerous UN missions around the world, in Bosnia, Sierra Leone, Liberia and all over the Middle East. Each was castigated by the international media and commentators for being inefficient, bureaucratic and ineffective, but such criticism always misses the point. Yes, the missions are sloppy and poorly focused, but that is precisely because the international community's attitude to complicated problems like the collapsing Yugoslavia, or rampaging west African rebels, is sloppy and poorly focused. When the United Nations Security Council addresses these international problems, the question it ends up answering is not 'What is the right thing to do?' but 'What is the least we can do?' UN missions around the world evolve at the pace of the lowest common denominator between the nations of the world, and that common denominator is pretty low when nations with interests as divergent as China and America both hold prominent positions in the UN Security Council.

Today's UN mission in the Congo developed along exactly these lines. When the most recent war started in 1998, aid groups and the international media reported the massive loss of life, demanding a response. The UN was understandably wary about sending troops back to the Congo. In 1960 UN peacekeeping cut its teeth in the Congo, trying to stop the chaotic aftermath of Belgium granting its colony independence. It was to be a grim experience for the international body, which had only been founded fifteen years earlier at the close of the Second World War. The UN's first Congo peacekeeping mission from 1960 to 1964 was a disaster, as peacekeepers ended up fighting pitched battles with white mercenaries and Congolese rebels backed by Belgium. The UN lost more peacekeepers in combat there than on any other peacekeeping mission, before or since. That early mission cost the life of the UN Secretary General, Dag Hammarskjöld, killed in a plane crash as he shuttled between rival Congolese factions in 1961.

So MONUC, the new Congo mission of the late 1990s, evolved slowly and cautiously. Its peacekeepers were deployed without adequate weapons or a clear chain of command, frankly powerless to stop the killing. But this simply reflected the lack of international willingness to genuinely do what was needed to end the fighting. MONUC was created so that the outside world could say something was being done about the Congo. The opprobrium of commentators would be better focused on world leaders, who use UN missions as scapegoats for their own lack of determination to deal with major international crises.

Ali told me a story that perfectly encapsulated the inefficiency and helplessness of MONUC. He was deployed on 'Pusher Number Ten' in Kisangani at the time of the Bukavu incident in June 2004 when mobs began to attack UN targets across Congo. He was onboard the boat, tied up alongside the dock, when smoke started to rise above Kisangani from burning UN cars and he heard on the local radio that UN personnel were being evacuated.

'The safest place for me and the boat was back out on the river. The local crew were scared too because they did not even come from Kisangani, so we unmoored and went back out onto the river.' He was grinning as he told the story, although it did not sound very amusing to me.

'We were busy for a few hours getting under way and moving a safe distance downstream, but the worst thing was when I got the satellite telex working and sent a message to our naval base in Kinshasa. I sat there waiting for a response for a few minutes, and then a few hours, and then a few days. Do you know what had happened? The entire naval command centre at UN headquarters had left because of the rioting and nobody had bothered to think about me and my command up at the other end of the river.' He was chortling quite loudly now.

'It's crazy. The ten pushers are the only major assets of the naval command and no-one from the operations room thought about them for a second!'

'So what did you do? How did you survive?' I had to wait a few minutes for Ali to regain his composure.

'Well, I keep enough water and food on the boat to last for weeks, so we went a safe distance downriver and tied up on a tree and I went fishing. I like fishing. It's my favourite hobby.

'After a few weeks I noticed a message arrived on the telex. It said something like "Where are you, Ali, we were worried." Obviously things had calmed down in Kinshasa and the operations room was back up and running, and someone had thought to ask what happened to Pusher Ten. It's crazy to think I could just have left Kisangani, evacuated with the other peace-keepers, and anything could have happened to this boat. But the really crazy thing is that nobody would have cared.'

My time on 'Pusher Number Ten' passed at its own strange pace.

My diary tells me we sailed for seven days, but it felt as if I travelled years back in time. After leaving Kisangani, we did not stop at any other town until Mbandaka, 1,000 kilometres downstream, and in between I felt as though I saw an Africa unchanged from that which Stanley saw.

Without any major towns all I saw was the endless forest, an unbroken screen of green that was reeled slowly past me. It would grow fat when we neared the water's edge and thin when our course took us far into the midstream, but for 1,000 kilometres it never quite broke. At first light the rising sun would colour in the forest with a rich spectrum of greens from emerald to lime, pea to peridot, before they steadily faded as the sun tracked upwards. By midday, the overhead sun would wash out all but the most vivid tints, before they were slowly restored as the sun dipped towards the western horizon.

And there was the river. Conrad's uncoiling serpent grew fatter and fatter each day that we descended. There are places where the river swells to a width exceeding five kilometres. We were constantly slaloming through eyots and islands, some of which were enormous, running to twenty kilometres or more in length. Every day we passed villages that had the same design Stanley described. There would be a clutch of thatched huts built on raised stilts to avoid the seasonal high water and, through the smoke from cooking fires, I would see people moving around wearing rags, while down on the river's edge a clutch of pirogues hung in the current.

For the first few days our progress was slow and cautious, as the Congolese skipper sat up in the wheelhouse barking at the helmsman to cut the revs, nudging the boat forward, while one of his crew stood right at the bow of the barge, more than forty metres away from the skipper, using an old branch to probe for a safe course through the sand banks. There was no sonar or depth sounder, just a branch broken off a riverside tree to save us from being marooned. The bowman had no radio or intercom, so our progress depended on wild gesticulations and the occasional scream. And after some days, as the chocolate-coloured waters deepened and the safe channel widened, the engine settled into the high-end rattle of full power and the bowman put down his stick and sat on a home-made wooden chair that hummed with the vibration coursing through the boat's superstructure.

I entered a zone of mental torpor. Normally I am the sort of person who needs to be doing something constantly. I am not a napper. But on that river passage, there was nothing I could do to influence our progress. We would reach our destination when we reached our destination and not a moment sooner, so I took off my wrist watch and let my days flow with the rhythm of the river.

At night the boat would stop. Night navigation was too dangerous, the navigable channel too tricky to follow in the dark. So just before sunset the skipper would look for a suitable section of river bank, steep enough to ensure we would not become beached. He would then gently kiss the bow of the barge up against it. By the time the bowman had jumped onto the bank and wrapped the large rusting anchor cable around a tree, the rest of the boat would have swung around in the current and now be hanging downstream. When the first Belgian-era steamboats started regular journeys on the Congo River, they used to pull over on the river bank just like this. Woodcutters would then be sent off into the forest to cut fuel overnight for the following day's steaming, while the white crew would struggle for sleep in the still heat under bombardment from mosquitoes.

It was exactly the same for me. When the boat tied up on the river bank each evening, the now motionless air would clot with heat and moisture. Insects would swarm to any flicker of torch-light so I clung to darkness, teaching myself how to feel my way around the boat, to the stern-plate to have a pee, to the store of jerrycans for a drink of clean water. Ali let me sleep on the carpeted floor of his cabin and I would huddle there in the dark, cocooned in my gossamer tent of mosquito netting, nervously fidgeting so that my skin never came into contact with its sides. Congo River mosquitoes are notorious. Conrad himself took six months to recover from the fever he caught during his single passage up and down the Congo River, and I knew the little bleeders were more than capable of biting through netting if I was foolish enough to let it come into contact with bare skin.

Ali was brought up in rural, tropical Malaysia and was clearly tougher than me in dealing with disease-carrying insects. His passion for fishing meant he would slip out of the cabin at night, wrapped in a hooded cagoule from which only his face pro- truded, and take up position on the side of the pusher, crouched over his fishing rod, constantly puffing on cigarettes to keep the insects from his face. In our time together he did not catch a single fish, but this did not deter him. Around midnight, as I thrashed in shallow sleep, he would tiptoe back into the room, shed his coat and, invariably, twang the web of strings I had set up to support my mosquito net.

Nights were grim and I would lie awake waiting for the first throaty cough of the diesel engines that marked dawn. The skipper liked to get away at first light and by the time the eastern sky was beginning to lighten, he would be back up in the wheelhouse ready for a day's passage. Once I had extricated myself from my straitjacket of sweat-sodden bedclothes and netting, the whole cabin would be vibrating as the engines powered the boat upstream to take the tension off the anchor line so that it could be retrieved by the bowman. Then the boat would pirouette and, once again, we would begin reeling in kilometre after kilometre of the green screen.

This was one of my favourite times of day. I had brought plenty of clean water for the trip and I would spend the first few hours of each day up on the top deck drinking mug after mug of black tea, enjoying the sensation of motion and the muggy waft of air moving across my face. My normal mindset would have found our progress infuriatingly slow. The boat rarely reached its top speed and even then it only managed 18 kph. But I had entered a Zen state and every metre we moved was a metre closer to the end of my ordeal.

I loved watching our wake. The mocha whirls of white water whipped up by the propeller would rush out from under the stern-plate, dancing and churning before growing steadily calmer and calmer. Slowly the creamy lather would lose its fizz and darken, merging into just another featureless reach of flat, brown water. But the thing I loved most about the wake was that it meant we were moving. A wake meant we were slightly closer to our destination. I loved watching our wake.

Out of boredom I found another way to monitor our progress. Up in the wheelhouse the skipper had a solitary navigational aid, a thirty-year-old map book. Each page was mouldy to the touch after years of exposure to the humid river air and the edges were as tattered as week-old leaves in a rabbit hutch. Grubby pencil messages, written and overwritten, had been scrawled on each page, as well as a dotted line that marked the navigable channel. I could see it had been rubbed out and redrawn numerous times. The entire route from Kisangani to Kinshasa, the descent of 1,734 kilometres, was covered by this old map book, so every time one of its sixty-four pages turned, I knew I was thirty kilometres or so nearer my destination.

By ten o'clock the morning heat was too much for me to stay out on deck. After crossing the Equator a short distance upstream from Kisangani, the Congo River prescribes a slow but momentous westward arc, eventually dipping back across the Equator for a second time at Mbandaka before its final run to Kinshasa, and thence the coast. The climate gets crueler and crueler with the descent. As altitude is lost, with it goes any hope of a cooling breeze. I found by late morning, even on a hazy day, the steel panels on the decks would be throbbing with heat. They were studded with rice-grain-sized bulges for grip, and through the soles of my sandals I could feel each one radiating warmth.

I would surrender to the heat by late morning, seeking shelter in the darkness of Ali's blacked-out cabin. Tired from the uncomfortable night's sleep, I would nap in between attempts to read some of the trashy novels Ali kept in his cabin.

I entered the same odd mental zone that I reach on overnight flights, the state of consciousness when I am awake enough to watch a film, but not awake enough to actually take anything in. Plane movies have a special quality. Within a few hours of watching them I never seem to be capable of remembering the smallest detail about the film – the name, the plotline, the actors. I felt exactly the same during my boat journey on the Congo. I would turn the pages of the book and my eyes would work through the paragraphs, but to this day I have no recall of what I read.

To pass the time I would drag out my daily ablutions, taking perverse pleasure in the slow process of boiling water for a meticulous, slow shave, before taking one of the world's most dangerous showers. The water for the shower came straight from the river. Against the creamy ceramic of an old shower cubicle, the water ran brown like tea. It reminded me of Scottish hill water tainted with peat, only it was much warmer and the chemicals that leached brown into the Congo River were more terrifying than those found in Highland soil. Somewhere to our north ran the Ebola River, a tributary of a tributary of the Congo River, but a name that is associated with a horrific medical condition. It was near this river that a virus was first discovered that caused its victims to die in a spectacularly horrible way, bleeding to death from every orifice. Several of the world's other spectacularly horrible haemorrhagic fevers were first discovered in the Congo. I kept my mouth tight shut whenever I showered.

Ali was a gracious host. He had kitted himself out with a Congo survival kit from the duty-free shop at Dubai airport while flying from Malaysia to Africa. He had brought himself a microwave, a kettle and a rice boiler. The diesel generators on the *Nganing* provided ample power, so he would provide me with meals of noodles and litres of water, boiled clean.

By late afternoon when the outside temperature had begun to dip, I would venture outside once more. Most days I would go all the way to the bow of the barge, picking my way over the straining hawsers and cables that connected the barge with the pusher, to join the Congolese bowman. His name was Pascal Manday Mbueta and he was entered on the crew list with the lowest possible grade of deckhand. Pascal lived inside the barge. He had no cabin and there was no furniture. He simply slept on the rusting metal, squashed up against a bulkhead. I peered through the hatch and down a ladder into his living space one day and winced at the smell. With the motion of the boat I could see a broken beer bottle floating down there in a malodorous swill of bilge water and God knows what else.

Pascal had the rheumy eyes of a confirmed drunk. He had brought a large stash of Primus beer from Kisangani but, if I got to him when he was sober, he was good company. Mostly we would sit in silence, listening to the hiss of the water working its way down the side of the barge. Occasionally he would blurt out something about how the river used to be.

'See there,' he would say, pointing at the river bank. 'There used to be a marker showing the safe channel. The authorities kept the channel clear and kept the markers in the right place, but all of that has gone. Now, you have to work by memory alone – 1,734 kilometres from memory alone. It's crazy.'

Our constant companion out on the river was water hyacinth. For each of the thousand kilometres of my river descent, floating alongside me in clumps that could be as small as a single tendril or as large as a tennis-court-sized raft, I was accompanied by the plant.

The story of the water hyacinth in the Congo is a wonderful allegory for the white man in this country. The plant's intended role was innocent enough. It was brought here as a garden ornament decades ago. According to one story, a Belgian colonialist who had seen it in its native South American environment imported the first seedlings to prettify a waterway near his remote colonial outpost. Another account blames an American Baptist missionary who was attracted by its delicate pastel flowers.

There was nothing innocent about the alien's behaviour once it took root in the Congo. It grew and grew and grew, spreading a deadly mat across much of the Congo River basin, suffocating the life out of ponds, lakes and slow-moving rivers and upsetting entire eco-systems. It is now categorised as a dangerous alien weed that should be eradicated before it clots even the main arteries of the river system. And I saw with my own eyes the extent of its grip on the Congo River. Downstream from Kisangani I barely saw a single stretch of river free from floating knots of water hyacinth.

As the sun neared the horizon, picking out the lilac blooms of the water hyacinth on their mattresses of matted tuber and leaf, the day's cycle would repeat itself. The skipper would look for a suitably steep river bank, Pascal would grab hold of the anchor line and I would return to the cabin and brace myself for another night of battle with mosquitoes.

It was while lying awake at night during the river passage that I thought about the world's changing attitude to the Congo. At the start of the twentieth century, the Congo was the dominant human-rights issue of the day. What Iraq, AIDS and globalisation are for today's campaigners, the Congo was for Edwardian human-rights groups. They were galvanised by the issue, launching unprecedented campaigns, both in Europe and America, to highlight the cruelty committed in the Congo Free State in the name of Leopold, focusing on the rubber industry and the violence unleashed by colonial agents to harvest it in the Congo. Just as campaigners today use the term Blood Diamonds to discredit gems produced in Africa's war zones, so their predecessors from a hundred years ago spoke of Red Rubber, publishing dramatic accounts of villagers being murdered or having their hands cut off to terrify their neighbours into harvesting more rubber. Leopold's representatives tried to suppress the flow of information emerging from the Congo and produced their own propaganda about the benign nature of the colony, but slowly and steadily, as information leaked out of the Congo over the years, smuggled out mainly by missionaries, they lost the public-relations battle.

Campaigners calling for Congo reform lobbied MPs at Westminster and Congressmen in Washington to debate the issue. Mass meetings were held and leaflets printed denouncing the evils of the Congo Free State. Conrad's *Heart of Darkness* was first published in 1899 and spoke directly to the message being promoted by the lobbyists. The campaign inspired Mark Twain, the American author famous for his strong anti-imperialist views, to mock the Belgian monarch in a small pamphlet he wrote entitled 'King Leopold's Soliloquy'. Roger Casement, a colourful British diplomat who was to end up being executed by Britain for treason, made his name in the Congo when he wrote an official consular report in 1904 on behalf of the British government, accusing the Belgian authorities of committing atrocities that led directly to three million deaths in the Congo. In the days before the Armenian genocide or the Nazi Holocaust, Casement's estimate was an extraordinary figure.

So successful was the campaign that in 1908 the Belgian king was forced to relinquish control of his African fiefdom. The Congo Free State passed into the hands of the Belgian state, no longer a plaything of the monarch, but a full colony to be known as the Belgian Congo, where the authorities were supposedly more committed to protecting the rights of local Congolese.

The international attention paid to the Congo around 1900 was matched decades later at independence. The first UN mission was covered intensely by the world's media, as was the assassination of Lumumba, the subsequent rebellions in eastern Congo and the mercenary wars, followed by the 1965 ascension of Mobutu.

But the thing that troubled me was why such scant attention is paid now to the Congo. According to the best estimates, since conflict began in 1998 around four million Congolese lives had been claimed (1,200 a day) and, in spite of the 2002 peace treaty, there has been no significant reduction in this daily loss of life. The international community seems to have developed a terrible Congo-fatigue, where deaths and suffering, even on the enormous scale reported by statisticians, somehow don't register. The world seems to view the Congo as a lost cause without hope of ever being put right.

Ali was a man happy with silence. We spent long hours in his cabin or out on deck without feeling the need to talk. But after a few days of silent bonding he took me into his confidence, showing me pictures of home in Malaysia, his wife, son and two daughters. He told me how much he was looking forward to his next leave and his plans to take his family on a beach holiday. It was only by accident that I found out he passed his thirty-ninth birthday while we were together on that boat.

When he did break his silence, he spoke with conviction.

'I don't know what it is about these Congolese people, or Africa in general, but look at this wasted opportunity,' he said one morning out on deck as I drank my tea, slowly coming round after another wretched night. He pointed at the river bank, which at that point was crowded with palm trees, the remnants of an abandoned plantation producing palm oil.

'In Malaysia, people make millions from palm oil. It is one of the most valuable commodities in the world right now. It's used in the best lipsticks and cosmetics, it is used for all sorts of food preparation and it is even used to make fuel that is more environmentally friendly than petrol. There are businessmen in

Malaysia who would give anything to get access to the palm plantations along this river.

'But the Congo people. They don't want to make money for themselves. They just wait to take money from others.'

I offered the standard explanation about the Congo's problems: that the Congolese had suffered under colonialism and, when independence came, the Congo was pulled apart by forces beyond its control, as the Cold War preoccupation of the West allowed Mobutu, under American patronage, to run the country into the ground.

'That is rubbish,' Ali said. During our trip I never saw him so animated. 'Malaysia was colonised for centuries too, most recently by the British, a colonial rule that was cruel and racist. We got independence at roughly the same time as the Congo in the early 1960s, and we were even drawn into a Cold War conflict for year after year as communist insurgents fought for control of Malaysia. But somehow Malaysia got through it and the Congo did not. Today, Malaysia is part of the rest of the world. People go on holiday in Malaysia. The world's business community does business in Malaysia. We even have a Grand Prix every year in Malaysia. The same is not true of the Congo. How can you explain the difference?'

Ali was almost shouting by the end of this outburst. His months in the Congo, exposed to all of its decay and waste, had clearly got to him. And he had distilled the quintessential problem of Africa that generations of academics, intellectuals and observers have danced around since the colonial powers withdrew. Why are Africans so bad at running Africa?

The Congo River was trapped in a zombie state, simultaneously dead and alive. We saw almost no other river-boat traffic in a week, but every day we would be intercepted by pirogues paddled by Congolese people from the riverside villages. They were desperate in their efforts to catch up with us. They were not just coming to trade. They were trying to leave behind a feral existence of mud-hut villages and connect with a different, modern world as symbolised by a moving motorboat.

The paddlers would take the most incredible risks as they tried to catch us. To stand any chance of success they needed at least two paddlers, one at the front of the pirogue and another at the rear. The flanks of the barge were too high and bare for them to get a hold of, so they had to wait patiently in their pirogues until the barge had passed, rocking dangerously over its wake before paddling like fury to come alongside the pusher. Its deck was much lower than the barge, enabling the lead paddler to jump aboard and whip some sort of rope attached to the pirogue to an anchor point on the pusher. It required split-second timing, strength and considerable bravery. Sometimes the lead paddler lost his footing and simply plunged into the river, lost in the water churned white by our propellers; at other times the rope line snapped, sending the pirogue darting backwards into our wake. If the lead paddler was still onboard, he would have to jump back over the side instantly or face an uncomfortably long swim. When more than one pirogue made the attempt at the same time the result could be chaos, with rival canoes clattering into each other, crews whacking each other with their paddles as they fought for a better position, their boats flapping in our wake, in constant danger of being overwhelmed.

The image of those who had been unsuccessful disappearing behind us comes back to me from time to time. Here were a people living alongside one of the great waterways of Africa, a potent economic asset that should have catapulted this entire region forwards, but who were left struggling on dugout canoes as the modern world steamed by.

The paddlers who were fortunate enough to make it onto our moving boat showed that their river communities still had life in them. They came to trade. They offered food mostly – cassava bread, fish, monkey and white grubs as fat and long as your thumb stored in tubs of damp moss. One enterprising seller made it onboard with a pirogue full of furniture: stools of whittled branches, tables of woven rattan.

It was tragic to watch the buyers' market drive the prices down. Our Congolese crew were the only customers and they could simply name a price, no matter how low, confident the seller would be desperate enough to accept. The sellers knew it would be months before the next river boat passed, so they had little choice.

Once business was concluded, the fish would be handed over, or the furniture tucked away in the hold of the barge, and the sellers would jump back onto their pirogues and face a long paddle back upstream.

I had an understandably hurried conversation with one of our visitors, Jerome Bilole. He said he was thirty-six and had been born near the now-ruined riverside town of Isangi.

'A boat like this is our only chance to earn any money. My village is like a community from the olden times, when people did not have clothes to wear. Your boat is our only lifeline.' He then hopped back into his pirogue and cast off. The last I saw of him was when our choppy wake had passed him by and he could balance on his paddle and count the few grubby Congolese notes he had earned.

In our 1,000-kilometre passage we passed what had once been large towns, places like Bumba. During the war Bumba fell into the hands of pro-Ugandan rebels with a reputation for being bloodthirsty. As we went by, some of its people came to the water's edge and gave us a macabre display. They threw their heads back and drew their fingers slowly across their throats.

'They tried to put some UN monitors into Bumba once, but it was too dangerous for them. They were pulled out and it does not look like the locals want them back any time soon. They don't like outsiders very much,' Ali explained.

And when we passed the town of Lisala, I looked for signs of its past grandeur. Mobutu was born in this town during the Belgian colonial period, and under his dictatorship it had benefited from his patronage. All signs of this had long gone. Without any mineral resources to fight over, the Congolese authorities had abandoned Lisala completely. All that could be seen on the river bank were some rusting hulks, shrouded in algae-covered fishing nets.

It was days before we finally saw another river boat. It was a sorry sight. A vast rusting barge, just like the one I had seen attached to the *Tekele* in Kisangani, was stationary in the middle of the river. I could see the current of the river was breaking around the barge's sides. It was stuck firmly on a sand bank.

On its deck hundreds of people sat under tarpaulins and pieces of plastic sheeting watching a tiny pusher, marked with the name *Mompoto*, as it tried in vain to shift the bigger vessel.

'They might have to wait for the rains to raise the water level,' Ali said.

'Do you ever stop to help them?' I asked.

'If they were sinking, we would of course stop to help. But we cannot stop for every boat that sets out overloaded or without the right amount of fuel. These people are only a day's pirogue from Lisala, so they will not starve. They must be patient.'

It was on the third day of the river journey that I began to feel sick. It started as nausea shortly after I took my morning malaria pill. During my trip I had learned that the pills had to be taken on a full stomach or they made me feel awful, but this time I felt grim even though I had already eaten. I was groggy from another bad night's sleep and thought at first that a day of shade and lots of tea would sort me out. I was wrong. My head started to throb, my limbs began to ache and in my heart I began to panic. We were days away from medical help.

I started to fantasise. I had killed a mosquito in the cabin one day. It was easy to swat precisely because it had fed well and was moving slowly, bloated with blood. It had left a bloom of livid red on the palm of my hand. I began to worry that I had been looking at my own, diseased blood. How long does the malaria pathogen take to develop? How long before the first dangerous symptoms? I knew from my time in Africa that incubation takes at least a week, often longer, but, in my fried mental state, common sense deserted me. I convinced myself this mosquito had made me ill.

Ali could not have been kinder, breaking open his medicine chest to give me painkillers, salt tablets and vitamin pills. But the feeling of sickness did not abate and I started saying no to meals and struggling to stomach water. By the seventh day of the journey I was a mess. I rarely ventured out of Ali's cabin, clinging to the shade in my puddle of sweat, willing the boat to reach Mbandaka.

By the time we eventually got there, a week after leaving Kisangani, it was all I could do to climb off the boat and back onto terra firma. The town sits almost smack on the Equator and has a grimly high attrition rate among its UN personnel, felled by malaria or dysentery or any of a host of other tropical diseases found in the town. Illness has clearly played a major role in Mbandaka's history. It was leprosy that brought Graham Greene here in the 1950s when he visited a local leprosarium while researching his novel *A Burnt-Out Case.*

The fabric of the town appeared to have been ravaged by disease. Like all the other Congolese towns I visited, Mbandaka lay in ruins, with potholed roads connecting tatty buildings. The only half-decent place was the UN headquarters, a two-storey disused factory that had been given a lick of paint and a strong perimeter fence. A few hundred metres from where our boat had tied up I could see a collection of rusting river hulks. Bracing myself against a throbbing headache, I made my way there gingerly to ask about river traffic to Kinshasa. The scene was exactly the same as the port in Kisangani. Crowds of Congolese sat on rusting decks, huddled around cooking pots, next to bundles of bedding, clothes and possessions, waiting in quiet desperation for news of a departure.

'There are no plans for any boats leaving here for Kinshasa. You will have to wait. It could be weeks, maybe longer,' I was told by a man who described himself as the Person Responsible for Mbandaka port.

I walked slowly back to Ali's boat. For the first time on my trip my determination to stick to Stanley's route downriver wobbled. I was feeling just too ill to face another delay of unknown duration. It had taken me two weeks in Kisangani before I had been lucky enough to find a place on the UN pusher. God knows how long I would have to wait here in Mbandaka for my next break.

As the sun began to dip, I gathered my strength for another walk. I needed to mull over my options. Like the other Congolese towns I had passed through, Mbandaka was little more than a sad collection of ruins. I felt a sense of déjà vu. The decay was just like what I had seen in Kalemie, Kabambarre, Kasongo, Kibombo, Kindu and elsewhere across the Congo. I tried to convince myself that I had already seen enough in my journey to understand what the Congo is really like. I had achieved more than I had thought possible before I started this trip. I had covered more than 2,000 kilometres on Stanley's route. Would my sense of achievement overcome the disappointment of skipping the next section?

I stewed all night, agonising over what to do. There was no hotel in Mbandaka, so the floor of Ali's cabin was the most comfortable place for me to stay. He was due to head back upstream in the next few days, and the prospect of being sick in Mbandaka without any tolerably clean place to stay tormented me. I could be trapped here, just like I was in Kisangani. I lay on the deck thrashing around in my mosquito net, churning the options in my head. I knew from Ali's contacts in the UN mission that a weekly helicopter shuttle to Kinshasa left the following day. I did not have much time to decide.

By morning I had made up my mind. Reluctantly, I would skip the river descent from Mbandaka to Kinshasa.

A day later, I found myself onboard a UN helicopter flying to Kinshasa. The shame I felt at temporarily abandoning Stanley's route was more than outweighed by a growing sense of relief that my ordeal was nearing its end. It took three hours to fly a distance that would have taken me weeks by river boat.

For most of the journey all I could see from the helicopter porthole was jungle. Then, just as we began our final approach to Kinshasa, I caught sight of the Stanley Pool where the Congo River gathers itself in a huge, lake-like expanse, twenty kilometres in width, before its final, tumultuous plunge to the sea. From the air all I could glimpse was an immense body of water, silver in the setting sun like the flank of a Goliath Tigerfish. I was disappointed to have missed this final section of the river, but all I could think about was the town of Boma, a few hundred kilometres off to the west, where my journey would finally end.

12.

Road Rage

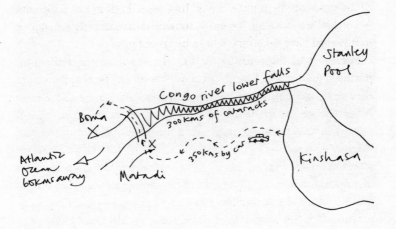

There can be no capital city in the world more unrepresentative of its country than Kinshasa. It has tarmac roads busy with traffic, shops selling imported goods, a music scene as prolific as any in Africa, even a swanky hotel where the doors are opened by swipe-cards. After all that I had seen on my journey, Kinshasa felt as if it did not even belong in the Congo.

Despite these first-world trappings, Kinshasa also has the chronic problems standard to many African capitals. Most of its nine-million-strong urban population crowd into squalid squatter camps without adequate drinking water, electricity, health care or basic services. Corruption corrodes every aspect of day-to-day life, forcing its people to rely on international organisations – the UN, aid groups, donors – to prop up the failing state. But by comparison with the country's medieval hinterland, Kinshasa is centuries ahead.

I found the disconnect between capital and country bewilder-ing when I arrived by UN helicopter. And it got worse after I was met by Maurice, the local representative of my cobalt-mining contact from Lubumbashi, and whisked away in his jeep. We passed city sights that I recognised from my earlier visit in 2001: the long central artery of the city, 'The 30th of June Boulevard', which locals boast of as the 'longest independence avenue in Africa'; the house where Patrice Lumumba briefly ran his doomed post-independence government before he was assas-sinated on the orders of Washington and Brussels; the stadium that staged the 'Rumble in the Jungle' boxing match; and the Belgian diplomatic compound where I met one of Mobutu's surviving cronies in 2001 and first discussed my plan to retrace Stanley's journey.

But it was not the fact that I was seeing familiar sights that confused me. It was the way that, in my mind, I could not connect these places with the Congo I had travelled through, a country where I had seen human bones lying too thick on the ground to be given a decent burial; where a stranger like me was implored to adopt a child to save him from a life of disease, hunger and misery; and where some people were so desperate they actually pined for the old and brutal order of Belgian colonial life.

My bewilderment was complete when Maurice dropped me at the Kinshasa headquarters of the mining company, a brand-new, luxury villa built on a prime piece of city-centre real estate fronting directly onto the Congo River. Armed guards nodded towards Maurice at the entrance to the exclusive, private estate and when they slammed the cast-iron gate behind us, there was an instant when I felt they had shut out the chaos of an entire continent. The estate would have looked at home in any major European city. There were well-tended gardens, cul-de-sacs curving between neatly laid-out kerbstones and family cars parked on driveways. The house Maurice led me to had features lifted straight from a Milanese loft apartment: polished wooden floors, stainless-steel designer kitchen units and a huge television screen wired into the most comprehensive satellite-television network money could buy. It was when I stepped into the shower and warm, clean water started to pulse from an array of nozzles in the glass cubicle for an all-over-body-massage that my compass went completely haywire. It was just too far removed from everything I had experienced.

I had entered the world of the Congo super-elite. It was a world of enormous wealth and power, made possible because of close connections to the regime of President Joseph Kabila. Without these links it would have been impossible to get modern kitchen units or any of the other expensive fittings into the country. As I experimented with the multi-setting, remote-controlled air-conditioning, I could see there was enough money sloshing around the Congo to make anything possible, given the right connections.

My contact's links with the Kabila regime could not have been stronger. When Joseph's father, Laurent, was assassinated in January 2001, the mining group helped ensure he was succeeded by his son, and not by a rival Congolese power broker. Within hours of the shooting, Laurent's body was secretly flown out of Kinshasa on the mining firm's private company jet. He was already dead, but to buy time a false story was put about that he had survived the attack and was receiving hospital treatment. This raised fears that rivals might stage another attempt to finish him off, so the mining firm even arranged for a second, dummy plane, supposedly carrying Laurent, to be seen landing at the airport in Harare, capital of Zimbabwe.

The ploy bought Joseph enough time to be made ready for succession. He was only in his twenties at the time and was completely unknown in Kinshasa, where his father's dictatorship had ruled for just four years since ousting Mobutu in 1997. The Kabila clan came from central Katanga, over on the other side of the country, where people speak Swahili and look more to the east, to the anglophone Indian Ocean nations of Kenya and Tanzania, than to francophone Kinshasa on the western side of the Congo. Joseph did not even speak Lingala, the language of the Congolese capital.

In those volatile days after the assassination, what Joseph needed most was time to allow his safe installation in Kinshasa. Coups are a common feature of the Congolese political landscape. I was in Kinshasa at that time and can remember the rumours of takeovers, counter-coups, mysterious forces marching on the presidential palace and secret military deployments.

Stability returned only after Joseph was seen in public for the first time, an occasion I witnessed. It was out at Kinshasa's main airport and he was meeting his father's coffin as it was flown back into the Congo. I remember how overwhelmed the young pretender looked. His ill-fitting dark suit swamped him and his eyes darted around as a line of tribal elders wearing leopardskin caps paid their respects to the world's then youngest head of state. Bodyguards and militiamen milled around with their weapons cocked. They included a large number of troops from Zimbabwe – the Kabila clan's closest international ally – and they were taking no chances. The road into his new capital was deemed too dangerous, so the new president was spirited to and from the airport by helicopter.

For its role in Joseph Kabila's succession, the mining company had been rewarded handsomely. It enjoyed large cobalt concessions for its mining operations in Katanga and export licences through the Katangan capital, Lubumbashi. But Lubumbashi lies 1,700 kilometres south-east of Kinshasa and, as Joseph started to spend more time in the capital, it became essential for the firm to maintain a presence there to iron out operational problems. The mining company rented this villa as a sort of forward operating base, so that its executives could fly in from time to time to deal with any glitches with the regime.

None of the cobalt miners were there when I stayed in the house, although I was not alone. After Maurice had dropped me off, I found a short, rather sinister-looking white man lying full-length on a plush leather sofa in the sitting room, cursing into a mobile phone, while his eyes followed muted coverage of the 2004 Ryder Cup golf competition on the satellite television. He had dark, slightly threatening eyes and, although he was in his forties, he was nuggety, without any flabby give in his weather-worn skin. Seeing televised sport for the first time in a month reminded me that the Athens Olympics had been about to start when I began my Congolese journey, so when he eventually ended his call I asked the man what had happened at the Games.

'They finished weeks ago,' he snapped impatiently. 'Where the hell have you been?'

I told him.

'You've come all the way from Lake Tanganyika. No way. That's not possible,' he said, swinging his legs onto the ground, clicking off the television and suddenly sounding much more approachable.

It took me a while to convince him I was not lying. I explained my route, overland through Katanga, and then along the upper Congo River to Kisangani and finally downstream by river boat to Mbandaka. He listened closely. When I finished, he exhaled in admiration, leaned forward to shake my hand, introduced himself as Johnny and began talking knowledgeably about Africa, and the Congo in particular.

His life story belonged in a Wilbur Smith novel. Born in Rhodesia, he was too young to enlist during the Rhodesian war of independence in the 1970s, when the white minority struggled against the black independence movement that would eventually transform the former British colony into Zimbabwe. This had not stopped him from being shot, however. He hoisted his shirt and showed me several scarred splash marks on his abdomen, explaining how he had been ambushed on a dirt road near his family's farm while motorbiking home from school. 'Ambushes were normal out in the rural areas back then, and I was hit four times. But we all carried guns, even us school children, so I shot back. Killed one of the "terrs",' he said, chuckling and using the abbreviated form of the word 'terrorist' favoured by white Rhodesians to describe their wartime enemy.

After Zimbabwean independence in 1980, he joined the South African armed forces and served in Angola, when South African troops became involved in the former Portuguese colony's tortuous and complex civil war. After some years he left the army, but returned to Angola, earning a living in the rich but chaotic diamond mines on the country's north-eastern frontier with the Congo. He described working closely with Jonas Savimbi, the bearded bush warrior who led the UNITA rebel force through thirty years of guerrilla fighting in Angola. It was diamond sales that kept UNITA going for so long, as well as financial and military support from the West. Like Mobutu in the Congo, Savimbi enjoyed generous backing from America and the West as his rebel force challenged the socialist MPLA government for control of Angola. Johnny had colourful stories of Savimbi entrusting him with bags of rough diamonds to be smuggled out of Angola, through the Congo, for sale at the diamond market in Antwerp. He chuckled when he described how a diamond mine he was working at was suddenly surrounded by MPLA soldiers, and he was forced to run for his life through the bush, surviving days out in the open before he reached safety.

There was something about Johnny's steely expression that convinced me he was not making any of this up. I let him continue.

In the late 1990s he started to spend more time in the Congo, working in the cobalt mines near Lubumbashi. Johnny was close to Zimbabwean businessmen with links to the first Kabila president, Laurent, and for a year or so they enjoyed bumper profits as the cobalt price boomed. And then his business contact fell out with Kabila, and Johnny ended up detained for several months by Kabila's troops. He was now back in the Congo plotting an ambitious diamond project down on the Congo–Angola frontier, using his close relationship with another Zimbabwean businessman well connected to the Kabila clan. As he enthused about his new diamond-mining operation, I heard echoes of Stanley and generations of other white adventurers who had come to the Congo over the previous 130 years and been enthralled by its economic promise.

'You would not believe the potential down near the border with Angola, on the Tshikapa River. It is amazing. It is just a matter of getting the equipment in place to be able to mine the diamonds,' he gushed.

The name Tshikapa rang a bell. When I had rented the satellite phone for my trip from a South African dealer back in Johannesburg and told him I was going to the Congo, he said something about Tshikapa. He described it as the densest source of satellite-phone communications on the planet, outside post-war Iraq. 'And all of those satellite phones are being used by people looking for diamonds.'

'People who say there is no money in Africa are talking complete bollocks,' Johnny said. 'I have seen with my own eyes that there has always been plenty of money, whether it's for diamonds, cobalt, safari hunting, whatever. And with China needing resources to keep up their current economic boom, there is more money around today for African raw materials than ever before. But the point is the money goes to only a few people, not to the country in general. If you think you can solve Africa's problems with money, then you are a bloody fool. You solve Africa's problems by creating a system of justice that actually works and by making the leaders accountable for their actions. If that happens, I guess things would get a lot more competitive for my business, but it would be good for Africa.'

When I flew into Kinshasa I was worried about my health. I was feeling weak and nauseous after the river-boat journey, but I was still 400 kilometres short of Boma, the place where Stanley completed his trip. It was only after two days of sleeping in a bed with laundered sheets, drinking clean water, eating healthy food and dosing myself with antibiotics in the comfort of the luxury house that I started to feel strong enough to contemplate attempting this final leg.

When Stanley's flotilla paddled across the huge expanse of the Stanley Pool in March 1877 they were in high spirits. Two of Stanley's three white companions had died of disease earlier in the expedition, but the last one, Francis Pocock, felt a surge of confidence when he saw tall, white cliffs rising up on the right bank of the river, because they reminded him of the cliffs at Dover near where he was brought up in Kent. 'I feel we are nearing home,' he enthused.

The confidence was premature. A short distance further west and the Stanley Pool narrowed dramatically, choked through a narrow rocky cleft, only a few hundred metres across. Stanley could have had no idea what other perils lurked beyond these first cataracts but he described how, in the space of just a few metres, the entire character of the Congo River was transformed:

It is no longer the stately stream whose mystic beauty, noble grandeur, and gentle uninterrupted flow . . . ever fascinated us, despite the savagery of its peopled shores, but a furious river rushing down a steep bed obstructed by reefs of lava, projected barriers or rock, lines of immense boulders, winding in crooked course through deep chasms, and dropping down over terraces in a long series of falls, cataracts and rapids.

Stanley decided on the same tactic he used 1,900 kilometres upriver when the expedition first encountered the Stanley Falls. He would approach as close to each cataract as was safe by boat, and then hack a track through the bush on one of the river banks so that the boats and expedition equipment could be dragged round to the next safe section of water. This had worked as a way to get round the Stanley Falls and he had no reason to doubt it would work on this lower section of river.

What he did not know was that the falls on the lower Congo River were a quantum level more hazardous than anything he had so far encountered. For the next 250 kilometres the river forms an almost unbroken chain of cataracts and rapids as it is funnelled through a tight fissure in the Crystal Mountains, a range separating the Atlantic Ocean from the Congo River basin. Hydrographers later charted thirty-two major sets of cataracts as the river snakes its way through the break in the mountainous plateau, but from Stanley's viewpoint, sitting low down on the water on his collapsible Thames river boat, the *Lady Alice*, he had no idea what he was embarking on when he gave the command for his boats to enter the gorge.

Stanley's description of this section grew ever more pathetic. As the cataracts became more dangerous, the river banks became increasingly rocky and more difficult to traverse. His expedition suffered from acute hunger, with local tribes reluctant to sell food. These tribes had been trading in European goods for hundreds of years – goods that had been shipped to the mouth of the Congo River, on the other side of the Crystal Mountains, ever since the Portuguese sailors first discovered the river in the fifteenth century. Stanley describes how the beads and wire that he had used to trade for food earlier in the expedition were no longer enough to impress the tribes on the lower Congo River, where tastes had grown more sophisticated:

Gunpowder was abundant with them, and every male capable of carrying a gun possessed one, often more. Delft ware and British crockery were also observed in their hands, such as plates, mugs, shallow dishes, wash-basins, galvanised iron spoons, Birmingham cutlery, and other articles of European manufacture.

The condition of his expedition plummeted. Disease became rampant, made worse by the gnaw of constant hunger and malnutrition. So many canoes were washed away by the river that the expedition had to camp for several weeks so that two suitable trees could be found, felled and turned into replacements. Ever faithful to the newspaper financiers of his expedition, Stanley named rivers feeding into this lower reach of the Congo River after his newspaper-editor sponsors, but his efforts to continue mapping and charting the river could not conceal the growing danger that the entire expedition might perish in those last few kilometres before the Atlantic Ocean. After three months of slogging through the gorge, Stanley lost his last white companion. With feet too damaged by ulcers to be able to walk around a particular set of falls, Pocock stayed onboard his canoe a moment too long. It was caught by the current, swept down some rapids and he was drowned.

The survivors struggled along the river for another two months, but with the cataracts getting no easier Stanley took one last gamble. The expedition would leave the river, abandon the boats and attempt to reach the trading station at Boma on foot. The river had been his handrail, guiding him for 2,500 kilometres across Africa, and by leaving it he risked getting lost and dying of starvation before the next food supplies could be found. He describes in emotional terms his parting from the *Lady Alice*:

> At sunset we lifted the brave boat after her adventurous journey across Africa, and carried her to the summit of some rocks . . . to be abandoned to her fate. On 31st July 1877, after a journey of nearly 7,000 miles up and down broad Africa, she was consigned to her resting-place above the Isangila Cataract, to bleach and to rot to dust!

In theory the journey from Kinshasa to Boma should have been the simplest part of my entire trip. The only functioning highway in the entire country traverses the Crystal Mountains in a south-westward arc for 350 kilometres from Kinshasa to the port of Matadi, built just below the lowest set of cataracts. The road then crosses the river on the Marshal Mobutu suspension bridge before continuing another 100 kilometres or so to Boma.

I naively thought I could do it in a single day round-trip. That was until I discussed the journey with Maurice.

'It's highly irregular for an outsider to want to travel there, you know,' he said. 'You will need written permission from both the national security service and the department of immigration.'

I remembered my rule for Congo: towns bad, open spaces good. Here in Kinshasa, the biggest city of all, I faced the worst pettifogging of my entire journey. Maurice heard my sigh of exasperation, but continued with the bad news.

'And how do you propose to travel there? There are no buses. You cannot take a taxi. There are no hire-cars. The old railway does not work. You have to remember that Kinshasa looks like a city, but it is largely an illusion. Things that you take for granted in other cities – like buses, taxis, hire-cars – just don't belong in Kinshasa.'

'Well, I thought I would be able to hitch a lift . . .' My voice trailed off. Even to myself, I sounded like a naive fool.

Maurice took pity on me. He explained he was part of a Katangan clique that had followed Laurent Kabila to Kinshasa when he took power in 1997. He said he had good connections with the various departments of immigration and national security, most of which were run by Katangans. If I gave him my passport, I was assured it would take just a day or two for the necessary paperwork to be prepared. And if I was willing to pay for a local driver, I could take the jeep that belonged to the mining company. His only condition was that one of his colleagues, Hippolite, must accompany me.

From the moment I saw Hippolite, I did not trust him. He was a big, lumbering oaf with a gormless expression. When I gave him my passport, I pointed out the yellow-fever certificate tucked between its pages and asked him to take particular care of it. Vaccination regulations are a common source of friction when travelling in Africa. If you don't have the right certificates you can find yourself being charged large sums by officials and proof of yellow-fever vaccination was often asked for. By the time Hippolite came back with my passport, the certificate was missing.

I stared at him angrily and asked what had happened. His gaze dropped to the ground and he mumbled something about not knowing what I was talking about, followed by a swift warning that I would need a yellow-fever certificate when I eventually left the country and a promise that, for a fee, he could arrange a replacement. I said we would sort it out later, but that exchange confirmed my first instinct about Hippolite's integrity.

We left early in the morning for the drive to Boma. There were three of us in the jeep: Roget, a locally hired driver, Hippolite in the front passenger seat and me, trying not to look conspicuous in the back. We would be passing through numerous checkpoints and I wanted to attract minimal attention from bribe-hungry officials. It took a long time to get past the city-centre traffic – we drove past a smart private school just as hundreds of children, offspring of politicians and aid workers, were being dropped off in limousines and 4×4s. I saw a traffic cop wearing the same uniform of yellow helmet and white gloves that I had seen weeks earlier in Kindu on the other side of the country. And, just as in Kindu, everyone ignored his gloved mime actions and whistles. It took us an hour to inch past the school.

Once we had left the city behind, our speed picked up and I felt the sensation of being in a car moving at full speed, something I had not done since arriving in the Congo six weeks earlier. The timing of my trip was lucky. Repairs on the trunk road between Kinshasa and Matadi had just been completed. The first half of it had been rebuilt with Chinese government assistance and the second half with European money. This is the main highway of the entire country, joining the capital city with the country's solitary deep-water port for ocean-going ships, Matadi, the main entry point for imports, and yet the government had to rely on foreign money to keep the road passable.

Now that traffic was moving again between Kinshasa and Matadi, another problem had developed – highway robbery. Armed gangs routinely robbed and killed people on the road. Most attacks happened after dark, but there had been a few during daylight hours. The situation was so bad that roadblocks were erected before sunset, stopping all overnight travel.

*

The only other vehicles on the road were trucks, which we saw every so often hauling containers to and from the port at Matadi. Along with their regular loads, almost all of them had a miserable human cargo. Maurice was right when he told me there were no taxis or buses on this route, so the container lorries were being used for public transport. The driving compartments would be crammed with people begging a ride, but they were the lucky ones. The unlucky ones were forced to risk their lives, clinging to the bare roof of the containers or perching precariously between the back of the cabin and the container. They had to stand there for hour after hour, with little to hold on to for safety. On some of the larger, articulated trucks the end of the container would shift towards them as they went round corners, threatening to squash them. Many of the lorries carried little signs banning passengers. Nobody paid any notice. I even saw policemen and soldiers taking their chances among the other passengers.

We came across a grizzly scene. A truck was jack-knifed across the road with a trail of blood, gore and body parts smeared across the tarmac in a line leading to its back axle. The truck had been forced to brake suddenly, some of the passengers had fallen off and the rear wheels had gone straight over them.

It made me think of Conrad's description of this same road. The Matadi–Kinshasa road had been a symbol of death and cruelty since Stanley returned to the Congo in the 1880s as Leopold's agent to set up the Belgian monarch's colony. Building a road, and later a railway, around the impassable rapids on the lower Congo River was key to the king's dream of opening up the Congo River system and Stanley set about the task with brutal determination. Local tribesmen were rounded up at gunpoint and forced to work in chain-gangs. Thousands died from disease, mistreatment and malnutrition. When Conrad came here in 1890 to serve on a steamboat on the river, he described the hellish trek along the primitive roadway over the Crystal Mountains, marked by grisly cairns made from the bones of dead labourers, some still wearing their shackles.

The jeep broke down four times on this leg of my journey and we were forced to stop and waste hours negotiating our way past checkpoints too numerous to remember. But crossing the Congo had made me accustomed to delay and I spent the time trying to make sense of what I had learned from my adventure.

In part my journey had been about gauging the scale of problems faced by the continent, and in this regard the Congo had been a revelation. In six harrowing weeks of travel I felt I had touched the heart of Africa and found it broken. While the Western world moves ahead with advances in medicine and technology, the people of the Congo are falling further and further behind. There was one sentence that stays with me after hearing it right across the country, from Lake Tanganyika in the east to the lower Congo River in the west. It came up in conversation with almost every Congolese person I met: villagers, priests, miners, fishermen. As I asked them about their situation they would, inevitably, tell me about some sort of disaster that had befallen them, whether it was an attack by rebels, a major flood or a political crisis, and, just as inevitably, they all finished with the same words: 'And we fled into the bush.'

I found it extraordinary that for millions of Congolese in the twenty-first century the rainforest offers the safest sanctuary.

And as the hours passed on my jeep ride, I thought more and more about Stanley and his role in creating the Congo of today. In the late nineteenth century he was heralded as a hero of the great age of African exploration – he was knighted by Queen Victoria in 1898 – but today's received historical wisdom is less flattering. His tactics in the Congo, especially the use of weapons to open fire on any tribesmen who got in his way, and his role in installing Leopold's rule, taint him as arch-colonial brute.

I was fully aware of Stanley's negative image when I started out, but my journey nevertheless taught me a grudging respect for my *Telegraph* predecessor. I had seen the scale of his achievement, the difficulty of the terrain he had crossed, the rigour of the climate and the constant threat from hunger and disease. The fact that he survived the three-year trek from one side of Africa to the other taught me respect for his determination, stamina and spirit. His three white companions all perished, but the little Welsh bastard toughed it out.

And I would disagree with those who dismiss him as an utter racist. When he reached the Atlantic, he had the chance to sail north to Europe to claim the fame and fortune he knew to be awaiting him following his feat of exploration. But instead of rushing home, he insisted on ensuring that his surviving African bearers made it safely back to their homes in Zanzibar. This decision meant it would be months before he returned to London as he sailed south, stopped over in Cape Town and eventually rounded the Cape of Good Hope to return his loyal expedition members to their island home in the Indian Ocean. This gesture suggests more empathy with Africans than he is normally given credit for.

But as I sat in the relative comfort of the jeep, driving in just two days a distance that it took Stanley five months to cover, inside me I felt an anger towards him welling up. His expedition could have been a positive turning point for Africa and its people. A continent cut off from the outside world could have benefited hugely from Stanley's achievement, as the positive aspects of the modern world – medicine, education, technology – were made available to Africa for the first time. But what enraged me was how Stanley's trip turned into one of the greatest missed opportunities of modern history.

Instead of bringing positive aspects of the developed world to Africa, it brought only the negative. For decades Leopold's apologists – Stanley being one of the loudest – described the Congo Free State as an exercise in civilising philanthropy, but in reality it was an exercise in asset-stripping. The colonialists took ivory, rubber, copper, timber and any other natural resource they could find, killing millions and millions of Congolese in the process. It took years of work by Edwardian human-rights campaigners to force the Belgian king to give up the Congo Free State and transform it into a full Belgian colony. Even after this transformation the Congo's enormous wealth of natural resources, such as diamonds, gold and copper, continued to be misappropriated, first by colonials and then by Mobutu's kleptocrats.

But the major lesson I learned on my trek through modern central Africa was that the most valuable asset stolen from the Congo was the sovereignty of its people.

Before Stanley and white rule, the people of the Congo genuinely enjoyed a sense of local power. Society was tribal, with authority lying in the hands of village chiefs and, above them, paramount chiefs. But local people enjoyed sovereign power to the extent that they could get rid of unpopular chiefs. No chief could afford to ignore totally the will of his subjects. Decisions had to be taken, at least in part, with the interests of the people in mind.

All of that changed with white rule, not just in the Congo, but across colonial Africa. All aspects of sovereignty were stripped from the people of Africa and they have never, to this day, fully got it back. One of the great fallacies about white rule in Africa was that when it ended, power was handed back to the people of Africa. I saw in the Congo how this simply is not true. At independence, colonial powers surrendered authority, but the point was that it never ended in the right place, back in the hands of the people. Instead it was hijacked by elites who publicly claimed they were working in the interests of their people, but were in fact only driven by self-interest. Mobutu's chartering of Concorde to deliver champagne to a palace specially built in the jungle is nothing but a colourful, extreme example of what African leaders do routinely right across the continent – enjoy grotesque luxury while ignoring the plight of their people.

I can think of no concept more abused in modern Africa than sovereignty. It is used by dictators and undemocratic regimes to fend off criticism of their rule and to conceal their own maladministration and corrupt pilfering. They cloak themselves in it to dismiss the right of any outsider to hold them to account. The greatest shame arising from Stanley's Congo journey was how it started this pattern of sovereignty-stripping, a process whereby the vast majority of Africans in the Congo and elsewhere have ended up not just without any say in the running of their country, but abused and exploited by their African leaders.

While outsiders led by Stanley can be blamed for creating this situation, the people of Africa must share responsibility for showing themselves unable to change it. The Malaysian naval officer on my river boat was right to ask why former European colonies in Asia have been able to develop since independence, while those in Africa have regressed. The cruelty and greed of African dictators is mostly to blame, but it is also true that the peoples of Africa have not been capable of working together to rein in the excesses of dictators. People power in Africa has a wretched record.

The challenge for the future must be to restore some sense of sovereignty and control to all in Africa, not just the elite. Elections are a necessary part of this, but by themselves they will not be sufficient. To make up for decades of misrule and exploitation, Africa needs help in installing meaningful legal systems that can hold leaders to account and ensure that national funds are spent on public projects and not funnelled into private bank accounts. This will need a fundamental change of attitude, not just from donors and foreign companies accepting a greater degree of transparency in their dealings with Africa, but also from the leaders and people of Africa, who must admit both how much they need help and that they are willing to compromise.

To save not just the Congo, but the entire continent of Africa, from its downward trajectory, a completely different way of thinking is needed. There are a few positive early signs. It is in the Congo that the International Criminal Court has begun pioneering work, investigating alleged atrocities committed in the war-ravaged east of the country. This admission by the Congolese authorities that it simply does not have the capability to ensure law and order by itself, and needs outside help, is a first step. But much more will need to be done to finally return authority to its rightful place, into the hands of the Congolese people themselves, and to right a wrong that Stanley did so much to perpetrate.

In August 1877 a messenger clambered half-dead down the seaward side of the Crystal Mountains. He was heading for the tiny port of Boma, the only European trading station for hundreds of kilometres on Africa's west coast, with orders to deliver a handwritten note addressed 'To Any Gentleman Who Speaks English'. The note was a desperate plea for help from Stanley:

> I have arrived at this place with 115 souls, men, women and children . . . We are now in a state of imminent starvation . . . We are in a state of the greatest distress; but if your supplies arrive in time, I may be able to reach Boma within four days . . . I want ten or fifteen man-loads of rice or grain to fill their pinched bellies immediately . . . Starving people cannot wait . . . The supplies must arrive within two days, or I may have a fearful time of it among the dying . . . What is wanted is immediate relief; and I pray you to use your utmost energies to forward it at once . . . For myself, if you have such little luxuries as tea, coffee, sugar and biscuits by you, such as one man can easily carry, I beg you on my own behalf that you will send a small supply . . . And add to the great debt of gratitude due to you upon the timely arrival of the supplies for my people.

Stanley signed the note, but he added a postscript. Boma was one of the world's most distant backwaters, but he nevertheless presumed that his reputation had reached there. Under his signature he wrote, 'You may not know me by name; I therefore add, I am the person that discovered Livingstone in 1871.'

For the traders, the wretched plight of the expedition described by Stanley was not the most dramatic aspect of the letter. What made the letter truly astounding was that it had arrived overland. For four centuries European traders had been regular visitors to Boma, but they had all arrived by ship and the African hinterland remained as much of a mystery to them in 1877 as it was in 1482 when the Portuguese explorer Diogo Cão first reached there. No white man had ever penetrated more than a few kilometres inland from Boma. And the few who had tried had all used Boma as a starting point, so the traders would have known of any recent mission. If this letter was to be believed, then the author must have come through territory widely held to be impassable.

The bearer with the message later recalled how a short, bespectacled white man came out from one of the wooden buildings at Boma demanding to see the letter. At first he could not believe what he was reading and hearing – the messenger was able to explain himself in English as he had been to a mission school on the island of Zanzibar, on the other side of Africa, thousands of kilometres away. His pathetic pleading for help backed up what the trader was reading.

The bearer reported how the sceptical white man fired a series of questions at him, wanting to know about the journey down to the smallest detail. Then the trader, believed to be John Harrison, the local agent for Hatton & Cookson, a Liverpool trading company, composed himself, ordered a meal for the messenger, and began preparations for a large relief convoy to rescue Stanley's expedition.

It set out the following morning with everything Stanley had requested, and more. The bearers carried sacks of rice, fish and potatoes, material for new clothes and even a five-gallon demijohn of rum. Stanley described the scenes of rapture when the relief column came into sight. One of the expedition's boys, he wrote, turned praise-singer, launching into a lyrical description of the hardships they had endured in crossing Africa, chanting about how they had survived the 'hell of hunger', defying cannibals and cataracts, snakes and starvation. Stanley wrote that the chorus was taken up loudly by the other members of his party, as they finally understood their ordeal was over:

> Then sing, O friends, sing; the journey is ended;
> Sing aloud, O friends, sing to this great sea.

He described how some of his party could not wait for the rice and fish to be cooked, stuffing their mouths with it raw, while others rushed about gathering firewood to prepare an immense feast. Bales of cloth had been included in the rescue package and Stanley described how eagerly they were used to cover the embarrassment of bare ribcages and protruding bones. As a journalist, he had a reputation for colourful exaggeration, but I am prepared to believe the childish delight he attributes to himself as he opened a swag-bag of goodies from the Boma traders:

Pale Ale! Sherry! Port wine! Champagne! Plum pudding! Currant, gooseberry, and raspberry jam! The gracious God be praised for ever! The long war we had maintained against famine and the siege of woe were over, and my people and I rejoiced in plenty! It was only an hour before we had been living on the recollections of the few peanuts and green bananas we had consumed in the morning, but now, in an instant, we were transported into the presence of the luxuries of civilisation. Never did gaunt Africa appear so unworthy and so despicable before my eyes as now, when imperial

Europe rose before my delighted eyes and showed her
boundless treasures of life, and blessed me with her stores.

After a day of gorging, his group continued its march and on 9
August 1877, exactly 999 days since his expedition set off from
the other side of Africa, it reached Boma. The traders came out to
meet Stanley's party, offering him – with no apparent sense of
irony – the freedom of the city, a city that ran to only six
stockaded buildings. The traders insisted that the explorer cover
the last part of the journey in a hammock borne by native bearers,
something he later complained about for giving the appearance of
being 'very effeminate'.

Within two days Stanley boarded a ship for the journey home.
As the boat headed out to sea he described his feelings at having
survived crossing the Congo:

Turning to take a farewell glance at the mighty River on
whose brown bosom we had endured so greatly, I saw it
approach, awed and humbled, the threshold of the watery
immensity, to whose immeasurable volume and illimitable
expanse, awful as had been its power, and terrible as had
been its fury, its flood was but a drop. And I felt my heart
suffused with purest gratitude to Him whose hand had
protected us, and who had enabled us to pierce the Dark
Continent from east to west, and to trace its mightiest River
to its Ocean bourne.

As we approached Boma my own sense of excitement grew.
Hippolite had been prattling on throughout our journey about
how he was well known in the area and how everyone there
respected him as an important man. I switched off and thought of
a Congo where people might one day prosper on merit and not,
like Hippolite, on tribal connections with an unelected dictatorship. Each time we were stopped at a checkpoint I would be

questioned about my motive for reaching Boma. By rote I would repeat my mantra: I am a historian interested in following the route used by Stanley before the colonial era, and please would the officials be so kind as to let me pass. I don't think they believed my story for a second. I am sure they suspected I was another white profiteer looking to exploit their country, but after an hour or so of toying with me, they would let me pass.

We were crossing a sparse landscape of mountain plateau. Bare hilltops rolled away to the horizon with just a thin covering of brown grass and an occasional splash of green from the odd cassava tree. Not far to the north of us was the narrow river ravine down which Stanley passed on those grim final days of his expedition. I asked Hippolite if he had heard of Isangila, the section of the river where Stanley described leaving the *Lady Alice*. He shrugged his shoulders and carried on talking about a prostitute in Boma whose number he had been given.

Eventually the road dropped down into Matadi and I caught sight of the river again. It was tens of metres beneath us, below the span of the Marshal Mobutu bridge. We were waiting at another checkpoint having my paperwork examined before I was to be allowed to use this strategic military asset, and I watched as a large ship struggled against the current heading upriver to Matadi's dockside. The bridge spans the river just below the lowest set of cataracts, and even from my high vantage point I could see the brown water was alive with eddies and undertows as it was squeezed through a steep-sided rocky gorge. If the hillsides had been covered in pines and the outside temperature about thirty degrees Celsius colder, I could have been looking at a Norwegian fjord.

By now I was on the edge of my seat. I had less than a hundred kilometres to go to reach Boma. This last stretch of road carried no container trucks and so it had not been repaired by foreign money. It was badly pitted and our speed dropped accordingly. Forest returned on either side of the road now that we were down off the mountain plateau, and every so often we would see villagers cutting timber or carrying baskets. As we passed a group of children, I watched as one of them, who appeared to be carrying a large pine cone, flicked his wrist extravagantly. The 'pine cone' uncoiled like a yo-yo, stretched out straight and then bundled itself back up into a ball. I shouted at Roget to stop the jeep. The children came running and I had a better look at what they were holding. It was a pangolin, a nocturnal forest animal that I had only ever read about and never seen. Like a hedgehog, it defends itself by rolling into a tight ball, but instead of a hedgehog's prickles it hides behind an armour of bony plates. 'You want to eat, you want to eat,' cried the pangolin's chief tormentor.

Finally we reached Boma. It has a sad, passed-over air. There are a few old colonial-era buildings close to the river's edge, but a modern town of dirty streets and shacks spreads up a hillside on high ground some way from the river. Stanley made Boma his capital when he came back here to set up the Congo Free State for Leopold and, after I had been interviewed at length by the town's chief immigration officer, I was eventually allowed to look around the relics of that period. There was a tiny Catholic church made completely from cast iron. A foundry in Belgium had moulded the wall panels, window frames, roof and spire before it was shipped out here and reassembled. I tried to go inside, but it was locked. On a hillock overlooking the church was the old governor's house and below it an abandoned hotel. A rather elegant gallery wrapped around the second storey, its edges decorated with filigree ironwork, red with rust.

I wanted to picture the scene when Stanley arrived here, half-dead from sickness and starvation after trekking from the other side of the continent. I tried to imagine the thrill he felt when he learned that Cameron, the Royal Navy officer who had set off two years before him, had not beaten him here and it was he who was the first outsider to chart the Congo River.

In my heart I also felt thrilled. When Stanley got here he was heralded as a hero by the Europeans manning the Boma trading station, because they knew how important his journey was. They knew it changed everything, solving a geographical mystery dating back hundreds of years and promising more visitors, trade and development. My thrill was more private. I had faced down the Congo, the most dangerous, chaotic, backward country in Africa.

I walked by myself down to the water's edge and thought about the river. Forty-four days earlier I had started my trip where Lake Tanganyika drains into the headwaters. From there I had watched the river gather strength through the savannah of Katanga and the thickening jungle of Maniema, before its sweep across equatorial Africa all the way to Boma. But the river did not just link me to the places passed through by Stanley. The river was the thread running through the continent's bloody history, connecting me not just to Stanley, but to Leopold, Conrad, Lumumba, Mobutu and other spectres from Africa's dark past.

Taking one last glance at the river before turning for home, I felt a lump in my pocket. It was a pebble I had picked up from the river shallows on my pirogue 2,000 kilometres upstream. Its surface was cracked and uneven. I rolled the stone between my fingers, imagining how the waters of the Congo River had washed over it year after year. I looked at it for a final time. It was the colour of dried blood.

Epilogue

In the two years since I completed my journey, much has happened in the Congo and yet little has changed.

In general the peace treaty of 2002 has held without a return to full-blown war. This does not mean the Congo has been free from violence. In southern Katanga, just weeks after I left, the town of Kilwa was seized by anti-government rebels, driving thousands of refugees across the border into neighbouring Zambia. Without any vehicles of their own, troops loyal to Kinshasa requisitioned jeeps from a nearby foreign-owned copper mine and descended on the town. According to eye-witnesses more than a hundred people, including women and children, were summarily executed as the soldiers ran amok.

Further north, rebels have continued to kill and cause mayhem across a large swathe of Congolese territory close to Uganda and Rwanda. MONUC, now the largest United Nations peacekeeping mission in the world, has adopted a much tougher posture than in my time, deploying attack helicopters and well-armed troops on combat patrols. They have been moderately successful at persuading some rebel groups to lay down their weapons, but this has not been without cost to the UN. In the worst incident in February 2005, nine Bangladeshi peacekeepers were ambushed and executed in the Ituri region of eastern Congo. Before they died they were tortured and mutilated.

So while the war remains officially over, the humanitarian crisis in the Congo claims lives on a staggering scale. The most recent assessment, published in January 2006 by the eminent British medical journal, *The Lancet*, suggests that 1,200 people die each day in the Congo as a direct result of endemic violence and insecurity.

Furthermore, the Congo's malign influence continues to leach across the region. An attempt in 2006 to persuade the Lord's Resistance Army in Uganda to accept a peace deal failed because many of their militia slipped across the border into the Congo, where they found sanctuary in its lawless jungle. And its influence has been felt in the worsening crisis in Sudan's Darfur region, where some rebel groups have financed their operations by selling ivory and rhino horn illegally poached from Sudan's southern neighbour, the Congo.

The most important single development in the Congo since my journey has been the attempt by the international community to install democracy. It cost more than four hundred million dollars, was boycotted by a major opposition party and took place two years behind schedule, but on 30 July 2006 the Congo held an election to choose both president and parliament. The first meaningful poll in the Congo since the 1960 general election that brought Lumumba to power, it was enthusiastically embraced by Congolese voters. Ballot boxes were delivered by dugout canoe, motorbike courier and helicopter to 46,693 polling stations across the vast country. Villagers trudged for days to take part amidst a mood of optimism that the election might just end decades of instability and reverse the spiral of decline.

It is too early to say if these hopes have been fulfilled, but the initial signs are not good. Fighting erupted in Kinshasa hours before the results were to be announced. Official reports said twenty-three people died on the streets of the capital, although other estimates put the death toll five times higher. The fighting was so bad that the head of the UN mission and fourteen foreign ambassadors were holed up in the house of a presidential candidate overnight before a special MONUC squad rescued them. The result was so close that a second round of voting had to be held in October 2006. Joseph Kabila was declared the winner, although the loser, Jean-Pierre Bemba, continues to dispute the result.

Where possible I have tried to keep in touch with many of the people I met on my journey. All of the foreign aid workers I met have moved on, as if duty in the Congo is a tough but necessary career rite of passage. Tom Nyamwaya, the Care International employee who made my trip possible by providing me with motorbikes through Katanga, left his post in Kasongo in 2004 and moved to a new aid job in Sudan. After Benoit's contract with Care International ended, he moved back to his home near the Congo's border with Rwanda, but his motorbiking partner Odimba remains in his birthplace, Kasongo. In Kalemie, Georges Mbuyu continues to work for his pygmy human-rights group in the ramshackle house he calls his headquarters. It became even more ramshackle in December 2005 when Kalemie was hit by a powerful earthquake registering 6.8 on the Richter scale.

When I got home to Johannesburg I was disappointed by the lack of interest in my journey from two of my most prominent Congolese contacts. Congo's ambassador to South Africa had talked enthusiastically about my journey when signing my laissez-passer before the trip, but when I tried to contact him to tell him how I had got on, he did not return my calls. And Adolphe Onusumba, the rebel leader I had courted before the journey, underwent a radical change. We had been exchanging emails and telephone calls regularly, but a few months after I got home all communication ended. I then found out that the former rebel had been co-opted into the government of his erstwhile enemy, President Kabila, as Defence Minister. I concluded that the ambassador and minister were too ashamed to hear what I had discovered about their failed state.

My own work took me to Jerusalem, from where I now cover the Middle East region for the *Telegraph*. I might have moved, but my obsession with the Congo – the daunting, flawed giant that

symbolises Africa's triumph of disappointment over potential –
remains stronger than ever.

Tim Butcher
Jerusalem, October 2006

Bibliography

Non-fiction

John and Julie Batchelor, *In Stanley's Footsteps – Across Africa From West to East*, 1990, Blandford

Colette Braeckman: *L'Enjeu Congolais*, 1999, Fayard

— *Les Nouveaux Prédateurs*, 2003, Fayard

Ritchie Calder: *Agony of the Congo*, 1961, Victor Gollancz

Verney Lovett Cameron: *Across Africa*, 1877, Daldy, Isbister and Company

Peter Forbath: *The River Congo*, 1977, Harper & Row

Alan Gallop: *Mr Stanley, I Presume? The Life and Explorations of Henry Morton Stanley*, 2004, Sutton Publishing

Guide Du Voyageur Au Congo Belge, 1951, Office of Tourism for the Belgian Congo, Brussels

Ernesto 'Che' Guevara: *The African Dream – The Diaries of the Revolutionary War in the Congo*, 2000, The Harvill Press

Richard Hall: *Stanley – An Adventurer Explored*, 1974, William Collins Sons & Company

Blaine Harden: *Africa, Dispatches From a Fragile Continent*, 1991, HarperCollins

Adam Hochschild: *King Leopold's Ghost*, 1998, Houghton Miffin Company

Mike Hoare: *Congo Mercenary*, 1967, Robert Hale

Richard Lawson: *Strange Soldiering*, 1963, Hodder and Stoughton

Sven Lindqvist: '*Exterminate All the Brutes*', 1997, Granta

Blaine Littell: *South of the Moon – On Stanley's Trail Through the Dark Continent*, 1966, Weidenfeld & Nicolson

Roger Louis and Jean Stengers: *E.D. Morel's History of the Congo*

Reform Movement, 1968, Clarendon Press

Frank McLynn: *Hearts of Darkness – The European Exploration of Africa*, 1992, Pimlico

— *Stanley: The Making of an African Explorer*, 1989, Constable and Company

— *Stanley: Sorcerer's Apprentice*, 1991, Constable and Company

Conor Cruise O'Brien: *To Katanga and Back*, 1962, Hutchinson & Company

Redmond O'Hanlon: *Congo Journey*, 1996, Hamish Hamilton

Thomas Packenham: *The Scramble for Africa*, 1991, Weidenfeld & Nicolson

André Pilette: *À Travers L'Afrique Équatoriale*, 1914, Oscar Lamberty

Colonel Jerry Puren: *Mercenary Commander*, 1986, Galago

Henry Morton Stanley: *Through the Dark Continent*, 1878, Sampson Low, Marston & Company

— *How I Found Livingstone*, 1872, Sampson Low, Marston, Low, and Searle

— *The Exploration Diaries of H.M. Stanley*, edited by Richard Stanley and Alan Neame, 1961, William Kimber & Company

Jeffrey Tayler: *Facing the Congo*, 2000, Little, Brown and Company

Marq de Villiers and Sheila Hirtle: *Into Africa*, 1997, Weidenfeld & Nicolson

Ludo de Witte: *The Assassination of Lumumba*, 2001, Jacana

Michela Wrong: *In the Footsteps of Mr Kurtz – Living on the Brink of Disaster*, 2000, Fourth Estate

Fiction

Joseph Conrad: *Heart of Darkness*, 1899, Blackwood's Magazine

Graham Greene: *A Burnt-Out Case*, 1961, Heinemann

Barbara Kingsolver: *The Poisonwood Bible*, 1998, HarperCollins

V.S. Naipaul: *A Bend in the River*, 1979, Andre Deutsch

Georges Simenon: *African Trio*, 1979, Hamish Hamilton

Acknowledgements

Blood River taught me how the seemingly solitary process of book-writing depends on many people.

Without the bravery and generosity I encountered from strangers in the Congo, the project would have failed. Those to whom I owe a particular debt include Georges Mbuyu, Benoit Bangana, Odimba Ngenda, Bishop Masimango Katanda, Dr Adolphe Onusemba Yemba, Clement Mangubu, Oggi Saidi, Brian Larson and his Care International Colleagues, Tom Nyamwaya and Lynn Heinisch, Tommy Lee and his International Rescue Committee colleague, Andrea De Domenico, Father Leon and his fellow Missionaries from the Order of the Sacred Heart of Jesus, and Michel Bonnardeaux and his colleagues from MONUC, Marie-France Hélière, Ann Barnes, Robert Powell, Commander Jorge Wilson and Lieutenant Commander Sazali Yusoff. I also owe thanks to others who cannot be named for reasons of security and whose names had to be changed in the text.

During my research I received help from many including Paul Salopek, Rae Simkin, Kate Nicholls, Jean de Dieu Wassoo, Robert Mwinyihali, Franck Meriau, Ambassador Bene M'Poko, Gaston Ntambo, Gerald Sadleir, Paul Connolly, John Loubser, Nick Alexander, James Astill and Jason Stearns.

And the long leg of the journey that began after I returned from the Congo was made possible by the love and support of Lisette and Stanley Butcher, Patrick and Marilyn Flanagan, Anthea Stephens and Stuart Huntley; the backing of kindred spirits at the *Daily Telegraph*; the courage of Camilla Hornby at Curtis Brown, and the skill of Rebecca Carter and Poppy Hampson at Chatto & Windus.

Finally, my eternal thanks and love to Jane for her unstinting enthusiasm and to Kit, who joined us halfway through the writing, for being such a good sleeper.

Credits:

p.30　Drawing of the *Lady Alice* taken from H.M. Stanley's *Through the Dark Continent*, 1878, Sampson Low, Marston & Company

p.52　Advertisements from *The Guide to South and East Africa (for the Use of Tourists, Sportsmen, Invalids and Settlers)*, 1915, Sampson Low, Marston & Company

p.118　Drawings of east Congolese hairstyles taken from H.M. Stanley's book, as above

p.154　Photograph of European explorer crossing eastern Congo, circa 1913, taken from André Pilette's *À Travers L'Afrique Équatoriale*, 1914, Oscar Lamberty

p.212　Drawing of Stanley Falls taken from H.M. Stanley's book, as above

p.232　Poster for the film *The African Queen*, 1951. With kind permission of ITC PLC (Granada Int'L)/LFI.

p.254　Drawing of the lowest cataract in the Stanley Falls, taken from H.M. Stanley's book, as above

p.292　Drawing of a Pike, taken from H.M. Stanley's book, as above

For more pictures, see www.bloodriver.co.uk

Index

Lose yourself
in a good
book with Galaxy

Curled up on the sofa,

Sunday morning in pyjamas,

just before bed,

in the bath or

on the way to work?

Wherever, whenever,
you can escape
with a good book!

So go on...
indulge yourself with

a good read and the

smooth taste of

Galaxy chocolate

www.vintage-books.co.uk